DECEIVED, DELUDED, DAMNED

DECEIVED, DELUDED, DAMNED

How Christianity Has Been Subtly Changed
From the Church Jesus Founded

Dan Beeson

Copyright © 2023 by Dan Beeson
Registered with the United States Copyright Office

All rights reserved. No part of this book may be reproduced or used in any manner without the written permission of the copyright owner, except for the scriptures contained herein, the brief quotations embodied in book reviews, and certain other noncommercial uses permitted by copyright law. For more information, email Dan at dan@vigilantvaliant.com.

First edition 2024
ISBN: 979-8-218-33454-3 (paperback)
www.vigilantvaliant.com   www.deceiveddeludeddamned.com

Unless otherwise noted, Scripture quotations are taken from The Holy Bible, KJV, the King James Version. Public domain.

Scripture quotations marked AMP are taken from the Amplified Bible, Copyright © 2015 by The Lockman Foundation, La Habra, CA90631 All rights reserved. Used by permission.

Scripture quotations marked BB1568 are taken from the Bishop's Bible, BB1568, the Bishop's Bible. Public domain.

Scripture quotations marked BSB are taken from the Berean Study Bible. Public domain as of April 30, 2023

Scripture quotations marked CB1535 are taken from The Coverdale Bible, CB1535, The Coverdale Bible. Public domain.

Scripture quotations marked (CEV) are from the Contemporary English Version Copyright © 1991, 1992, 1995 by the American Bible Society, Used by Permission.

Scripture quotations marked (CJB) are taken from the Complete Jewish Bible by David H. Stern. Copyright © 1998. All rights reserved. Used by permission of Messianic Jewish Publishers, 6120 Day Long Lane, Clarksville, MD 21029. www.messianicjewish.net.

Scripture quotations marked DARBY are taken from the Darby Bible Translation. Public domain.

Scripture quotations marked ESV are from the ESV® Bible (The Holy Bible, English Standard Version®), © 2001 by Crossway, a publishing ministry of Good News Publishers. Used by permission. All rights reserved.

Scripture quotations marked (GNT) are from the Good News Translation in Today's English Version, Second Edition. Copyright © 1992 by the American Bible Society. Used by permission.

Scripture quotations marked by the designation "GW" are taken from God's Word®. © 1995, 2003, 2013, 2014, 2019, 2020 by God's Word to the Nations Mission Society. Used by permission.

Scripture quotations marked LSB are taken from the (LSB®) Legacy Standard Bible®, Copyright © 2021 by The Lockman Foundation. Used by permission. All rights reserved. Managed in partnership with Three Sixteen Publishing Inc. LSBible.org and 316publishing.com.

Scripture quotations marked NASB are taken from the New American Standard Bible, Copyright © 1971 by The Lockman Foundation, La Habra, CA 90631 All rights reserved. Used by permission.

Scripture quotations marked NASB1995 are taken from the New American Standard Bible, Copyright © 1995 by The Lockman Foundation, La Habra, CA 90631 All rights reserved. Used by permission.

Scripture quotations marked NIV are taken from The Holy Bible, New International Version®, NIV® Copyright © 1973, 1978, 1984, 2011 by Biblica, Inc.® Used by permission. All rights reserved worldwide.

Scripture quotations marked NKJV are taken from the New King James Version®. Copyright © 1982 by Thomas Nelson. Used by permission. All rights reserved.

Scripture quotations marked NLT are taken from the Holy Bible, New Living Translation, copyright © 1996, 2004, 2015 by Tyndale House Foundation. Used by permission of Tyndale House Publishers, Inc., Carol Stream, Illinois 60188. All rights reserved.

Scripture quotations marked NRSVUE are taken from the New Revised Standard Version Updated Edition. Copyright © 2021 National Council of Churches of Christ in the United States of America. Used by permission. All rights reserved worldwide.

Scripture quotations marked TLV are taken from the Holy Scriptures, Tree of Life Version. Copyright © 2014, 2016 by the Tree of Life Bible Society. Used by permission of the Tree of Life Bible Society.

Scripture quotations marked YLT are taken from the 1898 Young's Literal Translation of the Holy Bible by J.N. Young, public domain.

Scripture quotations marked WEB are taken from the World English Bible. Public Domain.

Scripture quotations marked WNT are taken from the Weymouth New Testament, public domain.

Figures of BibleHub's Interlinear Bible verses are courtesy of BibleHub.com and Apostolic Bible Polyglot Interlinear.

Table of Contents

List of Figures viii
INTRODUCTION xi
PART I : Deceived, Deluded, Damned 1
Chapter 1: What Does It Mean to Be Deceived? 3
    How Easy It Is to Be Deceived 3
    Most of Humanity Has Been Deceived 7
    We Must Protect Ourselves from Being Deceived. ... 10
Chapter 2: What Does It Mean to Be Deluded? 13
    We Delude Ourselves 13
    Most of Mankind Is Deluded 14
Chapter 3: What Does It Mean to Be Damned? 17
    Most of Mankind Will Be Condemned 23
    There Is Good News 23
    There Is Bad News 24
Chapter 4: Condemned for What? 27
    Unbelief 27
    Disobedience 30
    Judgment Day Is Coming 38
    Summary of Part I 43
PART II: Escaping the First Deception 45
Chapter 5: What Is the First Deception We Must Escape? 45
    Will The Unrepentant Sinner Die? 45
    How Will the Condemned Be Punished? 46
    Is the Sentence Death or Eternal Torture Forever? .. 46
    To Love God, We Must Know God. 48
    Are You Worshipping the Wrong God? 50
    What Is the Punishment for Sin? 55
Chapter 6: Old Testament Hebrew for Soul and Spirit 61
    Do Humans Have an Immortal Spirit or Soul? 61
    The Word Soul in the Hebrew Old Testament 67
    Hebrew: Soul 67
    Hebrew: Living 68
    Hebrew: Spirit 80
Chapter 7: New Testament Greek for Soul and Spirit 105
    Greek: Soul 105
    Greek: Spirit 109
    Old Testament Scriptures with Soul and Spirit 113
    New Testament Scriptures with Soul and Spirit 117
Chapter 8: Do Humans Have a Soul That Will Live Forever?. 121
    Does the Bible Say Humans Are Immortal? 124
    Does the Bible Say Humans Are Mortal? 127
    Does the Bible Say Humans Have Eternal Life? 134

    How Do Humans Receive a Spirit? 138
    The Slam Dunk: The Mic Drop.............................. 151
Chapter 9: What Does the Bible Say Happens After Death?.. 155
    The First Death.. 156
    After death, we sleep until The Resurrection 156
    The Resurrections 166
    The First Resurrection... 167
    The Rapture of the Saved 171
    The Second Resurrection.. 172
    The Great White Throne Judgment......................... 176
    The Judgment Seat of Christ.................................... 180
    The Throne of His Glory 183
    The Book of Life... 186
    The Second Death... 189
    Verses That Say Souls Will Die in the Lake of Fire 191
Chapter 10: But What About Hell? 199
    What Is Hell?... 199
    Hell in the Old Testament 200
    Gehenna in the Hebrew Old Testament 209
    Hell in the New Testament.. 214
    Gehenna in the Greek New Testament 214
    Hades in the Greek New Testament........................ 216
    Tartarus in the Greek New Testament 218
Chapter 11: Will Humans Be Tortured for Ever? 219
    Eternal Torture Proof Texts Are Out of Context..... 219
    What Does For Ever Mean in the Bible? 221
    What Does Everlasting Mean in the Bible?............. 228
    What Does Unquenchable Mean in the Bible? 233
    Greek Fire.. 235
    Smoke Rises for Ever and Ever 242
    The Worm Dieth Not 244
    Verses That Say Souls Live For Ever in Hell 246
    The Great White Throne Judgment......................... 251
    Summary of Part II... 252
CONCLUSION... 253

List of Figures

    Figure 1.1: White Triangle 3
    Figure 1.2: Old Lady 4
    Figure 1.3: Frog 4
    Figure 1.4: Horse 6

    Figure 3.1: Mark 16:16 18
    Figure 3.2: Romans 14:23 18
    Figure 3.3: 2 Thessalonians 2:12 19

Figure 3.4: Matthew 23:33 20
Figure 3.5: Mark 3:29 21
Figure 3.6: Romans 3:8 22

Figure 5.1: Stargate Sarcophagus 47

Figure 6.1: Genesis 1:20 69
Figure 6.2: Genesis 1:21 70
Figure 6.3: Genesis 1:24 71
Figure 6.4: Genesis 2:7 73
Figure 6.5: Genesis 9:12 74
Figure 6.6: Leviticus 17:11 77
Figure 6.7: Exodus 12:16 78
Figure 6.8: Numbers 6:6 79
Figure 6.9: Genesis 1:2 81
Figure 6.10: Ecclesiastes 3:21 92
Figure 6.11: Psalm 104:4 93
Figure 6.12: Genesis 41:8 94
Figure 6.13: Genesis 7:15 95

Figure 7.1: Psalm 16:10 107
Figure 7.2: Acts 2:27 107
Figure 7.3: Revelation 16:3 109
Figure 7.4: Job 7:11 114
Figure 7.5: Job 12:10 115
Figure 7.6: Hebrews 4:12 119

Figure 9.1 : Romans 14:10 181
Figure 9.2 : 2 Corinthians 5:10 182

Figure 10.1: Joshua 15:8 211
Figure 10.2: Nehemiah 11:30 213

Figure 11.1: Greek Fire 235

INTRODUCTION

Who am I to write a book about spiritual things? I am nobody—a common man, a stumbling Christian, an everyday American. But, through all my failings and sins, I love God and want to be obedient to Him, though I can almost see Him rolling His eyes as I say that. My guardian angel has probably asked for hazardous duty pay or to be reassigned dozens of times. But, like you, I read the Bible and try to understand it. So I study it in my own way. This writing is an amalgamation of some of my studies.

I respect honest men and women of God and their right to interpret the Bible and teach it, but at the bottom line, we each need to believe God's word and Yeshua's words above human teachers.

What if the Scriptures seem contradictory? What if 60 verses say "x" and two seem to say "y?" If I cannot resolve the differences, it seems reasonable to me to go with the 60. Does that seem reasonable to you? I do not think God requires us to know Greek and Hebrew and somehow catch translation and transcription errors from a thousand years before we were alive. But I do think He expects us to do our best. He will take it from there. He will help us.

Most of my Bible studies attempt to have every scripture in the Bible on the topic. Some people have complained that there are just too many Bible verses. But my Bible studies are to learn the truth about what the Bible says—not what some denomination told me to believe, not what some person told me to believe, but what the Bible really says. I want all the Scriptures on the topic. I want the Scriptures that those with opposing beliefs use as their key Scriptures, so I can analyze them. I want to know their reason for believing the way they do and give that a fair hearing. How can we find the "Truth, the Whole Truth, and Nothing but the Truth" if we do not have all the data and all the information available? Since my studies are meant to learn what the Bible really says on a topic, I typically use nothing from outside the Bible. Outside sources may or may not be trustworthy. The only place we can read the words of Yeshua (Jesus in English) is in the Bible. So yes, I hope I have found every scripture on the topic. If I have missed a Scripture, if you find other Scriptures that address the question, or if you can in any way help me improve this writing or see a mistake, please email me and let me know at dan@vigilantvaliant.com. In this book, I have compiled the Scriptures I found on this topic. If you like it and it seems thorough and accurate, my other Bible studies may be found at www.vigilantvaliant.com.

I use the King James Version (KJV) of the Bible the most because it was by far the main English translation during my life. While there are other good translations of the Bible, I am using the one I am familiar with, the KJV. Yes, it is old-fashioned English, but it can also be poetic and beautiful. So, many Scriptures are quoted from the KJV Bible (King James Version), unless otherwise noted. Where the KJV English is hard to understand, I use mostly the New King James Version (NKJV), the World English Bible (WEB), or the Legacy Standard Bible (LSB). The LSB continues the quest of the NASB (1995) for being the most word-for-word accurate to the original Hebrew, Greek, and Aramaic, yet giving more readable English. All Scriptures will be indented and in italics. All Bolding, Underlining, Italicizing, parentheses, highlighting, and brackets, are done by me for emphasis. Be aware and realize that when I say any word is in the Bible X number of times, that means in the King James Version (KJV). If you look it up in another version, say the New International Version (NIV), the count may be different because they may use other words that mean the same thing, perhaps more modern words. This is not an error or flaw in the Bible, but just using different words, such as "day of his birth" in one version and "birthday" in another version. The meanings are the same, or should be.

PART I : Deceived, Deluded, Damned

Before we dive into our scriptures, let's address the elephant in the room. Damned! What a scary word!

Everyone has their own understanding of what it means to be damned. Everyone has their own idea of who should be damned. I would guess Hitler may be on most people's lists. But no one wants to think that they will be on anybody's list of those to be damned.

That anyone would be damned or condemned at all makes some people consider God to be harsh, possibly even cruel. How could a good, kind, and loving God condemn anyone? How could a loving God put anyone on His list of those to be damned? Well, I have good news for you! In all my Bible studies, I have never found it mentioned that God has a list of the damned! This twisted idea about God is all because of what I call the "First Deception." This book will show you scriptures that explain the first deception of mankind.

What the Bible says over and over is that God has a welcome list, the "Book of Life." This is God's list of those He, the King of Glory, will invite into His kingdom, the Kingdom of God. It is a place of only goodness, with no darkness or evil inside. It is His home, and He certainly has the absolute right to keep out people who would misbehave in His home. There are people you do not invite into your home, for the safety of your family and the peace and happiness of your loved ones. No matter how hospitable, congenial, and amiable you consider yourself to be, the long list of those you will welcome into your home does have an end. There are those who are not on your welcome list. What about the criminal who has committed multiple murders, has just broken out of prison, killed a number of guards, and is armed, dangerous, and on the run? If, in evading the police, he knocks on your door and you recognize him from police reports, are you going to invite him in to be with your spouse and children? Is he on your "welcome" list? You don't keep a "Not Welcome" list, but I think it is safe to say this criminal is not on your welcome list. Our situation is very similar to God's. The damned or condemned are those who will not be invited into the Kingdom of Heaven. They are not on God's welcome list, the Book of Life.

Is it being mean and cruel to keep the criminal out of your home? By not hiding him in your home, you are condemning him to be caught by the police and probably executed. Does this make you mean and cruel? If you are not being mean and cruel in this situation, how can anyone accuse God of being mean and cruel for doing the same thing? That is not fair. That is not good judgment.

If you and I make it into the Kingdom of God, do we want unrepentant, practicing murderers and rapists there? Should God invite in the devil, demons, and evil angels who hate Him and His family?

This book's title may sound harsh with the word "damned," but I don't think the words "unwelcome" or "uninvited" would have caught your eye. This book is not about a harsh god but about a loving, caring, gentle, and forgiving God. This book is about helping people keep their name on the good and kind God's guest list, the Book of Life. This does not mean earning our way into the Kingdom of God by being good. We try to be good and obedient because we love God and because of our gratitude to Him. A good child obeys his parents. A good child will not get their name erased from the invitation list by living a life of disobedience. We thank God, our Father, for sending Yeshua His Son to atone for our sins so that, by grace, we may be saved through faith in Yeshua Hamashiach, Jesus the Messiah.

Now let's get on with our study about our good, kind, loving, and forgiving God.

Chapter 1: What Does It Mean to Be Deceived?

According to the American Heritage Dictionary, the definition of "deceive" is:

Deceive, deceived, deceiving, deceives
1. To cause to believe what is not true; mislead
2. Archaic To catch by guile; ensnare
1. To practice deceit
2. To give a false impression:

How Easy It Is to Be Deceived.

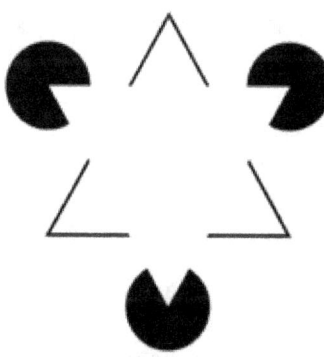

This is a Scripture search for the *"TRUTH."* Why? So I will not be beguiled, tricked, deluded, or deceived. We humans can be so easily deceived.

See the **White Triangle** in Figure 1.1, between the three black circles and upside down from the black triangle?

Figure 1.1: White Triangle
Attribution: "Kanizsa triangle" by Fibonacci
is licensed under CC BY-SA 3.0.

Great. Most people see it. But we are deceived. There is neither a white triangle, nor a black triangle, nor three black circles. This is an example of **Illusory Contours or Modal Completion.** Sure, now you understand it. Now you say you were never tricked by that image. You never saw a White Triangle? Look again.

See the old lady in Figure 1.2? Ah, now you are ready to catch this one. Maybe you see the old lady looking to our left with the big nose with a wart on it and a protruding chin. But just maybe you see the young lady, looking away from us, with a black neckband and her left ear peeking out from under her hair. Note that the young lady's ear is the old lady's eye. The young lady's neckband is the old lady's mouth. The young lady's little nose is the old lady's wart on her big, arched nose. This is an example of **Ambiguous Illusions**.

Figure 1.2: Old Lady
Attribution "My wife and my mother in law"
by Museo Ilusionario
licensed under CC BY-SA 2.0

Even after seeing the two, sometimes I have to think and focus to try to see the other again. I will get stuck on just seeing the old lady and have to really think about it to see the Young Lady again. Does this happen to you too?

The point of these images is how easily we are deceived or deluded. And how, even after having it explained to us and seeing one view, we can slip back into the other view.

How easily mankind can be beguiled, tricked, deluded, or deceived.

FROG

Glance at this drawing of a frog in Figure 1.3. It is perhaps a pencil sketch or a charcoal sketch. It is not a great drawing of a frog, but it may teach us something later.

Figure 1.3: Frog
Attribution: https://www.moillusions.com/frog

This is a Scripture search for the "***truth***." Is the truth that hard to find? Actually, the Bible says **yes**! Yeshua (Jesus in English) Himself says we can be beguiled, tricked, and deceived. Note the verses below.

> "11 **Many false prophets will arise and will deceive many.** 12 And because lawlessness is multiplied, most people's love will grow cold. 13 But the one who endures to the end, he will be saved. 14 And this gospel of the kingdom shall be proclaimed in the whole world as a witness to all the nations, and then the end will come." (Matthew 24:11-14 LSB)

> "23 Then if anyone says to you, 'Behold, here is the Christ,' or 'There He is,' do not believe him. 24 **For false christs and false prophets will arise and will show great signs and wonders, so as to deceive, if possible, even the elect.**" (Matthew 24:23-24 LSB)

The verses above are just a couple that show Yeshua warns His disciples about being deceived or deluded. You may think, "But could we be deceived through the Bible itself?" Read on.

> "1 Then Jesus was led up by the Spirit into the wilderness to be tempted by the devil. 2 And after He had fasted forty days and forty nights, He then became hungry. 3 And the tempter came and said to Him, "If You are the Son of God, command that these stones become bread." 4 But He answered and said, "It is written, 'Man shall not live on bread alone, but on every word that proceeds out of the mouth of God.'" 5 Then **the devil** *took Him into the holy city and had Him stand on the pinnacle of the temple, 6 and ***said to Him**, "If You are the Son of God, throw Yourself down; **for it is written, 'He will command His angels concerning You'; and 'On their hands they will bear You up, Lest You strike Your foot against a stone.'"** 7 Jesus said to him, "Again, it is written, 'You shall not put the Lord your God to the test.'" 8 Again, the devil *took Him to a very high mountain and *showed Him all the kingdoms of the world and their glory; 9 and he said to Him, "All these things I will give You, if You fall down and worship me." 10 Then Jesus *said to him, "Go, Satan! For it is written, 'You shall worship the Lord your God, and serve Him only." (Matthew 4:1-10 LSB)

The verses above show that the devil, and by extension, **people, can use the Scriptures improperly or twist the meaning of the Scriptures to try to deceive us**. So we must study the Scriptures carefully. It is extremely critical, particularly as Christians, that we keep our studies intellectually honest. There may be times we have to admit we are unable to draw a firm conclusion.

Consider this drawing of a Horse in Figure 1.4. You may have already seen my point. Our expectations, our mindset, and our preconceived ideas strongly influence what we think. Of course, this is exactly the same drawing of the frog as above. Maybe you caught this. Maybe it tricked you. This is called a Double Image Optical Illusion.

Figure 1.4: Horse
Attribution:www.moillusions.com /frog-or-horse/

"The glory which is built upon a lie soon becomes a most unpleasant encumbrance. **How easy it is to make people believe a lie, and how hard it is to undo that work again!**" This is from the Autobiographical dictation, 2 December 1906, Published in the Autobiography of Mark Twain, Volume 2 (University of California Press, 2013). This is the same idea as a quote attributed to Mark Twain, but that cannot be proven to be from him: "**It's easier to fool people than to convince them that they have been fooled.**" Once people have been deluded, it is very, very difficult to break them free of that delusion. It is like an addiction. It is my belief, based on my Bible studies, that the vast majority of Christians have been deluded. It is my belief that Christianity has been subtly changed over the years from the church Yeshua founded. Please read this book carefully, praying for the truth from Yahweh.

Every person who has copied Scriptures through the ages, every person who has translated Scriptures to another language, and every person who has made Scripture study notes that were made into a study Bible has been under delusions and had firmly ingrained beliefs, understandings, and points of view. Some were honest, God-fearing people. Some were not. We must be very careful in our study of Scripture. We must seek the best translations, founded on the most ancient documents, which have the very least chance of copy errors, typographical errors, translation errors, dogmatic indoctrination, or any other mode of error.

This is my attempt to discover the truth presented in the Bible and not be misled by tradition, statements, thoughts, opinions, etcetera from self-proclaimed experts. **I want to know the truth, the whole truth, and nothing but the truth. Don't you?** I believe

God is able to make His word clear to the masses, to normal men and women like you and me. He is able to safeguard His word so that the major translations today are trustworthy. Some translations may be purposefully changed to support a doctrine; some may be accidentally incorrectly translated, but I believe God is able to protect His word in its major distribution to mankind.

Most of Humanity Has Been Deceived.

The Devil Wants to Deceive Us.

> *"7 And there was war in heaven: Michael and his angels fought against the dragon; and the dragon fought and his angels, 8 And prevailed not; neither was their place found any more in heaven. 9 And the great dragon was cast out,* **that old serpent, called the Devil, and Satan, which deceiveth the whole world:** *he was cast out into the earth, and his angels were cast out with him." (Revelation 12:7-9)*

In fact, the Bible says straight out that the devil "**deceived the whole world.**" While Babylon is not the devil, it is clear that it was under the control of the devil and used by him to deceive **all the nations** of the Earth.

> *"21 Then a strong angel picked up a stone like a great millstone and threw it into the sea, saying, "So will Babylon, the great city, be thrown down with violence, and will not be found any longer. 22 And the sound of harpists and musicians and flute-players and trumpeters will not be heard in you any longer; and no craftsman of any craft will be found in you any longer; and the sound of a mill will not be heard in you any longer; 23 and the light of a lamp will not shine in you any longer; and the voice of the bridegroom and bride will not be heard in you any longer; for your merchants were the great men of the earth, because* **all the nations were deceived by your sorcery.** *24 And in her was found the blood of prophets and of saints and of all who have been slain on the earth."" (Revelation 18:21-24 LSB)*

In the same way, the beast of the end times and the false prophet are just tools of the devil and do all their work at his bidding.

*"20 And the beast was seized, and with him the false prophet who did the signs in his presence, **by which he deceived those** who had received the mark of the beast and those who worshiped his image. These two were thrown alive into the lake of fire which burns with brimstone." (Revelation 19:20 LSB)*

*"1 Then I saw an angel coming down from heaven, having the key of the abyss and a great chain in his hand. 2 And he laid hold of the dragon, the serpent of old, who is the devil and Satan, and bound him for a thousand years; 3 and he threw him into the abyss, and shut it and sealed it over him, **so that he would not deceive the nations any longer**, until the thousand years were finished. After these things he must be released for a short time." (Revelation 20:1-3 LSB)*

*"7 And when the thousand years are finished, Satan will be released from his prison, 8 **and will come out to deceive the nations** which are in the four corners of the earth, Gog and Magog, to gather them together for the war; the number of them is like the sand of the seashore. 9 And they came up on the broad plain of the earth and surrounded the camp of the saints and the beloved city, and fire came down from heaven and devoured them. 10 And the devil who deceived them was thrown into the lake of fire and brimstone, where the beast and the false prophet are also, and they will be tormented day and night forever and ever." (Revelation 20:7-10 LSB)*

*"8 Be of sober spirit, be watchful. **Your adversary, the devil,** prowls around like a roaring lion, **seeking someone to devour."** (1 Peter 5:8 LSB)*

There is no question that the great dragon, that old serpent, called the devil and Satan, is trying to deceive you, me, and the whole world.

Our Teachers and Friends Deceive Us.

"4 "Let everyone beware of his neighbor, And do not trust any brother, Because every brother surely supplants, And every neighbor goes about as a

> *slanderer. 5 **Everyone deceives his neighbor** And does not speak the truth; They have taught their tongue to speak lies; They weary themselves committing iniquity. 6 **Your habitation is in the midst of deceit;** Through deceit they refuse to know Me," declares Yahweh." (Jeremiah 9:4-6)*

Remember the thought behind these verses above? "Through deceit, they refuse to **know me**." If we are deceived about God, He says **we do not know Him.** We will see more about not knowing God later in this book.

> *"24 For there shall arise false Christs, and false prophets, and shall shew great signs and wonders; insomuch that, **if it were possible, they shall deceive the very elect.**" (Matthew 24:24)*

> *"18 For such men are slaves, not of our Lord Christ but of their own stomach, and **by their smooth and flattering speech they deceive the hearts of the unsuspecting**." (Romans 16:18 LSB)*

> *"14 That we henceforth be no more children, tossed to and fro, and carried about with every wind of doctrine, **by the sleight of men, and cunning craftiness, whereby they lie in wait to deceive;**" (Ephesians 4:14)*

> *"13 But evil men and impostors will proceed from bad to worse, **deceiving and being deceived.**" (2 Timothy 3:13)*

> *"10 For there are many unruly and **vain talkers and deceivers**, specially they of the circumcision:" (Titus 1:10)*

> *"26 If anyone thinks himself to be religious while not bridling his tongue **but deceiving his own heart,** this man's religion is worthless." (James 1:26 LSB)*

The verse above is Biblical proof that people can be very religious and still be condemned.

> *"7 For many deceivers are entered into the world, who confess not that Jesus Christ is come in the flesh. This is a **deceiver** and an antichrist." (2 John 1:7)*

*"19 I called to my lovers, **but they deceived me;** My priests and my elders breathed their last in the city While they sought food for themselves in order to restore their souls.." (Lamentations 1:19 LSB)*

*"7 All the men who have a covenant with you will send you forth to the border, and the men at peace with you **will deceive you** and overpower you. They who eat your bread will set an ambush for you. (There is no discernment in him.)" (Obadiah 1:7 LSB)*

We Must Protect Ourselves from Being Deceived.

***"16 Beware** lest your hearts **be deceived,** and you turn away and serve other gods and worship them," (Deuteronomy 11:16 LSB)*

*"31 Let him not believe in emptiness, **deceiving himself;** For emptiness will be his reward," (Job 15:31 LSB)*

*"8 For thus says Yahweh of hosts, the God of Israel, 'Do not let your prophets who are in your midst and your diviners **deceive you,** and do not listen to your dreams which you dream." (Jeremiah 29:8)*

*"4 And Jesus answered and said unto them, **Take heed that no man deceive you**. 5 For many shall come in my name, saying, I am Christ; **and shall deceive many**." (Matthew 24:4-5)*

*"5 And Jesus answering them began to say, **Take heed lest any man deceive you:** 6 For many shall come in my name, saying, I am Christ; **and shall deceive many**." (Mark 13:5-6)*

*"And he said, **Take heed that ye be not deceived**: for many shall come in my name, saying, I am Christ; and the time draweth near: go ye not therefore after them." (Luke 21:8)*

*"9 Or do you not know that the unrighteous will not inherit the kingdom of God? **Do not be deceived;***

neither the sexually immoral, nor idolaters, nor adulterers, nor effeminate, nor homosexuals, 10 nor thieves, nor the greedy, nor drunkards, nor revilers, nor swindlers, will inherit the kingdom of God." (1 Corinthians 6:9-10 LSB)

*"33 **Do not be deceived:** "Bad company corrupts good morals.""" (1 Corinthians 15:33 LSB)*

*"7 **Do not be deceived,** God is not mocked, for whatever a man sows, this he will also reap." (Galatians 6:7 LSB)*

*"8 See to it that no one **takes you captive through** philosophy and empty **deception,** according to the tradition of men, according to the elementary principles of the world, and not according to Christ." (Colossians 2:8 LSB)*

*"3 **Let no man deceive you by any means:** for that day shall not come, except there come a falling away first, and that man of sin be revealed, the son of perdition;" (2 Thessalonians 2:3)*

*"16 **Do not be deceived, my beloved brethren.** 17 Every good gift and every perfect gift is from above, and comes down from the Father of lights, with whom there is no variation or shadow of turning. 18 Of His own will He brought us forth by the word of truth, that we might be a kind of firstfruits of His creatures." (James 1:16-18 New King James Version NKJV)*

*"7 Little children, **let no one deceive you.** The one who does righteousness is righteous, just as He is righteous." (1 John 3:7 LSB)*

There are likely many more admonitions for us in the Bible, warning disciples not to be deceived.

Chapter 2: What Does It Mean to Be Deluded?

According to the American Heritage Dictionary, the definition of "delude" is:

Delude: deluded, deluding, deludes
1. To cause to hold a false belief; deceive thoroughly:

How is "deluded" different than "deceived"? While most thesauruses say they are synonyms, Hinative.com says, "While both words can be technically used interchangeably, delude is most often used when speaking of oneself. ' I deluded myself into thinking he liked me, but, in fact, he doesn't.'"
This is as opposed to someone else tricking us or deceiving us, as in "He deceived me into thinking that he truly liked me."
https://www.englishforums.com/ has some people that agree with that analysis. "They both mean roughly the same thing.
I would use "delude" when it is self-imposed (he is deluding himself) and deceive when it is someone else (she deceived him)."

We Delude Ourselves

> "18 **Let no man deceive himself.** If any man among you thinks that he is wise in this age, he must become foolish, so that he may become wise. 19 For the wisdom of this world is foolishness before God. For it is written, "He is the one who catches the wise in their craftiness";" (1 Corinthians 3:18-19 LSB)
>
> "3 For if anyone thinks he is something when he is nothing, **he deceives himself.**" (Galatians 6:3 LSB)
>
> 22 But become doers of the word, and not merely hearers **who delude themselves.**" (James 1:22 LSB)
>
> "13 suffering unrighteousness as the wages of their unrighteousness, considering it a pleasure to revel in the daytime—they are stains and blemishes, reveling in their deceptions, as they feast with you," (2 Peter 2:13 LSB)
>
> "8 If we say that we have no sin, **we deceive ourselves**, and the truth is not in us." (1 John 1:8)

> "9 Thus says Yahweh, 'Do not deceive yourselves, saying, "The Chaldeans will surely go away from us," for they will not go." (Jeremiah 37:9 LSB)
>
> "16 As for the terror of you, The arrogance of your heart **has deceived you**, O you who dwell in the clefts of the rock, Who seize the height of the hill. Though you make your nest as high as an eagle's, I will bring you down from there," declares Yahweh." (Jeremiah 49:16 LSB)
>
> "3 The arrogance of your heart **has deceived you**, You who dwell in the clefts of the cliff, In the height of your habitation, Who says in his heart, 'Who will bring me down to earth?'" (Obadiah 1:3 LSB)

Most of Mankind Is Deluded

Please read the following very carefully: God does not delude those seeking the truth. But those who turn from the truth and reject the truth open themselves up to believing something else. Something other than the truth must be a lie.

> "8 And then that lawless one will be revealed— whom the Lord Jesus will slay with the breath of His mouth and bring to an end by the appearance of His coming— 9 whose coming is in accord with the working of Satan, with all power and signs and false wonders, 10 and with all the **deception** of unrighteousness for those who perish, because they did not receive the love of the truth so as to be saved. 11 And for this reason God sends upon them a **deluding** influence so that they will believe what is false, 12 in order that they all may be judged who did not believe the truth, but took pleasure in unrighteousness. 13 But we should always give thanks to God for you, brothers beloved by the Lord, because God has chosen you as the first fruits for salvation through sanctification by the Spirit and faith in the truth. 14 It was for this He called you through our gospel, that you may obtain the glory of our Lord Jesus Christ." (2 Thessalonians 2:8-14 LSB)

Now before you think, "How mean of God to send them a delusion," consider carefully the following verses.

*"18 For the wrath of God is revealed from heaven against all ungodliness and unrighteousness of men who suppress the truth in unrighteousness, 19 **because that which is known about God is evident within them; for God made it evident to them.** 20 For since the creation of the world His invisible attributes, both His eternal power and divine nature, have been clearly seen, being understood through what has been made, so that **they are without excuse.** 21 For even though they knew God, they did not glorify Him as God or give thanks, but they became futile in their thoughts, and their foolish heart was darkened. 22 **Professing to be wise, they became fools, 23 and exchanged the glory of the incorruptible God for an image in the likeness of corruptible man and of birds and four-footed animals and crawling creatures.** 24 Therefore **God gave them over** in the lusts of their hearts to impurity, so that their bodies would be dishonored among them. 25 For they exchanged the truth of God for a lie, and worshiped and served the creature rather than the Creator, who is blessed [d]forever. Amen. 26 For this reason God gave them over to dishonorable passions; for their females exchanged the natural function for that which is unnatural, 27 and in the same way also the males abandoned the natural function of the female and burned in their desire toward one another, males with males committing indecent acts and receiving in their own persons the due penalty of their error. 28 **And just as they did not see fit to acknowledge God, God gave them over to an unfit mind,** to do those things which are not proper, 29 having been filled with all unrighteousness, wickedness, greed, evil; full of envy, murder, strife, deceit, malice; they are gossips, 30 slanderers, haters of God, violent, arrogant, boastful, inventors of evil, disobedient to parents, 31 without understanding, untrustworthy, unloving, unmerciful; 32 and although they know the righteous requirement of God, that those who practice such things are worthy of death, they not only do the same, but also give hearty approval to those who practice them." (Romans 1:18-32 LSB)*

The above verses show God gives us every chance to believe and be saved. It is people who turn against God. It is people who "changed the glory of the incorruptible God into an image." It is people who "changed the truth of God into a lie." He tried and tried, but some people rebelled and rebelled, and He finally "gave them over" or let them have what they wanted, which was to get rid of Him. "They are without excuse." **Let us, you and I, turn to God daily, and come out and stay out of the people that have turned against Him. Let us find out what God says, and believe and follow Him.**

Whether we are deceived by others trying to turn us from God or whether we are deluding ourselves by willingly believing a lie, we need to pray daily that our Father will protect us and guide us to the truth. If we do not believe the truth, we will be lost, condemned, and damned.

Chapter 3: What Does It Mean to Be Damned?

According to the American Heritage Dictionary, the definition of "damned" is:
1a. In various religions, condemned to eternal punishment
1b. Destined to an unhappy fate:
2. Informal; Deserving condemnation; detestable:

The word "damned" is found only three times in the King James Bible, all in the New Testament.

> "He that believeth and is baptized shall be saved; but **he that believeth not shall be damned**." (Mark 16:16)

> "And **he that doubteth is damned if he eat**, because he eateth not of faith: for whatsoever is not of faith is sin." (Romans 14:23)

> "**That they all might be damned who believed not the truth**, but had pleasure in unrighteousness." (2 Thessalonians 2:12)

Out of the 61 English Bible translations shown on BibleHub.com, the following alternate words are found the number of times shown:
47 = condemned
 7 = damned
 4 = judged
 3 = punished.

Let's examine the three verses above in Bible Hub's wonderful Interlinear Bible. It shows that the first two of the verses above have the same root word, G2632, "κατακρίνω", meaning "condemned." The third uses G2919, "κριθῶσιν."

Mark 16:16

3588 [e]	4100 [e]	2532 [e]	907 [e]	4982 [e]
ho	pisteusas	kai	baptistheis	sōthēsetai
ὁ	πιστεύσας	καὶ	βαπτισθεὶς	σωθήσεται ;
The [one]	having believed	and	having been baptized	will be saved

3588 [e]	1161 [e]	569 [e]	2632 [e]
ho	de	apistēsas	katakrithēsetai
ὁ	δὲ	ἀπιστήσας	κατακριθήσεται .
the [one]	however	having disbelieved	will be condemned

Figure 3.1: Mark 16:16
[Courtesy of BibleHub.com and Apostolic Bible Polyglot Interlinear.]

Romans 14:23

3588 [e]	1161 [e]	1252 [e]	1437 [e]	5315 [e]
ho	de	diakrinomenos	ean	phagē
ὁ	δὲ	διακρινόμενος ,	ἐὰν	φάγῃ ,
The [one]	however	doubting	if	he eats

2632 [e]	3754 [e]	3756 [e]	1537 [e]	4102 [e]	3956 [e]
katakekritai	hoti	ouk	ek	pisteōs	pan
κατακέκριται ,	ὅτι	οὐκ	ἐκ	πίστεως ;	πᾶν
has been condemned	because [it is]	not	of	faith	everything

1161 [e]	3739 [e]	3756 [e]	1537 [e]	4102 [e]	266 [e]	1510 [e]
de	ho	ouk	ek	pisteōs	hamartia	estin
δὲ	ὃ	οὐκ	ἐκ	πίστεως ,	ἁμαρτία	ἐστίν .
now	that [is]	not	of	faith	sin	is

Figure 3.2: Romans 14:23
[Courtesy of BibleHub.com and Apostolic Bible Polyglot Interlinear.]

◀ **2 Thessalonians 2:12** ▶

2443 [e]	2919 [e]	3956 [e]	3588 [e]	3361 [e]	4100 [e]
hina	krithōsin	pantes	hoi	mē	pisteusantes
12 ἵνα	κριθῶσιν	πάντες	οἱ	μὴ	πιστεύσαντες
in order that	should be judged	all	those	not	having believed

3588 [e]	225 [e]	235 [e]	2106 [e]	3588 [e]	93 [e]
tē	alētheia	alla	eudokēsantes	tē	adikia
τῇ	ἀληθείᾳ,	ἀλλὰ	εὐδοκήσαντες	τῇ	ἀδικίᾳ.
the	truth	but	having delighted	-	in unrighteousness

Figure 3.3: 2 Thessalonians 2:12
[Courtesy of BibleHub.com and Apostolic Bible Polyglot Interlinear.]

So the word "damned" as used in the Bible means to be judged (with a negative outcome), or to be condemned.

The word "damnation" is found 11 times in the King James Bible.

> "Woe unto you, scribes and Pharisees, hypocrites! For ye devour widows' houses, and for a pretence make long prayer: therefore **ye shall receive the greater damnation.**" (Matthew 23:14)

> "Which devour widows' houses, and for a pretence make long prayers: these shall receive **greater damnation.**" (Mark 12:40)

> "Which devour widows' houses, and for a shew make long prayers: the same shall receive **greater damnation.**" (Luke 20:47)

> "And shall come forth; they that have done good, unto the resurrection of life; and they that have done evil, unto **the resurrection of damnation.**" (John 5:29)

> "Whosoever therefore resisteth the power, resisteth the ordinance of God: and **they that resist shall receive to themselves damnation.**" (Romans 13:2)

*"For he that eateth and drinketh unworthily, **eateth and drinketh damnation to himself**, not discerning the Lord's body." (1 Corinthians 11:29)*

*"**Having damnation,** because they have cast off their first faith." (1 Timothy 5:12)*

*"And through covetousness shall they with feigned words make merchandise of you: whose judgment now of a long time lingereth not, **and their damnation slumbereth not.**" (2 Peter 2:3)*

Below, let's look more closely at the last three of the eleven verses that use the word damnation.

The King James Version of the Bible says:

*"Ye serpents, ye generation of vipers, how can ye escape the **damnation of hell**?" (Matthew 23:33)*

BibleHub's wonderful Interlinear Bible gives the following for the Greek of Matthew 23:33:

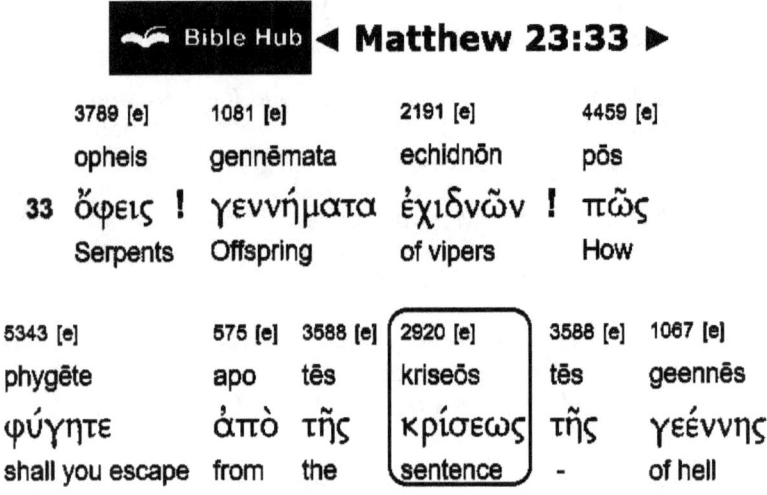

Figure 3.4: Matthew 23:33
[Courtesy of BibleHub.com and Apostolic Bible Polyglot Interlinear.]

The Strong's Concordance word G2920, "Krisis," is the base word used here and is defined as a "decision, a "judgment." Here it is translated "sentence."

The King James Version of the Bible says:

*"But he that shall blaspheme against the Holy Ghost hath never forgiveness, but is in danger of **eternal damnation.**" (Mark 3:29)*

BibleHub's Interlinear Bible gives the following for the Greek of Mark 3:29:

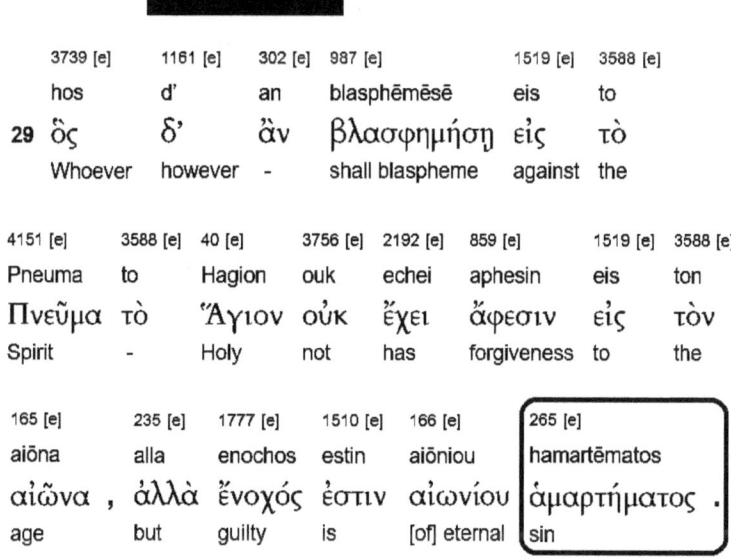

Figure 3.5: Mark 3:29
[Courtesy of BibleHub.com and Apostolic Bible Polyglot Interlinear.]

Strong's Concordance word G265 "hamartéma" is the base word used here and is defined as a fault, sin, or evil deed.

Here it is translated "sin."

The King James Version of the Bible says:

"And not rather, (as we be slanderously reported, and as some affirm that we say,) Let us do evil, that good may come? **Whose damnation is just."** *(Romans 3:8)*

BibleHub's Interlinear Bible gives this for the Greek.

2532 [e]	3361 [e]	2531 [e]	987 [e]		2532 [e]
kai	mē	kathōs	blasphēmoumetha		kai
καὶ	μὴ ,	καθὼς	βλασφημούμεθα ,		καὶ
And [is it]	not	as	we are slanderously charged		and

2531 [e]	5346 [e]	5100 [e]	1473 [e]	3004 [e]	3754 [e]
kathōs	phasin	tines	hēmas	legein	hoti
καθὼς	φασίν	τινες	ἡμᾶς	λέγειν	ὅτι ,
as	affirm	some [that]	us	to say	-

4160 [e]	3588 [e]	2556 [e]	2443 [e]	2064 [e]	3588 [e]
Poiēsōmen	ta	kaka	hina	elthē	ta
Ποιήσωμεν	τὰ	κακὰ ,	ἵνα	ἔλθῃ	τὰ
Let us do	things	evil	that	may come	the

18 [e]	3739 [e]	3588 [e]	2917 [e]	1738 [e]	1510 [e]
agatha	hōn	to	krima	endikon	estin
ἀγαθά ?	ὧν	τὸ	κρίμα	ἔνδικόν	ἐστιν .
good things	Their	-	condemnation	just	is

Figure 3.6: Romans 3:8
[Courtesy of BibleHub.com and Apostolic Bible Polyglot Interlinear.]

The Strong's Concordance word G2917, "krima," is the base word used here and is defined as a judgment, a verdict, or a condemnation. Here it is translated "condemnation."

In just these 3 examples, we have seen that the word "damnation" was used in the KJV to translate 3 different Greek words meaning slightly different things.

Out of 61 English Bible translations, the following alternate words for damnation are found the number of times shown:
20 = Judgment
18 = Condemned
 9 = Sentenced
 6 = Damnation
 2 = Penalty

So we have seen that in the original language, damned means condemned, judged, or sentenced.

Most of Mankind Will Be Condemned

Where does the Bible say most people will be sent on Judgment Day? Are most "saved" and go to live in eternal bliss with God, or are most damned, condemned, and thrown into the Lake of Fire? First, the good news!

There Is Good News

In the verses below, we see the good news! Yahweh wants everyone to be saved!

> "23 ***Do I have any pleasure in the death of the wicked***," declares Lord Yahweh, "is it not that he should turn from his ways and live?" (Ezekiel 18:23 LSB)

> "11 Say to them, 'As I live!' declares Lord Yahweh, '***I take no pleasure in the death of the wicked,*** but rather that the wicked turn from his way and live. Turn back, turn back from your evil ways! Why then will you die, O house of Israel?'" (Ezekiel 33:11 LSB)

> "3 This is good and acceptable in the sight of God our Savior, 4 **who desires all men to be saved** and to come to the full knowledge of the truth. 5 For there is one God, and one mediator also between God and men, the man Christ Jesus," (1 Timothy 2:3-5 LSB)

> "8 But do not let this one fact escape your notice, beloved, that with the Lord one day is like a thousand years, and a thousand years like one day. 9 The Lord is not slow about His promise, as some consider slowness, but is patient toward you, **not willing for any to perish but for all to come to repentance**. (2 Peter 3:8-9)

There Is Bad News

Nevertheless, the verses below show the bad news: that the majority, most of mankind, will reject Yahweh. Oh, they want to go to the good place, and they want to live forever, but they are unwilling to be obedient and shape themselves into the kind of people that Yahweh wants in heaven. It is a conscious choice to obey Yahweh or not. It is a conscious choice to believe what Yahweh says is true and to live like Yahweh says. Luckily, once that choice is made to obey, Yahweh takes our hands and helps us with guidance, training, forgiveness, mercy, and grace.

> "13 "Enter through the narrow gate; for **the gate is wide and the way is broad that leads to destruction, and there are many who enter through it.** 14 For the gate is narrow and the way is constricted that leads to life, and there are few who find it." (Matthew 7:13-14 LSB)

> "21 "**Not everyone who says to Me, 'Lord, Lord,' will enter the kingdom of heaven, but he who does the will of My Father who is in heaven will enter.** 22 Many will say to Me on that day, 'Lord, Lord, in Your name did we not prophesy, and in Your name cast out demons, and in Your name do many miracles?' 23 **And then I will declare to them, 'I never knew you; depart from Me, you who practice lawlessness.'** 24 "Therefore everyone who hears these words of Mine and does them, may be compared to a wise man who built his house on the rock. 25 And the rain descended, and the rivers came, and the winds blew and fell against that house; and yet it did not fall, for it had been founded on the rock. 26 And everyone hearing these words of Mine and not doing them, may be compared to a foolish man who built his house on the sand. 27 And the rain descended, and the rivers came, and the winds blew and slammed against

> *that house; and it fell—and great was its fall."''*
> *(Matthew 7:21-27 LSB)*

The verses above show that many religious people will not get into the Kingdom of Heaven. These are professing Christians, for they call Him Lord. They show surprise that they are not saved. They believe themselves to be saved by believing in Jesus.

But these words above are from the mouth of Yeshua. Note that Yeshua said one path leads to life and the other to destruction, not eternal torture.

> *"23 And someone said to Him, "Lord, are there just a few who are being saved?" And He said to them, 24 "Strive to enter through the narrow door, **for many, I tell you, will seek to enter and will not be able**." (Luke 13:23-24 LSB)*

> *"9 Or do you not know that **the unrighteous will not inherit the kingdom of God? Do not be deceived;** neither the sexually immoral, nor idolaters, nor adulterers, nor effeminate, nor homosexuals, 10 nor thieves, nor the greedy, nor drunkards, nor revilers, nor swindlers, will inherit the kingdom of God. 11 And such were some of you; but you were washed, but you were sanctified, but you were justified in the name of the Lord Jesus Christ and in the Spirit of our God." (1 Corinthians 6:9-11 LSB)*

> *"5 And He who sits on the throne said, "Behold, I am making all things new." And He *said, "Write, for these words are faithful and true." 6 Then He said to me, "They are done. I am the Alpha and the Omega, the beginning and the end. I will give to the one who thirsts from the spring of the water of life without cost. 7 He who overcomes will inherit these things, and I will be his God and he will be My son. 8 **But for the cowardly and unbelieving and abominable and murderers and sexually immoral persons and sorcerers and idolaters and all liars, their part will be in the lake that burns with fire and brimstone, which is the second death.**"'' (Revelation 21:5-8 LSB)*

In the above verses, Yeshua says twice that all who do not repent will perish. Perish means to DIE, not to be tortured forever.

We shall see later that "repent" in the Bible means to not just be sorry but to change your ways, to stop doing the wrong things and start doing the right things.

> *"1 Now at that same time there were some present who were reporting to Him about the Galileans whose blood Pilate had mixed with their sacrifices. 2 And Jesus answered and said to them, "Do you think that these Galileans were greater sinners than all other Galileans because they suffered these things? 3* **I tell you, no, but unless you repent, you will all likewise perish.** *4 Or do you think that those eighteen on whom the tower in Siloam fell and killed them were worse offenders than all the men who live in Jerusalem? 5* **I tell you, no, but unless you repent, you will all likewise perish.""**
> *(Luke 13:1-5 LSB)*

We don't have to be the worst people in the world to perish. We don't even have to be bad people to perish.

To know how to not perish, we must know why people will perish. So the question is, "Why?"

Why will the unrepentant perish? Why will they be condemned?

Chapter 4: Condemned for What?

The burning question now is, why? Why will those who have been deceived and deluded be condemned?

Unbelief

If we do not believe God, then we are calling Him a liar. What is your attitude toward someone who believes you lie to them? How horribly they are disrespecting you! By not believing God, how horribly we are disrespecting Him!

> "9 Now after He had risen early on the first day of the week, He first appeared to Mary Magdalene, from whom He had cast out seven demons. 10 She went and reported to those who had been with Him, while they were mourning and crying. 11 And when they heard that He was alive and had been seen by her, **they refused to believe it.** 12 After that, He appeared in a different form to two of them while they were walking along on their way to the countryside. 13 And they went away and reported it to the others, **but they did not believe them either.** 14 Afterward He appeared to the eleven themselves as they were reclining at the table; and **He reproached them for their unbelief and hardness of heart, because they had not believed those who had seen Him after He had risen.** 15 And He said to them, "Go into all the world and preach the gospel to all creation. 16 He who has believed and has been baptized shall be saved; but he who has disbelieved shall be condemned." (Mark 16:9-16 LSB)

> "14 And as Moses lifted up the serpent in the wilderness, even so must the Son of Man be lifted up; 15 **so that whoever believes will in Him have eternal life.** 16 "For God so loved the world, that He gave His only begotten Son, **that whoever believes in Him shall not perish, but have eternal life.** 17 For God did not send the Son into the world to judge the world, but that the world might be saved through Him. 18 **He who believes in Him is not judged; he who does not believe has been judged already, because he has not believed in the name of the only begotten Son of God. 19 And this is the judgment, that the**

> *Light has come into the world, and men loved the darkness rather than the Light, for their deeds were evil.* 20 For everyone who does evil hates the Light, and does not come to the Light lest his deeds be exposed." (John 3:14-20 LSB)

Yeshua says it three times in just a few verses, in one conversation. Can anyone honestly deny that He is serious about the need to believe?

Abraham was saved by acting on his faith in the Living God. The Bible says if he staggered or failed, it would have been because of unbelief. Faith is the opposite of unbelief.

> "18 **In hope against hope he believed,** so that he might become a father of many nations according to that which had been spoken, "So shall your seed be." 19 **And without becoming weak in faith** he contemplated his own body, now as good as dead since he was about a hundred years old, and the deadness of Sarah's womb; 20 yet, **with respect to the promise of God, he did not waver in unbelief but grew strong in faith,** giving glory to God, 21 and being fully assured that what God had promised, He was able also to do. 22 Therefore **it was also counted to him as righteousness.** 23 Now not for his sake only was it written that it was counted to him, **24 but for our sake also, to whom it will be counted, as those who believe upon Him who raised Jesus our Lord from the dead,** 25 He who was delivered over on account of our transgressions, and was raised on account of our justification." (Romans 4:18-25 LSB)

Unbelief is what can cause us to be rejected from the family of God.

> "16 And if the first piece of dough is holy, the lump is also; and if the root is holy, the branches are too. 17 But if some of the branches were broken off, and you, being a wild olive, were grafted in among them and became a partaker with them of the rich root of the olive tree, 18 do not boast against the branches. But if you do boast against them, remember that it is not you who supports the root, but the root supports you. 19 You will say then, "Branches were broken off so that I might be grafted in." 20 **Quite**

> *right!* ***They were broken off for their unbelief,*** *but you stand by your faith. Do not be haughty, but fear, 21 for if God did not spare the natural branches, He will not spare you, either. 22 Behold then the kindness and severity of God; to those who fell, severity, but to you, God's kindness, if you continue in His kindness; otherwise you also will be cut off. 23 And they also,* ***if they do not continue in their unbelief, will be grafted in,*** *for God is able to graft them in again. 24 For if you were cut off from what is by nature a wild olive tree, and were grafted contrary to nature into a cultivated olive tree, how much more will these who are the natural branches be grafted into their own olive tree?"* (Romans 11:16-24 LSB)

Unbelief keeps us from entering into God's "rest," the glory of eternal life with Him.

> *"7 Therefore, just as the Holy Spirit says, "Today if you hear His voice, 8 Do not harden your hearts as when they provoked Me, As in the day of trial in the wilderness, 9 Where your fathers tried Me by testing Me, And saw My works for forty years. 10 Therefore I was angry with this generation, And said, 'They always go astray in their heart, And they did not know My ways'; 11 As I swore in My wrath, 'They shall not enter My rest.'"* ***12 See to it brothers, that there not be in any one of you an evil, unbelieving heart that falls away from the living God.*** *13 But encourage one another day after day, as long as it is still called "Today," so that none of you will be hardened by the deceitfulness of sin. 14* ***For we have become partakers of Christ, if we hold fast the beginning of our assurance firm until the end,*** *15 while it is said, "Today if you hear His voice, Do not harden your hearts, as when they provoked Me." 16 For who provoked Him when they had heard? Indeed, did not all those who came out of Egypt led by Moses? 17 And with whom was He angry for forty years? Was it not with those who sinned, whose corpses fell in the wilderness? 18 And to whom did He swear that they would not enter His rest,* ***but to those who were disobedient? 19 So we see that they were not able to enter because of unbelief."*** (Hebrews 3:7-19 LSB)

*"6 Seeing therefore it remaineth that some must enter therein, and they to whom it was first preached **entered not in because of unbelief:** 7 Again, he limiteth a certain day, saying in David, To day, after so long a time; as it is said, To day if ye will hear his voice, harden not your hearts. 8 For if Jesus had given them rest, then would he not afterward have spoken of another day. 9 There remaineth therefore a rest to the people of God. 10 For he that is entered into his rest, he also hath ceased from his own works, as God did from his. 11 Let us labour therefore to enter into that rest, **lest any man fall after the same example of unbelief.**"* (Hebrews 4:6-11)

Disobedience

The word "disobedience" is used six times in the KJV Bible, all in the New Testament. The verses below show that **disobedience makes us sinners**, that disobedience brings us under the wrath of God, and that **every disobedience will be punished**!

*"18 So then as through one transgression there resulted condemnation to all men, even so through one act of righteousness there resulted justification of life to all men. 19 **For as through the one man's disobedience the many were appointed sinners, even so through the obedience of the One the many will be appointed righteous.** 20 Now the Law came in so that the transgression would increase, but where sin increased, grace abounded all the more, 21 so that, **as sin reigned in death,** even so grace would reign through righteousness to eternal life through Jesus Christ our Lord."* (Romans 5:18-21 LSB)

"2 I beg you that when I come I may not have to be as bold as I expect to be toward some people who think that we live by the standards of this world. 3 For though we live in the world, we do not wage war as the world does. 4 The weapons we fight with are not the weapons of the world. On the contrary, they have divine power to demolish strongholds. 5 We demolish arguments and every pretension that sets itself up against the knowledge of God, and we take

*captive every thought to make it obedient to Christ. 6 **And we will be ready to punish every act of disobedience, once your obedience is complete.**"* (2 Corinthians 10:2-6 NIV)

*"1 And you were dead in your transgressions and sins, 2 in which you formerly walked according to the course of this world, **according to the ruler of the power of the air, the spirit that is now working in the sons of disobedience**, 3 among whom we all also formerly conducted ourselves in the lusts of our flesh, doing the desires of the flesh and of the mind, and were by nature children of wrath, even as the rest. 4 But God, being rich in mercy because of His great love with which He loved us, 5 even when we were dead in our transgressions, made us alive together with Christ—by grace you have been saved— 6 and raised us up with Him, and seated us with Him in the heavenly places in Christ Jesus,"* (Ephesians 2:1-6 LSB)

*"1 Therefore be imitators of God, as beloved children, 2 and walk in love, just as Christ also loved us and gave Himself up for us, an offering and a sacrifice to God as a fragrant aroma. 3 But sexual immorality or any impurity or greed must not even be named among you, as is proper among saints; 4 nor filthiness and foolish talk, or coarse jesting, which are not fitting, but rather giving of thanks. 5 For this you know with certainty, that no one sexually immoral or impure or greedy, who is an idolater, has an inheritance in the kingdom of Christ and God. 6 **Let no one deceive you with empty words, for because of these things the wrath of God comes upon the sons of disobedience.** 7 Therefore do not be partakers with them, 8 for you were formerly darkness, but now you are light in the Lord; walk as children of light 9 (for the fruit of that light consists in all goodness and righteousness and truth), 10 trying to learn what is pleasing to the Lord. 11 And do not participate in the unfruitful works of darkness, but instead even expose them. 12 For it is disgraceful even to speak of the things which are done by them in secret."* (Ephesians 5:1-12 LSB)

*"1 Therefore, if you have been raised up with Christ, keep seeking the things above, where Christ is, seated at the right hand of God. 2 Set your mind on the things above, not on the things that are on earth. 3 For you died and your life has been hidden with Christ in God. 4 When Christ, who is our life, is manifested, then you also will be manifested with Him in glory. 5 Therefore, consider the members of your earthly body as dead to sexual immorality, impurity, passion, evil desire, and greed, which is idolatry. 6 **On account of these things, the wrath of God is coming upon the sons of disobedience,** 7 and in them you also once walked, when you were living in them. 8 But now you also, lay them all aside: wrath, anger, malice, slander, and abusive speech from your mouth. 9 Do not lie to one another, since you put off the old man with its evil practices, 10 and have put on the new man who is being renewed to a full knowledge according to the image of the One who created him— 11 a renewal in which there is no distinction between Greek and Jew, circumcised and uncircumcised, barbarian, Scythian, slave, and freeman, but Christ is all and in all."* (Colossians 3:1-11 LSB)

*"2 We must pay the most careful attention, therefore, to what we have heard, so that we do not drift away. 2 For since the message spoken through angels was binding, **and every violation and disobedience received its just punishment**, 3 how shall we escape if we ignore so great a salvation? This salvation, which was first announced by the Lord, was confirmed to us by those who heard him. 4 God also testified to it by signs, wonders and various miracles, and by gifts of the Holy Spirit distributed according to his will."* (Hebrews 2:1-4 NIV)

The word "disobedient" is used 13 times in the KJV Bible, twice in the Old Testament, and 11 times in the New Testament.

First, we start with a verse selection that does not actually use the word disobedient, but clearly shows how much God hates disobedience and requires all to be obedient.

*"18 "If any man has a **stubborn and rebellious son who will not obey his father or his mother,**

and when they discipline him, he will not even listen to them, 19 *then his father and mother shall seize him and bring him out to the elders of his city at the gateway of his hometown.* 20 *Then they shall say to the elders of his city, 'This son of ours is stubborn and rebellious; he will not listen to our voice; he is a glutton and a drunkard.'* 21 **Then all the men of his city shall stone him, and he will die; so you shall purge the evil from your midst,** *and all Israel will hear of it and fear.* 22 *"And if a man has committed a sin, the judgment of which is death, and he is put to death, and you hang him on a tree,* 23 *his corpse shall not hang all night on the tree, but you shall surely bury him on the same day (because cursed of God is he who is hanged), so that you do not make unclean your land which Yahweh your God gives you as an inheritance."* (Deuteronomy 21:18-23 LSB)

Yahweh, the Living God, the Almighty God, is not playing religious games. The disobedient will die!

Jeroboam was an evil king who promoted idol worship and appointed his own priests, who were not Levites. He made two golden calves (1 Kings 12:28) and placed them in the cities of Bethel and Dan, so people would worship these in his cities instead of going to the Temple in Jerusalem. He was worshipping the golden calf in Bethel by sacrificing to it on an altar he built. This story is so important that a large selection of Scriptures follow to give you the whole story.

"1 Now behold, **there came a man of God from Judah to Bethel by the word of Yahweh,** *while Jeroboam was standing by the altar to burn incense.* 2 **And he cried against the altar by the word of Yahweh,** *and said, "O altar, altar, thus says Yahweh, 'Behold, a son shall be born to the house of David, Josiah is his name; and on you he shall sacrifice the priests of the high places who burn incense on you, and human bones shall be burned on you.'"* 3 **Then he gave a miraculous sign the same day,** *saying, "This is the miraculous sign which Yahweh has spoken,* **'Behold, the altar shall be torn apart and the ashes which are on it shall be poured out.'"** 4 *Now it happened that* **when the king heard the word of the man of God,** *which he cried against the altar in Bethel,*

Jeroboam stretched out his hand from the altar, saying, "Seize him." But his hand which he stretched out against him dried up, so that he could not draw it back to himself. 5 The altar also was torn apart and the ashes were poured out from the altar, *according to the miraculous sign which the man of God had given by the word of Yahweh.* 6 ***Then the king answered and said to the man of God, "Please entreat Yahweh your God, and pray for me, that my hand may be restored to me." So the man of God entreated Yahweh, and the king's hand was restored to him,*** *and it became as it was before.* 7 ***Then the king said to the man of God, "Come home with me and refresh yourself, and I will give you a gift." 8 But the man of God said to the king, "If you were to give me half your house, I would not go with you, nor would I eat bread or drink water in this place. 9 For so it was commanded me by the word of Yahweh, saying, 'You shall eat no bread, nor drink water, nor return by the way which you came.'"*** *10 So he went another way and did not return by the way which he came to Bethel.* 11 ***Now an old prophet was living in Bethel;*** *and his sons came and recounted to him all the work which the man of God had done that day in Bethel; the words which he had spoken to the king, these also they recounted to their father. 12 And their father said to them, "Which way did he go?" And his sons had seen the way which the man of God who came from Judah had gone. 13 Then he said to his sons, "Saddle the donkey for me." So they saddled the donkey for him and he rode away on it.* 14 ***So he went after the man of God*** *and found him sitting under an oak; and he said to him, "Are you the man of God who came from Judah?" And he said, "I am."* 15 ***Then he said to him, "Come home with me and eat bread."*** *16 And he said, "I cannot return with you, nor go with you, nor will I eat bread or drink water with you in this place. 17 For a word came to me by the word of Yahweh, 'You shall eat no bread, nor drink water there; do not return by going the way which you came.'" 18 And he said to him, "I also am a prophet like you, and an angel spoke to me by the word of Yahweh, saying, 'Bring him back with you to your house, that he may* *eat bread and drink water.'" But he dealt falsely with him. 19 So he went back with him, and ate bread in his house and drank water.* 20 Now it happened as they were sitting down at the table, that the word of Yahweh came to the prophet who had brought him back; 21 and he called out to the man of God who came from Judah, saying, **"Thus says Yahweh, 'Because you have rebelled against the word of Yahweh, and have not kept the commandment which Yahweh your God commanded you, 22 but have returned and eaten bread and drunk water in the place of which He said to you, "Eat no bread and drink no water"; your body shall not come to the grave of your fathers.'"** 23 Now it happened after he had eaten bread and after he had drunk, that he saddled the donkey for him, for the prophet whom he had brought back. 24 **Then he went and on the way a lion met him and put him to death,** and his body was thrown on the road, with the donkey standing beside it; the lion also was standing beside the body. 25 And behold, men passed by and saw the body thrown on the road, and the lion standing beside the body; so they came and spoke about it in the city where the old prophet lived. 26 Then the prophet, who brought him back from the way, heard it and said, **"It is the man of God, who rebelled against the command of Yahweh;** therefore Yahweh has given him to the lion, which has mauled him and put him to death, according to the word of Yahweh which He spoke to him."" (1 Kings 13:1-26 LSB)

What a story! A good prophet does what God tells him, and his prophecy about the altar comes to pass. Then he even healed the evil king's hand when the king asked him to ask God to do so. The king asks the good prophet to come and eat with him as a way of thanking him for healing his hand. But the good prophet says God told him not to eat or drink but to go on his way. But, then a bad prophet asks the good prophet to eat and drink with him. The good prophet tells him God said not to. But then the bad prophet lied to the good prophet and said God told him that God had told him to feed the good prophet. He lied! But the good prophet believed him, was deceived, and went and ate. Then the lying prophet told the good prophet that God had now told him that the good prophet's body would not be buried with his fathers, as was the custom. And a lion killed the good but deceived prophet. To finish the story, the lying prophet buried the good prophet in the lying prophet's grave. So the word of the Lord came to be true.

Just how seriously does God take disobedience? Is being deceived an excuse to forgive the wrongs we have done?

This strong and eye-opening story above shows that being deceived is not a defense against sin. **God will not excuse us for being disobedient because we were deceived.**

The following is from the story starting in Nehemiah 2, where Artaxerxes was the king of Persia and Nehemiah was his trusted cupbearer. Artaxerxes allows Nehemiah to go to Jerusalem, his home city, to rebuild it. When the city was rebuilt, they had a gathering, and Ezra the priest opened the book of the law that had been lost and had it read to the people. Then some of the Levites reminded them how God had brought them from Egypt and given them the land of their enemies, but then let them be defeated and turned into slaves because they were disobedient.

> *"26 "But they became disobedient and rebelled against You, And cast Your law behind their backs And killed Your prophets who had testified to them So that they might return to You, And they committed great blasphemies. 27 Therefore You gave them into the hand of the ones who distressed them, and they afflicted them with distress, But at the time of their distress they cried to You, And You listened from heaven, and according to Your abundant compassion You gave them saviors and they saved them from the hand of the ones that distressed them. 28 But as soon as they had rest, they returned to do evil before You; Therefore You forsook them in the hand of their enemies, so they had dominion over them. Then they returned and cried to You. And You listened from heaven, And many times You delivered them according to Your compassion, 29 And testified to them in order to turn them back to Your law. Yet they acted presumptuously and did not listen to Your commandments but sinned against Your judgments, By which if a man does them, he shall live. And they gave a stubborn shoulder and stiffened their neck, and would not listen."*
> (Nehemiah 9:26-29 LSB)

In fact, the Law was made for disobedient people.

> *"5 But the goal of our command is love from a pure heart and a good conscience and an unhypocritical*

faith. 6 For some, straying from these things, have turned aside to fruitless discussion, 7 wanting to be teachers of the Law, even though they do not understand either what they are saying or the matters about which they make confident assertions. 8 ***But we know that the Law is good, if one uses it lawfully, 9 knowing this, that law is not made for a righteous person, but for those who are lawless and rebellious,*** *for the ungodly and sinners, for the unholy and godless, for those who kill their fathers or mothers, for murderers, 10 for sexually immoral persons, for homosexuals, for kidnappers, for liars, for perjurers, and whatever else is contrary to sound teaching,"* (1 Timothy 1:5-10 LSB)

So the Bible is clear: the condemnation of man will be for unbelief and disobedience.

When will the deceived and deluded be judged and condemned? God is absolutely just and fair. No one will be condemned without going to trial. Everyone will stand before the judge. This judge knows every single detail of our lives.

"3 ***The eyes of the Lord are in every place, beholding the evil and the good."*** (Proverbs 15:3)

"13 And there is no creature hidden from His sight, but all things are uncovered and laid bare to the eyes of Him to whom we have an account to give." (Hebrews 4:13 LSB)

"29 Are not two sparrows sold for a copper coin? And ***not one of them falls to the ground apart from your Father's will. 30 But the very hairs of your head are all numbered.*** *31 Do not fear therefore; you are of more value than many sparrows."* (Matthew 10:29-31 NKJV)

"1 O Yahweh, You have searched me and known me. 2 You know when I sit down and when I rise up; You understand my thought from afar. 3 You scrutinize my path and my lying down, And are intimately acquainted with all my ways. 4 Even before there is a word on my tongue, Behold, O Yahweh, You know it all." (Psalm 139:1-4 LSB)

> *"You keep track of all my sorrows. You have collected all my tears in your bottle. You have recorded each one in your book."* (Psalm 56:8 New Living Translation NLT)

> *"7 The angel of the Lord found Hagar near a spring in the desert; it was the spring that is beside the road to Shur. 8 And he said, "Hagar, slave of Sarai, where have you come from, and where are you going?" "I'm running away from my mistress Sarai," she answered. 9 Then the angel of the Lord told her, "Go back to your mistress and submit to her." 10 The angel added, "I will increase your descendants so much that they will be too numerous to count." 11 The angel of the Lord also said to her: "You are now pregnant and you will give birth to a son. You shall name him Ishmael,* **for the Lord has heard of your misery."** (Genesis 16:7-11 NIV)

> *"13 She gave this name to the Lord who spoke to her:* **"You are the God who sees me," for she said, "I have now seen the One who sees me."** (Genesis 16:13)

Every single good thing we have done, no matter how small, and every single bad thing we have done, no matter how small, is seen by God. Yahweh is called "El Roi," The God Who Sees. Our trial and our judgment will be extremely fair, and His judgment will be extremely just.

Judgment Day Is Coming

Throughout the entire Bible, both the Old and New Testaments, God repeatedly tells men that He has set a day of judgment on which all people will be judged. Following are just some of those verses.

The first one shows who the judge will be! Yahweh, The living God, has assigned that job of judgment to His Son, Yeshua, Jesus the Christ. It says we can be assured of this by the proof of His resurrection from the dead.

> *"29 Being then the offspring of God, we ought not to suppose that the Divine Nature is like gold or silver or stone, an image formed by the craft and thought of man. 30 Therefore having overlooked the times*

*of ignorance, God is now commanding men that everyone everywhere should repent, 31 **because He has fixed a day in which He will judge the world in righteousness through a Man whom He determined, having furnished proof to all by raising Him from the dead.***" (Acts 17:29-31 LSB)

*"22 For not even the Father judges anyone, but **He has given all judgment to the Son,** 23 so that all will honor the Son even as they honor the Father. He who does not honor the Son does not honor the Father who sent Him. 24 "Truly, truly, **I say to you, he who hears My word, and believes Him who sent Me, has eternal life, and does not come into judgment, but has passed out of death into life.**"* (John 5:22-24 LSB)

*"34 You brood of vipers, how can you, being evil, speak what is good? For the mouth speaks out of that which fills the heart. 35 The good man brings out of his good treasure what is good; and the evil man brings out of his evil treasure what is evil. 36 But I tell you that every careless word that people speak, **they shall give an accounting for it in the day of judgment.** 37 For by your words you will be justified, and by your words you will be condemned."* (Matthew 12:34-37 LSB)

*"44 And Jesus cried out and said, "He who believes in Me, does not believe in Me but in Him who sent Me. 45 And he who sees Me sees the One who sent Me. 46 I have come as Light into the world, so that everyone who believes in Me will not remain in darkness. 47 And if anyone hears My words and does not keep them, I do not judge him; for I did not come to judge the world, but to save the world. 48 He who rejects Me and does not receive My words, has one who judges him; **the word I spoke is what will judge him on the last day**."* (John 12:44-48)

*"10 **For we must all appear before the judgment seat of Christ;** that every one may receive the things done in his body, according to that he hath done, whether it be good or bad."* (2 Corinthians 5:10 ESV)

"11 For there is no partiality with God. 12 For all who have sinned without the Law will also perish without the Law, and all who have sinned under the Law will be judged by the Law. 13 For it is not the hearers of the Law who are just before God, but the doers of the Law will be justified. 14 For when Gentiles who do not have the Law naturally do the things of the Law, these, not having the Law, are a law to themselves, 15 in that they demonstrate the work of the Law written in their hearts, their conscience bearing witness and their thoughts alternately accusing or else defending them, 16 **on the day when, according to my gospel, God will judge the secrets of men through Christ Jesus."** (Romans 2:11-16 LSB)

"11 And I saw a great white throne, and him that sat on it, from whose face the earth and the heaven fled away; and there was found no place for them. 12 And I saw the dead, small and great, stand before God; and the books were opened: and another book was opened, which is the book of life: **and the dead were judged out of those things which were written in the books, according to their works.** 13 And the sea gave up the dead which were in it; and death and hell delivered up the dead which were in them: and they were judged every man according to their works." (Revelation 20:11-13)

"24 For Christ did not enter holy places made with hands, mere copies of the true ones, but into heaven itself, now to appear in the presence of God for us; 25 nor was it that He would offer Himself often, as the high priest enters the holy places year by year with blood that is not his own. 26 Otherwise, He would have needed to suffer often since the foundation of the world; but now once at the consummation of the ages He has been manifested to put away sin by the sacrifice of Himself. 27 And inasmuch as **it is appointed for men to die once and after this comes judgment,** 28 so Christ also, having been offered once to bear the sins of many, will appear a second time for salvation without reference to sin, to those who eagerly await Him." (Hebrews 9:24-28 LSB)

*"40 God raised Him up on the third day and granted that He appear, 41 not to all the people, but to witnesses who were chosen beforehand by God, that is, to us who ate and drank with Him after He arose from the dead. 42 And He commanded us to preach to the people, and solemnly to bear witness that **this is the One who has been designated by God as Judge of the living and the dead.**"* (Acts 10:40-42 LSB)

How to Not Be Deceived, Deluded, or Damned!

Before we consider what deceptions have misled the church, let's examine how we can break free of the deceptions we are trapped in. How can we stop deluding ourselves? How can we protect ourselves against being deceived and deluded in the future?

We must watch out! We must keep our eyes open!

"Watch and pray, that ye enter not into temptation: *the spirit indeed is willing, but the flesh is weak." (Matthew 26:41)*

Seek Him with all our heart!

*"11 For I know the plans that I have for you,' declares Yahweh, 'plans for peace and not for calamity, to give you a future and a hope. 12 Then you will call upon Me and come and pray to Me, and I will listen to you. 13 **You will seek Me and find Me when you search for Me with all your heart."** (Jeremiah 29:11-13 LSB)*

Keep our minds on Godly things. Do Godly things!

*"8 Finally, brothers, whatever is true, whatever is dignified, whatever is right, whatever is pure, whatever is lovely, whatever is commendable, if there is any excellence and if anything worthy of praise, consider these things. 9 **The things you have learned and received and heard and seen in me, practice these things, and the God of peace will be with you."** (Philippians 4:8-9 LSB)*

Search the Scriptures! While the following verse is spoken to unbelievers, the advice to search the Scriptures is certainly true for believers as well.

*"36 But the witness I have is greater than the witness of John; for the works which the Father has given Me to finish—the very works that I do—bear witness about Me, that the Father has sent Me. 37 And the Father who sent Me, He has borne witness about Me. You have neither heard His voice at any time nor seen His form. 38 And you do not have His word abiding in you, for you do not believe Him whom He sent. 39 **You search the Scriptures because you think that in them you have eternal life; it is these that bear witness about Me;** 40 and you are unwilling to come to Me so that you may have life." (John 5:36-40 LSB)*

Be a Berean, search the Scriptures daily, study, and pray.

*"10 And the brothers immediately sent Paul and Silas away by night **to Berea,** and when they arrived, they went into the synagogue of the Jews. 11 Now these were more noble-minded than those in Thessalonica, **for they received the word with great eagerness, examining the Scriptures daily to see whether these things were so.** 12 Therefore many of them believed, along with not a few prominent Greek women and men." (Acts 17:10-12 LSB)*

Rightly dividing (or accurately handling) the word of truth does not just happen while we sleep. We need to pray and study.

"15 Be diligent to present yourself approved to God, a worker who does not need to be ashamed, rightly dividing the word of truth." (2 Timothy 2:15 NKJV)

*"9 The coming of the lawless one will be in accordance with how Satan works. He will use all sorts of displays of power through signs and wonders that serve the lie, **10 and all the ways that wickedness deceives those who are perishing. They perish because they refused to love the truth** and so be saved. 11 For this reason God sends them a powerful delusion so **that they will believe the lie** 12 and so that all will be condemned **who have not believed the truth but have delighted in wickedness**." (2 Thessalonians 2:9-12 NIV)*

We must diligently seek the truth, love the truth, believe the truth, and live righteously, hating wickedness.

> *"11 And He Himself gave some as apostles, and some as prophets, and some as evangelists, and some as pastors and teachers, 12 for the equipping of the saints for the work of service, to the building up of the body of Christ, 13 until we all attain to the unity of the faith, and of the full knowledge of the Son of God, to a mature man, to the measure of the stature which belongs to the fullness of Christ, 14* **so that we are no longer to be children, tossed here and there by waves and carried about by every wind of doctrine, by the trickery of men, by craftiness in deceitful scheming,** *15 but speaking the truth in love, we are to grow up in all aspects into Him who is the head, that is Christ,,"* (Ephesians 4:11-15 LSB)

We must study to become perfect so that we are able to resist the "deceitful scheming" that evil entities use to try to deceive us.

Summary of Part I

So we have seen that people, including ourselves, are deceived and deluded about many things, and that we have to study the Word of God to see what He really says. We cannot trust tradition.

We have seen that people will be judged on their faithfulness and obedience.

We have seen the Bible make it clear that all humans will be judged and called to give an account to Yahweh, God the Father, of "every idle word." Happily, we can know and be sure that every little bit of good we have done will be taken into account.

> **"For whosoever shall give you a cup of water to drink in my name, because ye belong to Christ, verily I say unto you, he shall not lose his reward."** (Mark 9:41)

Sadly, we can know for sure that every little bit of bad we have done will also be taken into account.

We have seen that Yeshua, Jesus the Son of God, the Messiah, the Savior, has told Christians, His disciples, that they can be deceived, deluded, and damned.

And we have seen that He, Yeshua Hamashiach (in English, Jesus the Messiah), will be the judge on Judgment Day and that most people will be condemned.

Thank God, He has given us scriptures to help us discover our deceptions and break free of them.

PART II: Escaping the First Deception

Chapter 5: What Is the First Deception We Must Escape?

Will The Unrepentant Sinner Die?

Since we can be reasonably sure we are all deceived or deluded in some way, we need to study and pray to break free of all deceptions and delusions. But where do we start?

In my opinion, we should start at the very beginning of the Bible—the very beginning of mankind—in the book of Genesis. You all know this story. God created Adam and Eve, and then told them not to eat of the fruit of a certain tree. God said that if you eat it, you will die.

> *"17 but from the tree of the knowledge of good and evil, **you shall not eat from it; for in the day that you eat from it you will surely die.**" (Genesis 2:17 LSB)*

That is not that hard to understand. Then the old serpent, the devil, told Eve they would not die if they ate the fruit.

> *"4 And the serpent said to the woman, '**You surely will not die!** 5 For God knows that in the day you eat from it your eyes will be opened, and you will be like God, knowing good and evil.'" (Genesis 3:4-5 LSB)*

Think about that. We will examine these verses in depth later. They did eat the fruit. If God was telling the truth, that very day, they would lose the eternal life they were destined to receive. They would grow old and die.

If the devil was telling the truth, they would never die. Please try to put aside all the religious indoctrination you have been under and consider this. If you believe man has an immortal soul, spirit, or anything else, you are believing the devil, and you are calling the God of Glory a liar! If you think the first sin of mankind was to eat the forbidden fruit, consider this. Our actions are formulated by our thoughts. Adam and Eve sinned in thought first by not believing God. That led to them eating the fruit. We sin in thought first. The tenth commandment is about lusting and coveting in our thoughts and in our hearts. It is a sin, even if we do not act upon it.

This belief that man will not surely die is the very first deception of mankind. It then forces upon you the belief that unrepentant sinners will be tortured forever. Think how truly simple this is, how blatantly obvious it is, and how it is right in front of your face. Yet 95% of the Christian Church believes unrepentant sinners "shall not surely die," the very words from the mouth of Satan, the devil. 95% of the Christian Church **does not believe the only true God** who said, "You shall surely die."

It is hard not to go along with the crowd. It is hard to accept that we have been bamboozled, tricked, and deceived. And yet, the truth is just staring us in the face.

God says, "You will surely **die**."
Satan says, "You surely will **not** die."

If you believe the second statement, made by Satan, then you must believe the unrepentant sinner, the condemned, will be punished and tortured forever.

How Will the Condemned Be Punished?

This writing is for those who believe in the spiritual world and trust in the Bible as the truth. There are only two common outcomes that most Christians believe in for a sinner who dies. One is death. They believe the Bible says people dying in their sin, unrepented sin, will die. The other is eternal torture in a place called Hell. Which is it? Let's see what the Bible says.

Is the Sentence Death or Eternal Torture Forever?

Is the Sentence Eternal Torture?

Almost every human who believes in an afterlife believes in a place called Hell, where the condemned are tortured forever and ever. Dante's Inferno was published in 1314 A.D., and it describes the Nine Circles of Hell, each getting deeper and worse. The tortures there were depicted as lasting forever. This eternal torture in a horrendous place is how most Christians describe Hell, but it is Dante's hell, not God's.

This is why I am addressing a hell of eternal torture forever and ever as a false belief forced upon mankind by the first deception, "You will not surely die." It was the devil's first lie to mankind. Believing the devil was mankind's first sin. God told Adam and Eve they would die. The devil told them they would not die. This has made mankind imagine a place where they will live forever and ever, even though it is a place of fire and torment. Think of the picture this paints of Yahweh.

How can you love a person you think is horrible, cruel, mean, and unfair? How can you obey such a person? The answer to both questions is "you can't." You don't want to.

There is a science fiction movie named "Stargate." The main bad guys in the story are the Goa'uld. These very evil aliens lived in a feudal society as warlords. The most powerful warlord in an area had an army of slaves and a fleet of powerful spaceships. Their spaceships looked like the pyramids of Egypt, and they used the pyramids as landing docks. Their technology was so advanced and powerful that they demanded that their slaves call them gods. They would battle and wage wars with each other, trying to gain more power, more wealth, more slaves, more spaceships, etc. All these Goa'uld warlords were evil, and they killed people at will and even tortured people. Part of their technology was a device called a sarcophagus, which looked like an ancient Egyptian sarcophagus. It was a medical healing device of great power. If a person was shot or wounded, however grievously, if you opened the sarcophagus (left side of Figure 12.1) and placed them in it before they died, the sarcophagus would close (right side of Figure 12.1), stop the impending death, and heal them totally back to health.

Figure 5.1: Stargate Sarcophagus
Attribution: https://stargateresurgence.fandom.com/wiki/Sarcophagus
Creative Commons license CC BY-SA

But two of these evil warlords stand out as the very worst, hated by the other Goa'uld as the most evil of all.

Sokar was a powerful warlord who would slowly and painfully torture his captured enemies to the point of death, then place them in the sarcophagus and bring them back to health, only to torture them slowly again to the point of death and repeat the process over and over. Because of their technology, they never aged or died of old age. So Sokar tortured his captives over and over, forever and ever.

The other warlord captured the human hero, Jack O'Neill, and in order to extract secret military information, used this same technique of torturing him over and over forever and ever. His name was Ba'al. Sound familiar?

According to https://www.gotquestions.org/who-Baal.html, "Baal was the name of the supreme god worshiped in ancient Canaan and Phoenicia."

"Baal proved to be a highly adaptable god. Various locales emphasized one or another of his attributes and developed special "denominations" of Baalism. **Baal of Peor** (Numbers 25:3) and **Baal-Berith** (Judges 8:33) are two examples of such localized deities."

> *"11 Then the sons of Israel did what was evil in the eyes of Yahweh and served the **Baals**, 12 and they forsook Yahweh, the God of their fathers, who had brought them out of the land of Egypt, and followed other gods from among the gods of the peoples who were around them and bowed themselves down to them; thus they provoked Yahweh to anger. 13 So they forsook Yahweh and served **Baal** and the Ashtaroth."* (Judges 2:11-13 LSB)

Some use "Baalim" here. www.biblestudytools.com/dictionary/baalim/ "**Baalim** [N] [H] [S]: **plural of Baal;** images of the god Baal."

According to https://www.gotquestions.org/who-Baal.html, "In Matthew 12:27, Jesus calls Satan "Beelzebub," linking the devil to **Baal-Zebub**, a Philistine deity (2 Kings 1:2). The **Baal**im of the Old Testament were nothing more than demons masquerading as gods, and all idolatry is ultimately devil worship (1 Corinthians 10:20)."

So the creators of this movie series (and TV series) named this most evil of the evil ones after the devil himself.

I have recounted this part of the Stargate movies to a number of people. The invariable response is horror, and agreement that this is the most evil thing anyone could do. These were certainly the most evil of the most evil aliens!

A couple of people stopped short when they realized **this is exactly what they think Yahweh, the Living God, does,** keeps people alive just to torture them. Yahweh the good God, Yahweh the loving God, Yahweh the just God, Yahweh the merciful God—this is what they think He is capable of.

How can you love a god like that? How can you love an evil, mean, cruel, unfair, and unjust god?

If this is what you think of God, you do not know the God of the Bible!

To Love God, We Must Know God.

There are many Scriptures about God wanting us to know Him and the Messiah He sent to us.

*"3 **Know that Yahweh, He is God;** It is He who has made us, and not we ourselves; We are His people and the sheep of His pasture."* (Psalm 100:3 LSB)

*"3 **And by this we know that we have come to know Him, if we keep His commandments.**"* (1 John 2:3 LSB)

*"8 **The one who does not love does not know God, because God is love.**"* (1 John 4:8 LSB)

*"3 These things they will do **because they did not know the Father or Me**."* (John 16:3 LSB)

*"29 But Jesus answered and said to them, "You are mistaken, **not understanding the Scriptures nor the power of God.**"* (Matthew 22:29 LSB)

*"10 The fear of Yahweh is the beginning of wisdom, **And the knowledge of the Holy One is understanding**."* (Proverbs 9:10 LSB)

*"10 **that I may know Him and the power of His resurrection** and the fellowship of His sufferings, being conformed to His death,"* (Philippians 3:10 LSB)

*"10 so that you may walk in a manner worthy of the Lord, to please Him in all respects, bearing fruit in every good work **and multiplying in the full knowledge of God;**"* (Colossians 1:10 LSB)

*"17 that the God of our Lord Jesus Christ, the Father of glory, may give to you the Spirit of wisdom **and of revelation in the full knowledge of Him**,* (Ephesians 1:17 LSB)

*"4 **The one who says, "I have come to know Him," and does not keep His commandments, is a liar,** and the truth is not in him;"* (1 John 2:4 LSB)

*"20 And **we know that the Son of God has come,** and has given us understanding **so that we may know Him who is true**; and we are in Him who is true, in His Son Jesus Christ. This is the true God and eternal life."* (1 John 5:20 LSB)

> "8 However at that time, **when you did not know God,** you were slaves to those which by nature are no gods." (Galatians 4:8 LSB)

> "2 Grace and peace be multiplied to you **in the full knowledge of God and of Jesus our Lord**; (2 Peter 1:2 LSB)

> "60 **so that all the peoples of the earth may know that Yahweh is God;** there is no one else." (1 Kings 8:60 LSB)

> "18 but **grow in the grace and knowledge of our Lord and Savior Jesus Christ.** To Him be the glory, both now and to the day of eternity. Amen." (2 Peter 3:18 LSB)

> "5 Then you will understand the fear of Yahweh **And find the knowledge of God.**" (Proverbs 2:5 LSB)

> "1 Listen to the word of Yahweh, O sons of Israel, **For Yahweh has a contention against the inhabitants of the land, because there is no truth or lovingkindness Or knowledge of God in the land.**" (Hosea 4:1 LSB)

> "34 Become righteously sober-minded, and stop sinning; **for some have no knowledge of God. I speak this to your shame."** (1 Corinthians 15:34 LSB)

Finally, it is clearly stated that to gain eternal life, **we must know the only true God,** Yahweh, and His Messiah, Yeshua Hamashiach.

> "3 And this is eternal life, **that they may know You, the only true God, and Jesus Christ** whom You have sent." (John 17:3 LSB)

If you do not **know the God of the Bible**, then how can you worship and serve Him?

Are You Worshipping the Wrong God?

Imagine you had an acquaintance you thought was a friend. They called you a friend. They helped you sometimes and asked you for help sometimes. But one day you are called into court, and you find out this person has accused you of torturing people to the point of death, then reviving and healing them, then torturing them all over again. Even if these people were petty criminals, small-time thieves, and the like, no one deserves this punishment. This so-called friend says you hung them up in chains in your hidden torture chamber, over a fire that would not kill them quickly but very, very slowly.

What would you think? Is this person a true friend? Or would you think, "How can you even think such a horrible thing of me?" "Clearly, **you don't know me**; you never knew me." "And **I never knew you**." "Torturing people **never entered into my mind**." Well, that is exactly what God says!

> "22 Many will say to Me on that day, 'Lord, Lord, in Your name did we not prophesy, and in Your name cast out demons, and in Your name do many miracles?' 23 And **then I will declare to them, 'I never knew you; depart from Me, you who practice lawlessness.'** 24 "Therefore everyone who hears these words of Mine and does them, may be compared to a wise man who built his house on the rock." (Matthew 7:22-24 LSB)

Three English versions are below to give feeling to God's repulsion at the very idea of torture in fire.

> "35 And they built the high places of Baal that are in the valley of Ben-hinnom **to cause their sons and their daughters to pass through the fire to Molech, which I had not commanded them, nor had it come upon My heart that they should do this abomination,** to cause Judah to sin. " (Jeremiah 32:35 LSB)

> "35 They built high places for Baal in the Valley of Ben Hinnom to sacrifice their sons and daughters to Molek, though I never commanded—**nor did it enter my mind—that they should do such a detestable thing** and so make Judah sin." (Jeremiah 32:35 NIV)

> "35 They built the high places [for worship] of Baal in the Valley of Ben-Hinnom (son of Hinnom) **to make their sons and their daughters pass through the fire** to [worship and honor] Molech— which I had not commanded them **nor had it**

entered My mind that they should do this repulsive thing, to cause Judah to sin." (Jeremiah 32:35 AMP)

If you truly believe in your heart that Yahweh, the God of love, would torture humans in fire for eternity, you have been **deceived**! You don't know me, says God! You must break free of the first deception that the world and the devil have tricked you into believing.

If you don't know Him, you are praying to and worshipping someone else, a false, man-imagined god.

To worship Him in spirit and in truth, you must know him first.

Study the Bible diligently and get to know the real God, the Living God, the only true Eternal God, the Holy One of Israel!

Start worshipping and obeying the One True God.

How do you break free of this first great deception of mankind? As we explained above, study the Bible and pray, pray and study. Pray that God, the Almighty Father, the Living God, will guide you, open your eyes, and break you free of every deception you are under. Say His name! Yahweh! Pray to Him, Yahweh!

Is the Sentence Death?

What does the Bible say about what happens to humans when they die? The Bible says Yahweh loves us, the common people. The Bible says Yahweh is love.

*"16 "**For God so loved the world,** that He gave His only begotten Son, **that whoever believes in Him shall not perish, but have eternal life.** 17 For God did not send the Son into the world to judge the world, but that the world might be saved through Him." (John 3:16-17 LSB)*

*"7 Beloved, let us love one another, **for love is from God;** and everyone who loves has been born of God and knows God. 8 The one who does not love does not know God, **because God is love.**" (1 John 4:7-8 LSB)*

Consider a little preteen girl (above the age of reason) who never really got any Bible teaching or even heard of Yeshua (Jesus), who lived a normal life as a good kid, and who dies at a young age. Does it make any sense at all that Yahweh loves her, but based on her not accepting Him as her savior in those few years she lived past the age of reason, He will torture her eternally, for ever and ever, in a horrifying, terrifying existence? Does the punishment fit the crime for her? I am not asking if He will take her to His home in Heaven, or give her eternal life. But will Yahweh really take a normal, reasonably decent person who lived a reasonably good life and torture them for ever and ever, burning in fire continually, screaming in unfathomable pain, unable to die to end the agony?

You and I wouldn't do that to the most evil murderer. And all of us have enough not-so-nice vindictive vengeance in us to sentence an evil murderer to a really bad sentence. Clearly, Yahweh is better than us in mercy, grace, and love. Don't you believe Yahweh is good—really, really good? And don't you believe Yahweh is loving—very, very loving?

> *"17 And He said to him, "Why are you asking Me about what is good? **There is only One who is good;** but if you wish to enter into life, keep the commandments.""* (Matthew 19:17 LSB)

So if He won't save her, and that's a fair choice, and if He won't torture her forever, as some have been told the Bible says, then what will Yahweh do with her? What will He do with you and me if He doesn't save us?

We not-so-nice humans have some sense of fairness. Abraham bargained with Yahweh and proved that Yahweh is also fair. He is fair far beyond our ability to be fair.

> *"20 So Yahweh said, "The outcry of Sodom and Gomorrah is indeed great, and their sin is exceedingly grave. 21 I will go down now and see whether they have done entirely according to its outcry, which has come to Me; and if not, I will know." 22 Then the men turned away from there and went toward Sodom, while Abraham was still standing before Yahweh. 23 Then Abraham came near and said, "Will You indeed sweep away the righteous with the wicked? 24 Suppose there are fifty righteous within the city; will You indeed sweep it away and not spare the place for the sake of the fifty righteous who are in it? **25 Far be it from You to do such a thing, to put to death the righteous***

> **with the wicked,** *so that the righteous and the wicked are treated alike. Far be it from You!* **Shall not the Judge of all the earth do justice?**" *26 So Yahweh said, "If I find in Sodom fifty righteous within the city, then I will spare the whole place on their account." 27 And Abraham answered and said, "Now behold, I have ventured to speak to the Lord, although I am but dust and ashes. 28 Suppose the fifty righteous are lacking five, will You destroy the whole city because of five?" And He said, "I will not destroy it if I find forty-five there." 29 Then he spoke to Him yet again and said, "Suppose forty are found there?" And He said, "I will not do it on account of the forty." 30 Then he said, "Oh may the Lord not be angry, and I shall speak; suppose thirty are found there?" And He said, "I will not do it if I find thirty there." 31 And he said, "Now behold, I have ventured to speak to the Lord; suppose twenty are found there?" And He said, "I will not destroy it on account of the twenty." 32 Then he said, "Oh may the Lord not be angry, and I shall speak only this once; suppose ten are found there?" And He said,* "**I will not destroy it on account of the ten.**" *33 And as soon as He had finished speaking to Abraham, Yahweh departed, and Abraham returned to his place." (Genesis 18:20-33 LSB)*

"Shall not the Judge of all the earth do justice?" Abraham had a sense of fairness. And Abraham asked Yahweh outright, face-to-face, if the Most High God, the Judge of all the Earth, would do right. Would Yahweh be fair? And of course, Yahweh was fair.

Does the little girl mentioned above get tortured forever and ever? Is this fair? Would Abraham not bargain strongly for this little girl? "Shall not the Judge of all the earth do right?" The little girl did not hurt anybody, affected no one else, only lived for a few years, and was of the age of reason for only a few years. Will she receive torture forever as punishment? Really? Do you really believe Yahweh would do that? Does that sound even remotely fair? Does that sound at all like justice? Does that sound like love? Our God, the Living God, Yahweh, says this.

> *"24 But let justice roll on like a river, and righteousness like an ever-flowing stream." (Amos 5:24 Berean Study Bible BSB)*

Does that sound like Yahweh will not judge justly or fairly?

Why would the forces of evil deceive people about hell? Imagine the evangelist telling the unbeliever about God. He says, "Believe in our God; He is a merciful God, a patient God, a kind God, and a loving God." The unbeliever asks, "What if I don't believe in Him?" The evangelist says, "Then he will torture you with horrendous tortures, as you scream in pain, forever and ever and ever." Can't you almost hear the unbeliever say, "Thanks, but you can keep your 'loving' God." How many might have come to the real God if they had not been horrified at the mean and cruel god the "Christian" told them about? What harm has this done to the effort of evangelization?

People already know they are going to die. I believe the truth the Bible tells us is this: "Believe in our holy, loving, and good God, and He will give you eternal life." "What if I don't?" "Then you won't gain eternal life, and you will die." To which I think most people will say, "Fair enough. Tell me more about how to gain eternal life."

But we cannot base our understanding of Yahweh on our feelings, our emotions, or our understanding of justice. To know the truth, we must hear it from the mouth of Yahweh. The closest thing we have to that nowadays, short of personal revelation, is the Bible.

So what happens to the people who die in their sins, unconfessed, and have not accepted Yeshua Hamashiach, Jesus the Messiah, as their Savior? We will search both the Old Testament and the New Testament to get the entire Biblical teaching on the wages of sin.

What Is the Punishment for Sin?

The Wages of Sin Are Death!

Following are 35 verses where the Bible says the wages of sin are death. It does not say eternal torture forever and ever. God is not the author of confusion. Any confusion you have on the wages of sin is from man and traditions, not from Yahweh, The living God. Do you really think the Almighty and All-knowing God, cannot make such a simple idea clear? Do you think He wants people to be confused about the wages of sin? Read it for yourself. Don't try to hide the fact that you have been deceived and deluded. You have been tricked. Don't try to make far-fetched excuses for what God's clear words really mean because someone told you something different. "Oh, die and death means to be tortured forever and ever." Really? "Oh, to be destroyed with nothing left of them means to be tortured forever and ever." Really? Are you buying that? Read the words of the living God and believe Him. He is the good God. He is the loving God. He will grant many people eternal life if they believe and are obedient. The others die. He does not torture anyone. The English Standard Version just sounds clearer than the King James Version in some of these cases. Read them in whatever version you like best. They will have exactly the same meaning: **death**.

> "17 But of the tree of the knowledge of good and evil you shall not eat, for **in the day that you eat of it you shall surely die**." (Genesis 2:17 ESV)

Those words are directly from the mouth of God! If you sin, you die.

> "19 I call heaven and earth to witness against you today, that **I have set before you life and death,** blessing and curse. Therefore **choose life, that you and your offspring may live**," (Deuteronomy 30:19 ESV)

> "20 **But the wicked will perish**; the enemies of the Lord are like the glory of the pastures; **they vanish—like smoke they vanish away**." (Psalm 37:20 ESV)

> "14 Like sheep **they are appointed for Sheol; death shall be their shepherd,** and the upright shall rule over them in the morning. **Their form shall be consumed in Sheol**, with no place to dwell." (Psalm 49:14 ESV)

> "48 **What man can live and never see death? Who can deliver his soul from the power of Sheol**? Selah" (Psalm 89:48 ESV)

> "7 As when one plows and breaks up the earth, **so shall our bones be scattered at the mouth of Sheol**." (Psalm 141:7 ESV)

> "20 The Lord preserves all who love him, but **all the wicked he will destroy**." (Psalm 145:20 ESV)

> "12 There is a way that seems right to a man, **but its end is the way to death**." (Proverbs 14:12 ESV)

*"4 Behold, all souls are mine; the soul of the father as well as the soul of the son is mine: **the soul who sins shall die.**" (Ezekiel 18:4 ESV)*

*".13b . . shall he then live? **He shall not live.** He has done all these abominations; **he shall surely die;** his blood shall be upon himself." (Ezekiel 18:13b ESV)*

*"18 As for his father, because he practiced extortion, robbed his brother, and did what is not good among his people, behold, **he shall die for his iniquity**." (Ezekiel 18:18 ESV)*

*"20 **The soul who sins shall die**. The son shall not suffer for the iniquity of the father, nor the father suffer for the iniquity of the son. The righteousness of the righteous shall be upon himself, and the wickedness of the wicked shall be upon himself." (Ezekiel 18:20 ESV)*

*"23 **Have I any pleasure at all that the wicked should die**? Saith the Lord God: and not that he should return from his ways, and live?" (Ezekiel 18:23)*

*"26 When a righteous person turns away from his righteousness and does injustice, **he shall die for it; for the injustice that he has done he shall die.**" (Ezekiel 18:26 ESV)*

*"31 Cast away from you all the transgressions that you have committed, and make yourselves a new heart and a new spirit! **Why will you die,** O house of Israel? 32 For **I have no pleasure in the death of anyone, declares the Lord God; so turn, and live."** (Ezekiel 18:31-32 ESV)*

*"24 As for his father, because he practiced extortion, robbed his brother, and did what is not good among his people, behold, **he shall die for his iniquity**." (Ezekiel 21:24 ESV)*

*"14 **I shall ransom them from the power of Sheol; I shall redeem them from Death. O Death, where are your plagues? O Sheol, where is your***

sting? *Compassion is hidden from my eyes." (Hosea 13:14 ESV)*

"1 For behold, the day is coming, burning like an oven, ***when all the arrogant and all evildoers will be stubble. The day that is coming shall set them ablaze, says the Lord of hosts, so that it will leave them neither root nor branch."*** *(Malachi 4:1 ESV)*

"28 And ***do not fear those who kill the body but cannot kill the soul. Rather fear him who can destroy both soul and body in hell."*** *(Matthew 10:28 ESV)*

"3 No, I tell you; but ***unless you repent, you will all likewise perish.****" (Luke 13:3 ESV)*

"16 For God so loved the world, that he gave his only Son, that ***whoever believes in him should not perish*** *but have eternal life." (John 3:16 ESV)*

"12 Therefore, just as ***sin came into the world through one man, and death through sin,*** *and so death spread to all men because all sinned." (Romans 5:12 ESV)*

"21 So that, as ***sin reigned in death,*** *grace also might reign through righteousness leading to eternal life through Jesus Christ our Lord." (Romans 5:21 ESV)*

"16 Do you not know that if you present yourselves to anyone as obedient slaves, you are slaves of the one whom you obey, ***either of sin, which leads to death,*** *or of obedience, which leads to righteousness?" (Romans 6:16 ESV)*

"23 ***For the wages of sin is death,*** *but the free gift of God is eternal life in Christ Jesus our Lord." (Romans 6:23 ESV)*

"1 There is therefore now no condemnation for those who are in Christ Jesus. 2 For the law of the Spirit of life has set you free in Christ Jesus from ***the law of sin and death****." (Romans 8:1-2 ESV)*

> "22 For as **in Adam all die**, so also in Christ shall all be made alive." (1 Corinthians 15:22 ESV)

> "1 And **you were dead in the trespasses and sins**." (Ephesians 2:1 ESV)

> "9 **They will suffer the punishment of eternal destruction,** away from the presence of the Lord and from the glory of his might," (2 Thessalonians 1:9 ESV)

> "15 Then desire when it has conceived gives birth to sin, and **sin when it is fully grown brings forth death**." (James 1:15 ESV)

> "7 But by the same word the heavens and earth that now exist are stored up for fire, being kept until the day of **judgment and destruction of the ungodly.**" (2 Peter 3:7 ESV)

> "9 The Lord is not slow to fulfill his promise as some count slowness, but is patient toward you, **not wishing that any should perish,** but that all should reach repentance." (2 Peter 3:9 ESV)

> "17 All wrongdoing is sin, but **there is sin that does not lead to death**." (1 John 5:17 ESV)

If there is some sin that is forgivable and does not lead to death, all other sins lead to **death**.

> "14 Then Death and Hades were thrown into **the lake of fire. This is the second death**, the lake of fire." (Revelation 20:14 ESV)

> "8 But as for the cowardly, the faithless, the detestable, as for murderers, the sexually immoral, sorcerers, idolaters, and all liars, **their portion will be in the lake that burns with fire and sulfur, which is the second death.**" (Revelation 21:8 ESV)

Could God make it any clearer? The unrepentant sinner, the person who dies in their sin, dies not only the first physical death but also the death of the soul, the death of their entire being.

Chapter 6: Old Testament Hebrew for Soul and Spirit

Do Humans Have an Immortal Spirit or Soul?

If they are going to be tortured forever and ever, they must be immortal. This has made people believe in the immortal spirit of a human being, or the immortal soul. But what exactly does the Bible overwhelmingly say?

For unrepentant sinners who die in their sin, being tortured forever and ever requires that they be immortal. To be actively tortured for eternity, some part of the human being must survive. That would be an immortal part—not mortal and able to die, but unable to die.

Does the Bible say any part of a human immortal? Let's start our Bible search with the Old Testament.

When we are searching for Bible truth, often the best place to start is at the beginning. And that is exactly where the first problem with humans occurred. We have glanced at this before. God made a man, Adam, and a woman, Eve, and placed them in the beautiful Garden of Eden.

Yahweh, The Living God, gave humans one rule, one commandment.

> *"17 but from the tree of the knowledge of good and evil, **you shall not eat from it; for in the day that you eat from it you will surely die**." (Genesis 2:17 LSB)*

God was very clear. You eat, you die.

You all know the story. The old serpent, the devil, then told Eve they would not die if they ate the fruit but instead would become wise, knowing good and evil.

> *"4 And the serpent said to the woman, **"You surely will not die!** 5 For God knows that in the day you eat from it your eyes will be opened, and you will be like God, knowing good and evil.""* (Genesis 3:4-5 LSB)

So Eve ate some of the fruit and gave it to Adam, and he ate it. The Bible defines sin as the breaking of God's Law, so this was the first sin.

The Bible does not show the first of men to be troglodytes, or unintelligent brutish beasts, but fully thinking creatures. Nowhere is there a record of Adam and Eve saying to God the morning after they sinned, "Look, God. It's the next day, and we are still alive." Surely they realized this sentence of Yahweh was that the day, probably the moment, they ate the forbidden fruit, they had lost eternal life and would just live the physical bodily life, then they would die and return to the dust from which they were made.

> *"19 By the sweat of your face You will eat bread, Till you return to the ground, Because from it you were taken;* **For you are dust, And to dust you shall return."."** *(Genesis 3:19 LSB)*

Adam and Eve had lost the gift of eternal life for humankind. The Almighty God said they would not live but die. He explained His sentence on them, saying they would now have to work hard and sweat for their food and would end up dying, not living forever. The devil said they would not die but would live forever. Did Adam die?

> *"5 And all* **the days that Adam lived** *were nine hundred and thirty years:* **and he died**.*" (Genesis 5:5)*

What do almost all Christian churches teach today about dying? My experience is that they know from practical experience that all bodies will die; they cannot deny that, so they believe that a human's soul or spirit will live forever, either in the Kingdom of Heaven or in Hell. They teach that the essential part of humans will not die; only the body dies, and the essential part of you, your soul or spirit, will live forever.

Another Scripture selection that helps us make up our minds about what kind of death Yahweh is speaking of is in Ezekiel 18 below. Is God speaking of the physical death of the body or the death of our entire being— a final, non-reversible death?

> *"1 Then the word of Yahweh came to me, saying, 2 "What do you mean by using this proverb concerning the land of Israel, saying, 'The fathers eat the sour grapes, But the children's teeth are set on edge'? 3 As I live," declares Lord Yahweh, "you are surely not going to use this proverb in Israel anymore. 4* **Behold, all souls are Mine;** *the soul of the father as well as the soul of the son is Mine.* **The soul who sins will die.** *5 "But if a man is righteous and does justice and righteousness, 6 and does not eat at the mountain shrines or lift up his eyes to the idols of the house of Israel, or defile his neighbor's wife or approach a woman during her*

menstrual period— 7 if a man does not mistreat anyone, but returns to the debtor his pledge, does not commit robbery, but gives his bread to the hungry and covers the naked with clothing, 8 if he does not lend money on interest or take increase, if he turns his hand from injustice and does true justice between man and man, 9 **if he walks in My statutes and My judgments and is careful to do the truth—he is righteous and will surely live,"** *declares Lord Yahweh. 10 "Then he may have a violent son who sheds blood and who does any of these things to a brother 11 (though he himself did not do any of these things), that is, he even eats at the mountain shrines and defiles his neighbor's wife; 12 he mistreats the afflicted and needy, commits robbery, does not return a pledge, but lifts up his eyes to the idols and does abominations; 13 he lends money on interest and takes increase; will he live?* **He will not live!** *He has done all these abominations;* **he will surely be put to death; his blood will be on himself.** *14 "Now behold, he has a son who has seen all his father's sins which he has done. And he saw this but does not do likewise. 15 He does not eat at the mountain shrines or lift up his eyes to the idols of the house of Israel, or defile his neighbor's wife 16 or mistreat anyone, or retain a pledge or commit robbery, but he gives his bread to the hungry and covers the naked with clothing; 17 he turns his hand away from the afflicted, does not take interest or increase, but does My judgments and walks in My statutes;* **he will not die for his father's iniquity;** **he will surely live.** *18 As for his father, because he practiced extortion, robbed his brother, and did what was not good among his people, behold,* **he will die for his iniquity.** *19 "Yet you say, 'Why should the son not bear the punishment for the father's iniquity?' But the son has done justice and righteousness and has kept all My statutes and done them.* **He shall surely live.** *(Ezekiel 18:1-19 LSB)*

The verse selection above is important to us because it is another example of what God said to Adam and Eve in the Garden of Eden. Reading verse 13: "**He shall surely die;** his blood shall be upon him" reminds us that in Genesis 2, in the Garden of Eden, God told Adam and Eve, "**You surely will not die.**" We have already covered that it is impossible in the Genesis account that God is speaking of physical bodily death **because Adam and Eve do not die that day.** They lived many more years. Those who believe these verses to mean the physical, biological death of the body believe the devil, who said, "Ye shall not surely die."

God says, "In the day that thou eatest thereof, you will surely die." The devil says, "You surely will not die."

Adam lived for about 930 more years, having many sons and daughters, and then his biological body died. If God was talking about Adam's biological body, then God lied, and the devil told the truth because Adam did not physically die the same day he ate the forbidden fruit. If you believe in Yahweh, the Almighty God of the Bible, it is not possible that He lied. **God cannot lie.**

*"19 God is not a man, that He should lie, Nor a son of man, that He should repent; Has He said, and will He not do it? **Or has He spoken, and will He not establish it?**" (Numbers 23:19 LSB)*

So it was God who told the truth and the devil who lied, in that he said the opposite of what God said would happen. Therefore, if we believe the Almighty Eternal Creator of all things, we have proved that God was not talking about Adam and Eve's physical biological bodies.

Reading verse Ezekiel 18:13 above, we note it says, **"His blood will be upon himself**. This may seem like He is talking about the biological death of a flesh-and-blood body. But think more deeply about that. If we are very literal, it seems that God means the person will be cut open and his blood will pour all over him. Does this mean the person's liquid red blood will be all over him? Or, does it mean the fault will be his; the fault will be upon him? God says, I have warned you clearly. If you do this, you will die. If you do this, your death will be your own fault, not mine. How often, even in modern English, do we say or hear, "Hey, that's on you!" Don't people mean that's your fault; the consequences of your act are on you, not me? "Don't blame me for that."

So while verse 13 may, at first glance, indicate physical blood on a physical body, that does not truly fit well in the context of the entire chapter of Ezekiel 18.

Another proof that this is not talking about physical death is the hearer's own experience. Whether in ancient Israel or in the modern world, sinners do not die sooner than good people. Common people of every era have bemoaned that evil people get away with their evil and live fat, rich, and happy.

In fact, during the reign of King David, Asaph wrote Psalm 73.

*"1 **Surely God is good to Israel**, To those who are pure in heart! 2 But as for me, my feet had almost stumbled, My steps had almost slipped. 3 For I was envious of the boastful, **I saw the peace of the wicked. 4 For there are no pains in their death, And their body is fat. 5 They are not in trouble as other men, And they are not stricken along with the rest of mankind.** 6 Therefore lofty pride is their necklace; The garment of violence covers them. **7 Their eye bulges from fatness;** The delusions of their heart overflow. 8 They scoff and wickedly speak of oppression; They speak from on high. 9 They have set their mouth against the heavens, And their tongue goes through the earth. 10 Therefore his people return here, to his place, And waters of fullness are drunk by them. 11 They say, "How does God know? And is there knowledge with the Most High?" 12 **Behold, these are the wicked; And always at ease, they have increased in wealth.** 13 Surely in vain I have kept my heart pure And washed my hands in innocence; 14 For I have been stricken all day long And reproved every morning. 15 If I had said, "I will recount thus," Behold, I would have betrayed the generation of Your children. 16 When I gave thought to know this, It was trouble in my sight"* (Psalm 73:1-16 LSB)

Asaph was bemoaning that evil people seem to get away with their evil; they prosper and grow rich. Yes, now and then a bad person is jailed, but even in America today, very few criminals are executed. Yes, some are killed by others of their own kind in gang wars or by backstabbing. But it is common experience that sinners do not die before everybody else and that good people do not outlive everybody else. It just doesn't happen that way.

In fact, there is a song about it, "Only the Good Die Young" by Billy Joel.

With this being the reality of life, if God was talking about physical death for Adam and Eve in the Garden of Eden or for the Children of Israel through Ezekiel, then God was wrong. Can Yahweh, the Living God, the All-Knowing God, ever be wrong? Obviously, no! Let's read Numbers 23:19 again.

*"**19 God is not a man, that He should lie,** Nor a son of man, that He should repent; Has He said, and will He not do it? **Or has He spoken, and will He not establish it?**" (Numbers 23:19 LSB)*

Can you honestly believe that God meant only the physical body when He said sinners would die? If He does not, then He is talking about the death of a human, of the entire being. That means that humans are born without an immortal soul.

God said, "You will surely die." The devil said, "You surely will not die." You make up your own mind about who to believe—God, or the devil.

Being forced to acknowledge that bad and good men all die physically, yet wanting support for this belief (or hope) of living forever, mainline Christian churches imagine an immortal soul or spirit in humans that never dies. But did they learn that from the Bible?

What happens to humans who die in their unrepented sin depends on whether they have an immortal part or not. Let's see what the Bible really says about a human's soul or spirit.

One of the problems we will run into is the wide range of meanings for the words "soul and "spirit." So let's look at the modern English definition of spirit from the Merriam-Webster Dictionary.

https://www.merriam-webster.com/dictionary/spirit
SPIRIT noun
"Spir·it | \ ˈspir-ət \
Definition of "spirit" (Entry 1 of 2)
1: an animating or vital principle held to give life to physical organisms
2a: a supernatural being or essence, such as a capitalized Holy Spirit.
2b: Soul in the sense of 2a above.
2c: an often malevolent being that is bodiless but can become visible. Specifically: ghost as in sense 2.
2d: a malevolent being that enters and possesses a human being.
3: temper or disposition of mind or outlook, especially when vigorous or animated and in high spirits.
4: the immaterial, intelligent, or sentient part of a person
5a: the activating or essential principle influencing a person to act in a spirit of helpfulness
5b: an inclination, impulse, or tendency of a specified kind, mood
6a: a special attitude or frame of mind; "the money-making spirit was, for a time, driven back."

6b: the feeling, quality, or disposition characterizing something undertaken in a spirit of fun
7: a lively or brisk quality in a person or a person's actions
8: a person having a character or disposition of a specified nature
9: a mental disposition characterized by firmness or assertiveness, "denied the charge with spirit."
10a: Distillate, sense 1: such as
(1): the liquid containing ethanol and water that is distilled from an alcoholic liquid or mash (often used in plural)
(2): any of various volatile liquids obtained by distillation or cracking (as of petroleum, shale, or wood)—often used in plural
10b: a usually volatile organic solvent (such as an alcohol, ester, or hydrocarbon)
11a: prevailing tone or tendency, "spirit of the age."
11b: general intent or real meaning, "spirit of the law."
12: an alcoholic solution of a volatile substance, "spirit of camphor."
13: enthusiastic loyalty, "school spirit."
14 capitalized, Christian Science: God sense 1b"

Wow, you can see the many, many meanings attached to the word "spirit."

Also, we are quite familiar with meanings like "school spirit," "high spirits," "inclination," "mental disposition," and more of the like.

So what are we looking for? Our quest is to find out if any Scriptures definitively state that there is an immortal soul or spirit in a human from birth. If we find none, then we have our answer!

One definition of "spirit" is "soul," so "soul" and "spirit" are often used interchangeably. Because of this interchangeability, we will examine both the words "spirit" and "soul" in the Hebrew of the Old Testament and the Greek of the New Testament.

The Word Soul in the Hebrew Old Testament

Because the words "soul" and "spirit" are often used interchangeably, we are examining the Hebrew word for "soul."

The quest here is to see if any verse of Scripture in the Old Testament proves the existence of an immortal soul or spirit existing in a human from birth.

For understanding this word "soul" from Scripture, knowing the Hebrew word "nepes" may help clear up misunderstandings. It is often used with the word "living," so we will also look at the Hebrew word "Hay."

Hebrew: Soul

https://www.blueletterbible.org/lexicon/h5315/kjv/wlc/0-1/
Strong's H5315 - nep̄eš
נֶפֶשׁ
Part of Speech=feminine noun
Root Word (Etymology)
From נָפַשׁ (H5314)
KJV Translation Count—Total: 753x
"The KJV translates Strong's H5315 in the following manner: soul (475x), life (117x), person (29x), mind (15x), heart (15x), creature (9x), body (8x), himself (8x), yourselves (6x), dead (5x), will (4x), desire (4x), man (3x), themselves (3x), any (3x), appetite (2x), miscellaneous (47x)."

This word is used for animals and mankind and is the life force in them. **This is not an immortal spirit or soul.** Note from above that it is used a total of 753 times in the Bible and is translated as "**soul" 475 times,** as "**life" 117 times**, and as other things like person, mind, heart, creature, man, and more.

Strong's H2416 is also used with "nepes" or "nephesh" for the phrase "living creature."

Hebrew: Living

https://www.blueletterbible.org/lexicon/h2416/kjv/wlc/0-1/
Strong's H2416 - ḥay
חַי
Part of Speech = adjective, feminine noun, masculine noun
The KJV translates Strong's H2416 in the following manner: live (197x), life (144x), beast (76x), alive (31x), creature (15x), running (7x), living thing (6x), raw (6x), miscellaneous (19x).
Root Word (Etymology)
From חָיָה (H2421)
KJV Translation Count: Total: 501x
"The KJV translates Strong's H2421 in the following manner: live (153x), alive (34x), save (13x), quicken (14x), revive (12x), surely (10x), life (9x), recover (8x), miscellaneous (9x)."

The first time the word creature (or soul, being, or thing) is used in the Bible is in the very beginning, in Genesis 1:20. From Genesis 1:20-21 below, you can see **it is used of animals**.

> *"20 Then God said, "Let the waters swarm with swarms of living creatures, and let birds fly above the earth across the face of the expanse of the heavens." 21 And God created the great sea monsters and every **living creature** that moves,*

with which the waters swarmed after their kind, and every winged bird after its kind; and God saw that it was good." (Genesis 1:20-21 LSB)

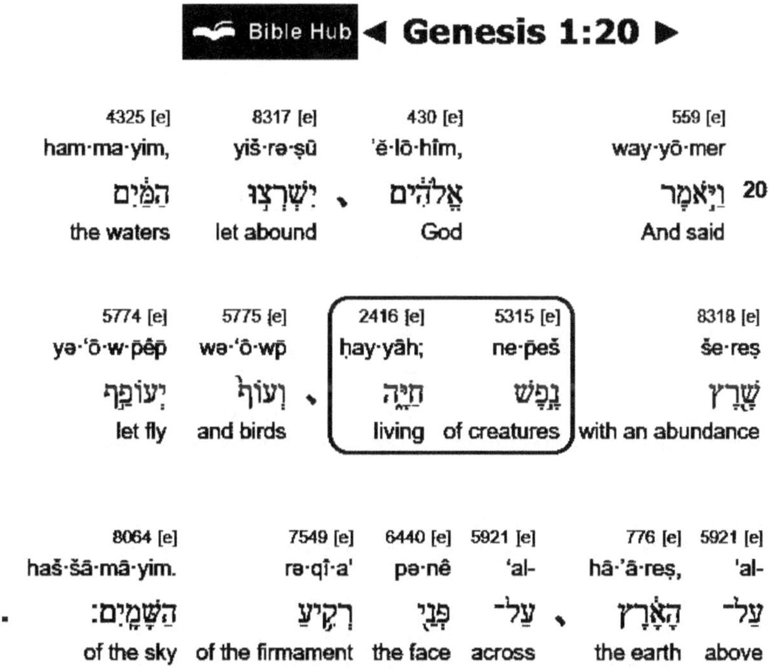

◀ Bible Hub ◀ Genesis 1:20 ▶

4325 [e]	8317 [e]	430 [e]	559 [e]
ham·ma·yim,	yiš·rə·ṣū	'ĕ·lō·hîm,	way·yō·mer
הַמַּיִם	יִשְׁרְצוּ ׀	אֱלֹהִים	וַיֹּאמֶר 20
the waters	let abound	God	And said

5774 [e]	5775 [e]	2416 [e]	5315 [e]	8318 [e]
yə·'ō·w·p̄êp̄	wə·'ō·wp̄	ḥay·yāh;	ne·p̄eš	še·reṣ
יְעוֹפֵף	וְעוֹף ׀	חַיָּה	נֶפֶשׁ	שֶׁרֶץ
let fly	and birds	living	of creatures	with an abundance

8064 [e]	7549 [e]	6440 [e]	5921 [e]	776 [e]	5921 [e]
haš·šā·mā·yim.	rə·qî·a'	pə·nê	'al-	hā·'ā·reṣ,	'al-
הַשָּׁמָיִם׃	רְקִיעַ	פְּנֵי	עַל־ ׀	הָאָרֶץ	עַל־
of the sky	of the firmament	the face	across	the earth	above

Figure 6.1: Genesis 1:20
[Courtesy of BibleHub.com and Apostolic Bible Polyglot Interlinear.]

◄ Genesis 1:21 ►

1254 [e]	430 [e]	853 [e]	8577 [e]	1419 [e]
way·yiḇ·rā	'ĕ·lō·hîm,	'eṯ-	hat·tan·nî·nim	hag·gə·ḏō·lîm;
וַיִּבְרָא 21	אֱלֹהִים	אֶת־	הַתַּנִּינִם	הַגְּדֹלִים
So created	God	-	sea creatures	great

853 [e]	3605 [e]	5315 [e]	2416 [e]	7430 [e]	834 [e]	8317 [e]
wə·'êṯ	kāl-	ne·p̄eš	ha·ḥay·yāh	hā·rō·me·śeṯ	'ă·šer	šā·rə·ṣū
וְאֵת	כָּל־	נֶפֶשׁ	הַחַיָּה ׀	הָרֹמֶשֶׂת	אֲשֶׁר	שָׁרְצוּ
and	every	thing	living	that moves	with which	abounded

4325 [e]	4327 [e]	853 [e]	3605 [e]	5775 [e]	3671 [e]
ham·ma·yim	lə·mî·nê·hem,	wə·'êṯ	kāl-	'ō·wp̄	kā·nāp̄
הַמַּיִם	לְמִינֵהֶם	וְאֵת	כָּל־	עוֹף	כָּנָף
the waters	according to their kinds	and	every	bird	winged

4327 [e]	7200 [e]	430 [e]	3588 [e]	2896 [e]
lə·mî·nê·hū,	way·yar	'ĕ·lō·hîm	kî-	ṭō·wḇ.
לְמִינֵהוּ	וַיַּרְא	אֱלֹהִים	כִּי־	טוֹב׃

Figure 6.2: Genesis 1:21
[Courtesy of BibleHub.com and Apostolic Bible Polyglot Interlinear.]

In Genesis 1:24, we see the word Strong's H2416 Hayyah used as a phrase with "nepes" or "nephesh" to mean **"living creature" or "living thing."**

> "24 Then God said, "Let the earth bring forth **living creatures** after their kind: cattle and creeping things and beasts of the earth after their kind"; and it was so." (Genesis 1:24 LSB)

Figure 6.3: Genesis 1:24
[Courtesy of BibleHub.com and Apostolic Bible Polyglot Interlinear.]

In Genesis 1:24 above, the same word "nepes" or "nephesh" is translated as soul when speaking of whales, other sea life, and winged fouls. In Genesis 2:7 below, it is also translated as soul when speaking of mankind. **It is clear that it is not an immortal soul or spirit.**

> *"7 And the Lord God formed man of the dust of the ground, and breathed into his nostrils the breath of life; and **man became a living soul.**"* (Genesis 2:7 KJV)

Comparing Genesis 2:7 from the KJV above with the NKJV below, note that the KJV uses the English word "soul," while the NKJV uses the English word "being."

> *"7 And the Lord God formed man of the dust of the ground, and breathed into his nostrils the breath of life; and man became a **living being.**"* (Genesis 2:7 NKJV)

Note that the first five Bible versions from BibleHub's Parallel Bibles have four different phrases for Genesis 2:7.

New International Version
"7 Then the LORD God formed a man from the dust of the ground and breathed into his nostrils the breath of life, and the man became a **living being.**" (Genesis 2:7 NIV)

New Living Translation
"7 Then the LORD God formed the man from the dust of the ground. He breathed the breath of life into the man's nostrils, and the man became a **living person.**" (Genesis 2:7 NLT)

English Standard Version
"7 Then the LORD God formed the man of dust from the ground and breathed into his nostrils the breath of life, and the man became a **living creature.**" (Genesis 2:7 ESV)

Berean Study Bible
"7 Then the LORD God formed man from the dust of the ground and breathed the breath of life into his nostrils, and the man became a **living being**." (Genesis 2:7 BSB)

King James Bible
"7 And the LORD God formed man of the dust of the ground, and breathed into his nostrils the breath of life; and man became a **living soul.**" (Genesis 2:7 KJV)

From the BibleHub.com Interlinear Bible, in the figure below, note the words that are circled. In Genesis 2:7, the words are Strong's H5315 and Strong's H2416. These are "Le nepes hayyah." Remember, Hebrew reads from right to left. The word "Le" translates to "a," so it is translated "a living being."

Genesis 2:7

6083 [e]	120 [e]	853 [e]	430 [e]	3068 [e]		3335 [e]
'ā·p̄ār	hā·'ā·ḏām,	'eṯ-	'ĕ·lō·hîm	Yah·weh		way·yî·ṣer
עָפָר֙	הָֽאָדָ֔ם	אֶת־	אֱלֹהִ֤ים	יְהוָ֨ה		וַיִּיצֶר֩ 7
[from] the dust	man	-	God	Yahweh		And formed

5397 [e]	639 [e]		5301 [e]	127 [e]	4480 [e]
niš·maṯ	bə·'ap·pāw		way·yip·paḥ	hā·'ă·ḏā·māh,	min-
נִשְׁמַ֣ת	בְּאַפָּ֖יו		וַיִּפַּ֥ח ׃	הָ֣אֲדָמָ֔ה	מִן־
the breath	into his nostrils		and breathed	the ground	of

2416 [e]	5315 [e]	120 [e]		1961 [e]	2416 [e]
ḥay·yāh.	lə·ne·p̄eš	hā·'ā·ḏām		way·hî	ḥay·yîm;
חַיָּֽה׃	לְנֶ֥פֶשׁ	הָֽאָדָ֖ם		וַֽיְהִ֥י —	חַיִּ֑ים
living	a being	the man		and became	of life

Figure 6.4: Genesis 2:7
[Courtesy of BibleHub.com and Apostolic Bible Polyglot Interlinear.]

Some consider the human "soul" to be different from the animal "soul" and different from the angel "soul." Compare Genesis 2:7 above, with Genesis 9:12 below. Their Hebrew wording is the same, but their English wording is different. In Genesis 9:12 below, hayyah nepes is translated "living creature."

> "12 Then God said, "This is the sign of the covenant which I am giving to be between Me and you and every **living creature** that is with you, for all successive generations;" (Genesis 9:12 LSB)

In the figure of Genesis 9:12 below, the same Hebrew words are used as in Genesis 2:7: H5351 and H2416.

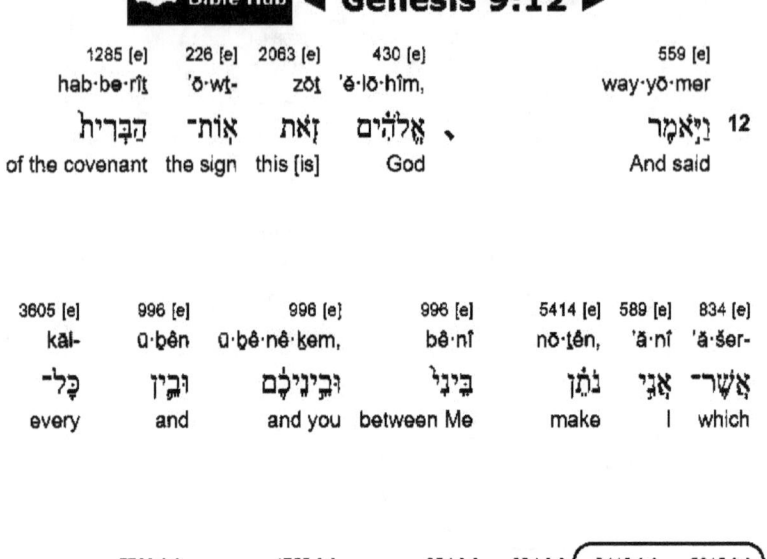

Figure 6.5: Genesis 9:12
[Courtesy of BibleHub.com and Apostolic Bible Polyglot Interlinear.]

So the same words, "hayyah nepes," are used for "living creature," "living person," "living being," and "living soul." There is no difference in meaning when the same words are used. Below, a Scripture with the same word, Strong's H5315 nephesh, shows this is the **life-force** leaving Rachel, as she died.

> *"17 Now it happened that when she was in severe labor the midwife said to her, "Do not fear, for now you have another son." 18 **Now it happened as her soul was departing (for she died),** that she named him Ben-oni; but his father called him Benjamin. 19 So Rachel died and was buried on the way to Ephrath (that is, Bethlehem)."* (Genesis 35:17-19 LSB)

As a result, the term "soul" does not refer to an "immortal soul or spirit," but rather to a "living creature." **Soul is used for animals and humans. It is the breath given by Yahweh that**

gives animals and men life. When it departs, it goes back to God, and the animal or human dies.

In the verses below, with the phrase "living creature," the same Hebrew words "hayyah nepes" are used.

> *"21 And God created the great sea monsters and every **living creature** that moves, with which the waters swarmed after their kind, and every winged bird after its kind; and God saw that it was good.."* (Genesis 1:21 LSB)

> *"24 Then God said, "Let the earth bring forth **living creatures** after their kind: cattle and creeping things and beasts of the earth after their kind"; and it was so."* (Genesis 1:24 LSB)

> *"19 And out of the ground Yahweh God had formed every beast of the field and every bird of the sky, and He brought each to the man to see what he would call it; and whatever the man called a **living creature**, that was its name."* (Genesis 2:19 LSB)

> *"10 and with every **living creature** that is with you, the birds, the cattle, and every beast of the earth with you; of all that comes out of the ark, even every beast of the earth."* (Genesis 9:10)

> *"12 Then God said, "This is the sign of the covenant which I am giving to be between Me and you and every **living creature** that is with you, for all successive generations;"* (Genesis 9:12 LSB)

> *"15 and I will remember My covenant, which is between Me and you and every **living creature** of all flesh; and never again shall the water become a flood to destroy all flesh."* (Genesis 9:15 LSB)

Below, God is speaking of The Day of Atonement being a Holy Day and a Sabbath, and no one can do work. He says a soul can work and a soul can be destroyed. Both occurrences of the word "soul' below are translated from Strong's H5315 nephesh.

> *"30 And **whatsoever soul it be that doeth any work** in that same day, **the same soul will I destroy** from among his people."* (Leviticus 23:30)

If a soul can do physical work, it is not a spirit. If the soul can be destroyed, it is not an immortal soul. Can a physical sword be any threat to an immortal soul or spirit? No!

> **"20 Deliver my soul from the sword,** My only life from the power of the dog." (Psalm 22:20 LSB)

King David did not regard his "soul" as an immortal spirit or soul.

Below, the New Revised Standard Version shows more detail than the LSB, so both are shown. Remember, the same root word, Strong's H5315 nephesh, is used for soul 475 times and for life 117 times, so in Hebrew it is the same as "takes the soul" of that person."

> "11 But if someone at enmity with another lies in wait and attacks and **takes the life of that person** and flees into one of these cities, 12 then the elders of the killer's city shall send to have the culprit taken from there and handed over to the avenger of blood to be put to death.' (Deuteronomy 19:11-12 NRSVUE New Revised Standard Version Updated Edition)

> "11 "But if there is a man who hates his neighbor and lies in wait for him and rises up against him **and strikes down his life so that he dies,** and he flees to one of these cities, 12 then the elders of his city shall send and take him from there and give him over into the hand of the avenger of blood, that he may die." (Deuteronomy 19:11-12 LSB)

So if a man can take another person's soul by killing it, it is not an immortal soul or spirit.

In Deuteronomy 12:20 below, "soul" is used twice, saying the "soul" would desire to eat meat. Both words are from Strong's H5315 nephesh.

> "20 When Yahweh your God enlarges your border, as he has promised you, and you say, "I want to eat meat," because **your soul desires to eat meat,** you may eat meat, after **all the desire of your soul."** (Deuteronomy 12:20 WEB)

Because the soul craves savory meat, it cannot be an immortal spirit.

Ecclesiastes 6:7 speaks of a man wanting to satisfy his appetites, particularly his mouth or belly. The KJV just says "appetite" when the word is again from Strong's H5315 nephesh for "soul."

King James Version
*"7 All the labour of man is for his mouth, and yet the **appetite is not filled.***" (Ecclesiastes 6:7 **KJV**)

New King James Version
*"7 All the labor of man **is for his mouth**, and yet the **soul is not satisfied**.*" (Ecclesiastes 6:7 **NKJV**)

Young's Literal Translation
*"7 All the labour of man **is for his mouth**, and yet the **soul is not filled**.*" (Ecclesiastes 6:7 **YLT**)

For the soul to be satisfied by physical food, it cannot be an immortal spirit.

See Leviticus 17:11 from BibleHub.com's excellent Interliner Bible.

◀ Leviticus 17:11 ▶

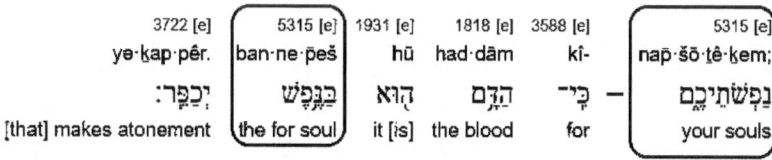

Figure 6.6: Leviticus 17:11
[Courtesy of BibleHub.com and Apostolic Bible Polyglot Interlinear.]

Note that the word Strong's H5315 Nephesh is first translated as "life," then twice as "soul." Does an immortal spirit or soul need to eat physical food? Obviously not, for that would mean it could die of starvation. Can an angel starve to death? Obviously, they cannot, for angels do not need to eat physical food. Below is a verse that says the soul must eat, **showing beyond the shadow of a doubt that the human soul is not immortal.** The verse below speaks of the Passover Holy day, and says that you must not work on this Holy Day, except for preparing the food you need to eat. The word "man" is again Strong's H5315 nephesh, which means soul.

*"16 Now on the first day there shall be a holy convocation, and on the seventh day there shall be a holy convocation for you; no work at all shall be done on them, **except what must be eaten by every person**, that alone may be done by you."* (Exodus 12:16 LSB)

◀ Bible Hub ◀ **Exodus 12:16** ▶

6944 [e]	4744 [e]	7223 [e]	3117 [e]
qō·ḏeš,	miq·rā-	hā·ri·šō·wn	ū·ḇay·yō·wm
קֹדֶשׁ	מִקְרָא־	הָרִאשׁוֹן	וּבַיּוֹם 16
holy	[there shall be] a convocation	first	And On the day

	1961 [e]	6944 [e]	4744 [e]	7637 [e]	3117 [e]
lā·ḵem;	yih·yeh	qō·ḏeš	miq·rā-	haš·šə·ḇî·'î,	ū·ḇay·yō·wm
לָכֶם ׃	יִהְיֶה	קֹדֶשׁ	מִקְרָא־	הַשְּׁבִיעִי	וּבַיּוֹם
for you	there shall be	holy	a convocation	seventh	and on the day

834 [e]	389 [e]		6213 [e]	3808 [e]	4399 [e]	3605 [e]
'ă·šer	'aḵ	bā·hem,	yê·'ā·śeh	lō-	mə·lā·ḵāh	kāl-
אֲשֶׁר	אַךְ ׃	בָּהֶם	יֵעָשֶׂה	לֹא־	מְלָאכָה	כָּל־
[that] which	but	on them	shall be done	No	of work	manner

6213 [e]	905 [e]	1931 [e]	5315 [e]	3605 [e]	398 [e]
yê·'ā·śeh	lə·ḇad·dōw	hū	ne·p̄eš,	lə·ḵāl	yê·'ā·ḵêl
יֵעָשֶׂה	לְבַדּוֹ	הוּא ׃	נֶפֶשׁ	לְכָל־	יֵאָכֵל
may be prepared	only	that	person	every	must eat

Figure 6.7: Exodus 12:16
[Courtesy of BibleHub.com and Apostolic Bible Polyglot Interlinear.]

So the human soul, "nepes" or "nephesh," "must eat." This is most emphatically not an immortal soul!

In the following verse from Job, speaking of people being chastised by God, they get so sick they do not even want to eat food. The word translated "soul" is again a form of Strong's H5315 nephesh.

> "19 "Man is also reproved with pain on his bed, And with unceasing contention in his bones, 20 So that his life loathes bread, **And his soul favorite food."** (Job 33:19-20 LSB)

If the soul has favorite foods, it is obviously not an immortal soul or spirit.

Numbers 6:6 below shows the nephesh, or soul, can die, for it talks of those who would separate themselves from a worldly life and could not touch a dead body, or soul. Note that Strong's H5315 nephesh is translated as body here.

> "'Throughout the period of their dedication to the LORD, the Nazirite must not go near a dead **body**." (Numbers 6:6 NIV)

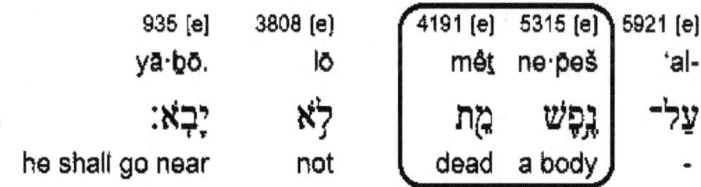

Figure 6.8: Numbers 6:6
[Courtesy of BibleHub.com and Apostolic Bible Polyglot Interlinear.]

There are probably hundreds more examples in the Bible of how the authors of the Scriptures did not think man's soul was either spiritual or immortal.

We have seen beyond the shadow of a doubt that the words "Hayyah Nepes" or other phrases based on "nephesh" do not mean immortal soul or spirit.

Let us now consider another word that some believe means immortal soul or spirit.

Is it true that man has an immortal soul or spirit, according to the Bible?

Some believe that when Yahweh made man, He breathed into him an immortal soul or spirit. But what the Bible says is that He breathed into them "the breath of life."

> *"7 Yahweh God formed man from the dust of the ground, and breathed into his nostrils the **breath of life;** and man became **a living soul.**"* (Genesis 2:7 WEB)

In the section above, we saw the translation of that word as soul, being, or creature, and it is used of both men and animals. So let's look now at the Hebrew word for spirit.

Hebrew: Spirit

From Strong's Exhaustive Concordance:
"Strong's H7307 - rûaḥ חרו
Transliteration rûaḥ"
"The KJV translates Strong's H7307 in the following manner: Spirit or spirit (232x), wind (92x), breath (27x), side (6x), mind (5x), blast (4x), vain (2x), air (1x), anger (1x), cool (1x), courage (1x), miscellaneous (6x)."

The word "spirit" is used in the Old Testament 236 times. We will not examine all those occurrences, but those that show the different usages.

The very first occurrence of the word "spirit" in the Old Testament is in Genesis 1:2. It is referring to the "Spirit of God." Using one of my favorite Bible study tools, BibleHub.com's Interlinear Bible, we see the Hebrew word "ruah," Strong's H7303. It is used to mean a non-corporeal, non-physical being, but also the "breath" of life, as in animals.

6440 [e]	5921 [e]	2822 [e]	922 [e]	8414 [e]	1961 [e]	776 [e]
pe·nê	'al-	we·ḥō·šek	wā·ḇō·hū,	ṯō·hū	hā·ye·ṯāh	we·hā·'ā·reṣ,
פְנֵי	עַל־	וְחֹשֶׁךְ	וָבֹהוּ	תֹהוּ	הָיְתָה	וְהָאָרֶץ 2
the face	[was] over	and darkness	and void	formless	was	And the earth

		4325 [e]	6440 [e]	5921 [e]	7363 [e]	430 [e]	7307 [e]	8415 [e]
		ham·mā·yim.	pe·nê	'al-	me·ra·ḥe·p̄eṯ	'ĕ·lō·hîm,	we·rū·aḥ	ṯe·hō·wm;
.		הַמָּיִם׃	פְנֵי	עַל־	מְרַחֶפֶת	אֱלֹהִים	וְרוּחַ	תְהוֹם
		of the waters	the face	over	was hovering	of God	And the Spirit	of the deep

Figure 6.9: Genesis 1:2
[Courtesy of BibleHub.com and Apostolic Bible Polyglot Interlinear.]

The second occurrence of the word "spirit" is in Genesis 6:3, and it is used in the same way, as God being a non-material being.

> "3 Then Yahweh said, **"My Spirit shall not strive with man** forever because he indeed is flesh; nevertheless his days shall be 120 years.""
> (Genesis 6:3 LSB)

However, it is not the Spirit of God we are studying but whether there is an immortal soul or spirit in mankind when he is born. So, we will now only look at the word "spirit" when used for humankind.

The third occurrence of the word spirit is in Genesis 41:8, where it speaks of the spirit of Pharaoh being troubled by dreams. The same Hebrew word, H7307, is used.

> "8 And it came to pass in the morning that **his spirit was troubled;** and he sent and called for all the magicians of Egypt, and all the wise men thereof: and Pharaoh told them his dream; but there was none that could interpret them unto Pharaoh."
> (Genesis 41:8)

The meaning here is the same as being troubled in your heart or mind. Note above that "mind" is one of the meanings Strong's gives for this word. Nothing in the text suggests that Pharaoh has an immortal soul or spirit.

The fourth occurrence of spirit is in Genesis 41:38, where Pharaoh is praising Joseph for interpreting his dream. Pharaoh says the "Spirit of God" is in Joseph and is declaring that as unusual. Yeshua did the same when He stated that many are called, but few are chosen, and in response to the question, "Lord, are there few that will be saved?"

> *"23 And someone said to Him, "Lord, are there **just a few who are being saved?**" And He said to them, 24 "Strive to enter through the narrow door, for many, I tell you, will seek to enter and **will not be able.**"* (Luke 13:23-24 LSB)

> *"38 And Pharaoh said unto his servants, Can we find such a one as this is, a man **in whom the Spirit of God is**?"* (Genesis 41:38)

So while God gives a part of His Spirit to men for certain purposes, this verse itself makes it clear that this is unusual, so this cannot be scriptural proof that all of humankind innately possesses an immortal soul or spirit before they are "born-again" and receive the Holy Spirit of God.

Often, when we see the "spirit" in man spoken of in the Bible, it is the Spirit of God that has been placed in an individual.

> *"16 Yahweh said to Moses, "Gather to me seventy men of the elders of Israel, whom you know to be the elders of the people and officers over them; and bring them to the Tent of Meeting, that they may stand there with you. 17 I will come down and talk with you there. **I will take of the Spirit which is on you, and will put it on them;** and they shall bear the burden of the people with you, that you don't bear it yourself alone."* (Numbers 11:16-17 WEB)

> *"24 Moses went out, and told the people Yahweh's words; and he gathered seventy men of the elders of the people, and set them around the Tent. 25 **Yahweh came down** in the cloud, and spoke to him, **and took of the Spirit that was on him**, and **put it on the seventy elders.** When the Spirit rested on them, they prophesied, but they did so no more."* (Numbers 11:24-25 WEB)

Yahweh took some of the "spirit" He had given Moses, perhaps the spirit of wisdom and good judgment, and put some of it on the 70 elders so they could help Moses judge the people.

God puts some of His spirit in certain people to do certain jobs.

> *"1 And Yahweh spoke to Moses, saying, 2 "See, I have called by name Bezalel, the son of Uri, the son of Hur, of the tribe of Judah. 3 And **I have filled him with the Spirit of God** in wisdom, in discernment, in knowledge, and in all kinds of craftsmanship, 4 to devise artistic designs for work in gold, in silver, and in bronze, 5 and in the cutting of stones for settings, and in the carving of wood, in order for him to work in all kinds of craftsmanship."*
> (Exodus 31:1-5 LSB)

The verses above and below show that God imparts a part of His spirit, similar to the breath of life He gives even to animals, to some people to finish a task for Him. He gives special knowledge, talent, and innate understanding to some people for the good of mankind.

> *"30 Then Moses said to the sons of Israel, "See, Yahweh has called by name Bezalel the son of Uri, the son of Hur, of the tribe of Judah. 31 And **He has filled him with the Spirit of God,** in wisdom, in discernment, and in knowledge, and in all craftsmanship; 32 to devise designs for working in gold and in silver and in bronze, 33 and in the cutting of stones for settings and in the carving of wood, so as to do well in every work of thoughtful design. 34 He also has put in his heart to teach, both he and Oholiab, the son of Ahisamach, of the tribe of Dan. 35 He has filled them with wisdom in their heart to do every work of an engraver and of a designer and of an embroiderer, in blue and in purple and in scarlet material and in fine linen, and of a weaver, as those who do every work and make designs."* (Exodus 35:30-35 LSB)

> *"15 Then Moses spoke to the Lord, saying, 16 "May the Lord, **the God of the spirits of all flesh**, appoint a man over the congregation, 17 who will go out and come in before them, and who will lead them out and bring them in, so that the congregation of the Lord will not be like sheep which have no shepherd." 18 So the Lord said to Moses, **"Take Joshua the son of Nun, a man in whom is the Spirit,** and lay your hand on him; 19 and have him stand before Eleazar the priest and before all the congregation, and commission him in*

their sight. 20 You shall put some of your authority on him, in order that all the congregation of the sons of Israel may obey him." (Numbers 27:15-20 NASB1995)

*"9 Then the sons of Israel cried to Yahweh, and Yahweh raised up a savior for the sons of Israel to save them, Othniel the son of Kenaz, Caleb's younger brother. 10 **And the Spirit of Yahweh came upon him,** and he judged Israel. And he went out to war, and Yahweh gave Cushan-rishathaim king of Mesopotamia into his hand. So his hand was strong against Cushan-rishathaim. 11 Then the land was quiet for forty years. And Othniel the son of Kenaz died."* (Judges 3:9-11 LSB)

*"30 However, You bore with them for many years, And testified to them **by Your Spirit by the hand of Your prophets,** Yet they would not give ear. So You gave them into the hand of the peoples of the lands."* (Nehemiah 9:30 LSB)

*"1 Then Job continued to lift up his discourse and said, 2 "As God lives, who has removed my justice, And the Almighty, who has embittered my soul, 3 **For as long as breath is in me, And the spirit from God is in my nostrils,** 4 My lips certainly will not speak unrighteousness, Nor will my tongue utter deceit."* (Job 27:1-4 LSB)

The Midianites and Amalekites were preparing to attack Israel, so God put some of His Spirit on Gideon to make him a leader of Israel.

*"33 Then all the Midianites and the Amalekites and the children of the east assembled themselves together; and they passed over, and encamped in the valley of Jezreel. 34 But **Yahweh's Spirit came on Gideon,** and he blew a trumpet; and Abiezer was gathered together to follow him. 35 He sent messengers throughout all Manasseh, and they also were gathered together to follow him. He sent messengers to Asher, and to Zebulun, and to Naphtali; and they came up to meet them."* (Judges 6:33-35 WEB)

> *Judges chapters 6 and 7 are very exciting reading, so when you are looking for an encouraging reading time, read the story of Gideon in Judges 6 and 7.*

> *"28 But the king of the sons of Ammon did not listen to the words which Jephthah sent him. 29 Now **the Spirit of Yahweh came upon Jephthah**, so that he passed through Gilead and Manasseh; then he passed through Mizpah of Gilead, and from Mizpah of Gilead he went on to the sons of Ammon."* (Judges 11:28-29 LSB)

The story of Samson is an interesting part of the Bible to read through for excitement, valor, deceit, betrayal, and final victory! It is another good example of how Yahweh, the Living God, can place His spirit on people for a certain task or purpose but then remove it at will. As with the other verses above and below, this use of "spirit" does not indicate an immortal soul or spirit in mankind from birth.

> *"24 Then the woman gave birth to a son and named him Samson; and the child grew up, and Yahweh blessed him. 25 And **the Spirit of Yahweh began to stir him** in Mahaneh-dan, between Zorah and Eshtaol."* (Judges 13:24-25 LSB)

> *"5 Then Samson went down to Timnah with his father and mother, and they came as far as the vineyards of Timnah; and behold, a young lion came roaring toward him. 6 **And the Spirit of Yahweh came upon him mightily,** so that he tore it as one tears a young goat, though he had nothing in his hand; but he did not tell his father or mother what he had done.* (Judges 14:5-6 LSB)

> *"19 Then **the Spirit of Yahweh came upon him** mightily, and he went down to Ashkelon and struck down thirty of them and took their spoil and gave the changes of clothes to those who told the riddle. And his anger burned, and he went up to his father's house. 20 But Samson's wife was given to his companion who had been his friend."* (Judges 14:19-20 LSB)

> *"14 When he came to Lehi, the Philistines shouted as they met him. And **the Spirit of Yahweh came upon him** mightily so that the ropes that were on*

his arms were as flax that is burned with fire, and his bonds dropped from his hands. 15 And he found a fresh jawbone of a donkey, so he sent forth his hand and took it and struck down 1,000 men with it. 16 Then Samson said, "With the jawbone of a donkey, Heaps upon heaps, With the jawbone of a donkey I have struck down 1,000 men."" (Judges 15:14-16 LSB)

Below, Samuel tells Saul that God will put His Spirit on him and make him king.

*"6 Then **the Spirit of Yahweh will come upon you mightily**, and you shall prophesy with them and be changed into another man. 7 Now it will be when these signs come to you, do for yourself whatever your hand finds to do, for God is with you."* (1 Samuel 10:6-7 LSB)

Note that in the verse above, Saul receives the Spirit of God, but later, after disobedience, God withdraws His Holy Spirit from Saul and places it on David.

*"13 Then Samuel took the horn of oil and anointed him in the midst of his brothers; and **the Spirit of Yahweh came mightily upon David from that day forward**. And Samuel arose and went to Ramah. 14 Now **the Spirit of Yahweh departed from Saul,** and an evil spirit from Yahweh terrorized him."* (1 Samuel 16:13-14 LSB)

King Belshazzar, king of Babylonia and son of King Nebuchadnezzar, was having a party, and a spiritual hand appeared and wrote words on the wall. No one could interpret them, and the king became despondent. But the queen then reminded him of Daniel, who could interpret dreams. So she tells Belteshazzar the following:

*"11 There is a man in your kingdom **in whom is a spirit of the holy gods;** and in the days of your father, illumination, insight, and wisdom like the wisdom of the gods were found in him. And King Nebuchadnezzar, your father, your father the king, set him as chief of the magicians, conjurers, Chaldeans, and diviners. 12 **This was because an extraordinary spirit, knowledge and insight, interpretation of dreams, explanation of***

> **enigmas, and solving of difficult problems were found in this Daniel,** *whom the king named Belteshazzar. Let Daniel now be summoned, and he will declare the interpretation.""* (Daniel 5:11-12 LSB)

Yahweh poured out His Spirit on men to be leaders, warriors, artisans, or whatever was needed for the good of the people.

> *"1 Now **the Spirit of God came on Azariah** the son of Oded, 2 and he went out to meet Asa and said to him, "Listen to me, Asa, and all Judah and Benjamin: Yahweh is with you when you are with Him. And if you seek Him, He will be found; but if you forsake Him, He will forsake you."* (2 Chronicles 15:1-2 LSB)

> *"10 So now, behold, the sons of Ammon and Moab and Mount Seir, whom You did not let Israel invade when they came out of the land of Egypt (they turned aside from them and did not destroy them), 11 and behold, they are rewarding us by coming to drive us out from Your possession which You have caused us to possess. 12 O our God, will You not judge them? For we are powerless before this great multitude who are coming against us; and we do not know what we should do, but our eyes are on You." 13 Now all Judah was standing before Yahweh, with their little ones, their wives, and their children. 14 Then in the midst of the assembly **the Spirit of Yahweh came upon Jahaziel** the son of Zechariah, the son of Benaiah, the son of Jeiel, the son of Mattaniah, the Levite of the sons of Asaph; 15 and he said, "Pay attention, all Judah and the inhabitants of Jerusalem and King Jehoshaphat: thus says Yahweh to you, 'Do not fear or be dismayed because of this great multitude, for the battle is not yours but God's."* (2 Chronicles 20:10-15 LSB)

> *"20 Now **the Spirit of God clothed Zechariah** the son of Jehoiada the priest; and he stood above the people and said to them, "Thus says God, 'Why do you trespass against the commandments of Yahweh and do not succeed? Because you have*

> *forsaken Yahweh, He has also forsaken you.'"'* (2 Chronicles 24:20 LSB)

> *"28 And it will be afterwards That **I will pour out My Spirit on all mankind;** And your sons and your daughters shall prophesy; Your old men will dream dreams; Your young men will see visions. 29 **Even on the male slaves and female slaves I will in those days pour out My Spirit.**"* (Joel 2:28-29 LSB)

God giving a part of His Spirit to people in the form of knowledge and skill as artisans, leaders, or prophets in no way supports the existence of an immortal soul or spirit in mankind from birth.

The fifth occurrence of the word spirit is in Genesis 45:27. It speaks of the "spirit of Jacob," who had been despondent since the loss of his son Joseph but was revived when his other sons found Joseph alive in Egypt.

> *"27 Yet they told him all the words of Joseph that he had spoken to them, and he saw the wagons that Joseph had sent to carry him. Then **the spirit of their father Jacob revived**."* (Genesis 45:27 LSB)

> *"26 So **the God of Israel stirred up the spirit of Pul,** king of Assyria, even the spirit of Tilgath-pilneser, king of Assyria, and he took them away into exile, namely the Reubenites, the Gadites, and the half-tribe of Manasseh, and brought them to Halah, Habor, Hara, and to the river of Gozan, to this day."* (1 Chronicles 5:26 LSB)

Again, this is used as the mind, heart, or feelings, with no indication of being an immortal soul or spirit.

Another example of "spirit" being used as a synonym for attitude or heart is found in Isaiah.

> *"2 For My hand made all these things, Thus all these things came into being," declares Yahweh. "But to this one I will look, **To him who is humble and contrite of spirit,** and who trembles at My word."* (Isaiah 66:2 LSB)

Obviously, God is not proclaiming here that man has an immortal spirit from birth.

We do not need to examine all 236 occurrences, but will note from here on only those of significant importance. If you find one I have missed that is germane to this study, please contact me and let me know.

Strong's H7307 is also used in phrases such as the following: the anguish of spirit, the spirit of wisdom, familiar spirits, the spirit of jealousy, and more, none of which indicate an immortal soul or spirit in man.

> "16 Then Samson said, "With the jawbone of a donkey, Heaps upon heaps, With the jawbone of a donkey I have struck down 1,000 men." 17 Now it happened that when he had finished speaking, he threw the jawbone from his hand; and he named that place Ramath-lehi. 18 Then he became very thirsty, and he called to Yahweh and said, "You have given this great salvation by the hand of Your slave, but now shall I die of thirst and fall into the hands of the uncircumcised?" 19 So God split the hollow place that is in Lehi and water came out of it. Then he drank, **and his spirit returned, and he revived.** Therefore he named it En-hakkore, which is in Lehi to this day." (Judges 15:16-19 LSB)

This cannot have been an immortal soul or spirit that left him and came back into him, but his emotional state, as in "After being depressed for many weeks, the party with his friends revived his spirit." This "spirit" was revived when he drank water. This is not an immortal spirit.

Numbers 16:22 may be of significance in this search. Korah and many people with him sinned, and Moses and Aaron prayed to God not to hold the whole congregation of the Children of Israel guilty for the sins of these few.

> "22 But they fell on their faces and said, "O God, **God of the spirits of all flesh**, when one man sins, will You be angry with the entire congregation?"" (Numbers 16:22 LSB)

Note that a very popular translation of the Bible, the New International Version (NIV), translates "ruah" as "breath," as does the New Living Translation.

New International Version
> "22 But Moses and Aaron fell facedown and cried out, "O God, the God who **gives breath to all living things,** will you be angry with the entire

assembly when only one man sins?" (Numbers 16:22 NIV)

New Living Translation
> *"22 But Moses and Aaron fell face down on the ground. "O God," they pleaded, "you are the God who **gives breath to all creatures.** Must you be angry with all the people when only one man sins?"* (Numbers 16:22 NLT)

> *"8 There is **no man that hath power over the spirit to retain the spirit;** neither hath he power in the day of death: and there is no discharge in that war; neither shall wickedness deliver those that are given to it."* (Ecclesiastes 8:8)

Which is more appropriate in the verse above, the spirit or the breath of life? Both are possible translations. It depends on your inclinations.

Also, the other translations almost all agree on the phrase "spirits of all flesh," which includes animals. This does not imply that man is born with an immortal soul or spirit.

Understand also from this example above that the interpretation of a word was at the inclination, understanding, prejudice, or whim of the translator. Of course, I appreciate the many excellent interpreters who were doing their very best to be honest and accurate in translating the exact meaning of the ancient languages.

Most of these translators were probably well-meaning, honest men trying to do what was right and good. So was Uzzah. The following Scripture reference is not for baby Christians or lukewarm Christians.

> *"3 And they drove the ark of God on a new cart that they might bring it from the house of Abinadab which was on the hill; and Uzzah and Ahio, the sons of Abinadab, were leading the new cart. 4 So they brought it with the ark of God from the house of Abinadab, which was on the hill; and Ahio was walking ahead of the ark. 5 Now David and all the house of Israel were celebrating before Yahweh with all kinds of instruments made of fir wood, and with lyres, harps, tambourines, castanets, and cymbals. 6 Then they came to the threshing floor of Nacon. And **Uzzah reached out toward the ark of God and took hold of it,** because the oxen nearly upset it. 7 And the anger of Yahweh burned against*

Uzzah, and God struck him down there for his irreverence; and he died there by the ark of God."
(2 Samuel 6:3-7 LSB)

Uzzah was trying to save the Ark of the Covenant. Uzzah probably had only good intentions in his heart. Uzzah was probably an honorable man in that he was chosen as a driver for the cart that would carry the Ark of the Covenant to Jerusalem. Uzzah was doing a good thing, and God killed him.

But wait! Before you start worrying about our God being unreasonably harsh, consider all the facts. Yahweh had given very specific instructions about how to move the Ark of the Covenant. There were rings on each side and two long poles to be slid through the rings to allow it to be carried by men. The Ark of the Testimony was not to be thrown on a cart like garbage being taken to the dump. It was extremely holy. Note: 2 Samuel 6:7 says it was for his error that he died. Uzzah died as a result of his failure to know or obey the truth.

Imagine a scientist makes a high-voltage power supply for an experiment, and in the instructions it says "Do not touch or this will kill you," and he puts warning signs on it, "Deadly, High Voltage, Do Not Touch." He puts rings on the sides and makes long wood insulating poles with instructions that that is how it can be safely carried. The technicians carefully follow the instructions as they load it on a moving cart. As it is being carted from the room in which it was constructed to a different room for the experiment, a scientist sees it start to fall off the cart. Through reflex action, he reaches out to stabilize it and is instantly electrocuted. This is not the wish of the designer. He tried to make it safe. He gave many warnings.

A more careful reading will expose that "the anger of the Lord was kindled against Uzzah." My Bible studies have proven to me that Our Father is a kind, forgiving, and loving God. He does not get angry without cause.

That means that Uzzah certainly knew it was wrong to touch the Ark, that God had forbidden it, and that God had set the penalty at death. Uzzah either just didn't think and reacted, didn't believe all the hype about the Ark, or had some other thoughts but did not force himself to be obedient to God. There is a penalty for sin. Being ignorant of the law does not make you innocent of wrongdoing. Try that tactic in a legal courtroom and see what happens.

Not knowing the truth does not free us from having to obey the law. We are supposed to study and learn the truth with God's help.

Note that in Ecclesiastes 3:21, below, the same word, H7307, is used for the "spirit" of animals and the "spirit" of man, proving that this word does not indicate an "immortal soul or spirit." Remember that Hebrew is read from right to left.

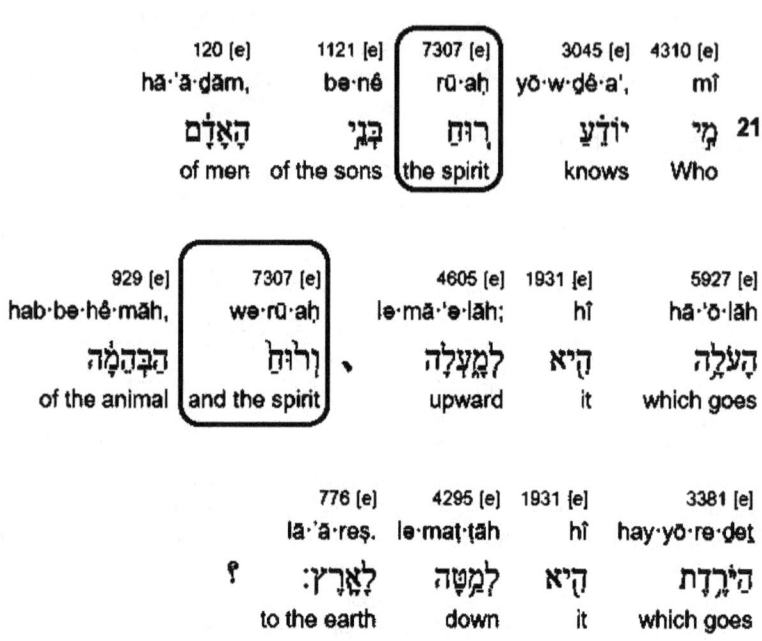

Figure 6.10: Ecclesiastes 3:21
[Courtesy of BibleHub.com and Apostolic Bible Polyglot Interlinear.]

Consider this example:
ECCLESIASTES 12:7 in various translations:
KJV: "Then shall the dust return to the earth as it was, and the **spirit** shall return unto God who gave it."
CEB: "Before dust returns to the earth as it was before and the **life-breath** returns to God who gave it."
CEV: "So our bodies return to the earth, and the **life-giving breath** returns to God."
GW: "Then the dust of mortals goes back to the ground as it was before, and the **breath of life** goes back to God who gave it"
GNT: "Our bodies will return to the dust of the earth, and the breath of life will go back to God, who gave it to us."
LEB: "And the dust returns to the earth as it was, and the breath returns to God who gave it."
NOG: "Then the dust of mortals goes back to the ground as it was before, and the breath of life goes back to Elohim who gave it."
NABRE: "And the dust returns to the earth as it once was, and the life breath returns to God who gave it."

NET Bible: "And the dust returns to the earth as it was, and the life's breath returns to God who gave it."
NRSV: "And the dust returns to the earth as it was, and the **breath** returns to God who gave it."
NRSVA: "And the dust returns to the earth as it was, and the breath returns to God who gave it."
NRSVACE: "And the dust returns to the earth as it was, and the breath returns to God who gave it."
NRSVCE: "And the dust returns to the earth as it was, and the breath returns to God who gave it."

Above, twelve translations of the Bible say the "breath" returns to God, Yahweh, though the KJV and many others say "spirit."

They are looking back at Genesis 2:7 for the definition.

*"7 Then Yahweh God formed man of dust from the ground and breathed into his nostrils the **breath of life**; and so the man became a living being."* (Genesis 2:7 LSB)

Below, it is used of angels, as in angels being ministering spirits. While almost everyone assumes the angels are innately immortal, try to prove through Scripture that the fallen angels are immortal. There is one Scripture that says the angels in heaven with God do not die. But I can find no Scripture that says that of the disobedient, fallen angels.

Figure 6.11: Psalm 104:4
[Courtesy of BibleHub.com and Apostolic Bible Polyglot Interlinear.]

Below, the word "spirit" is used for a human, the Pharaoh of Egypt. We glanced at this verse above, but here it is using BibleHub.com's wonderful study tool, their Interlinear Bible.

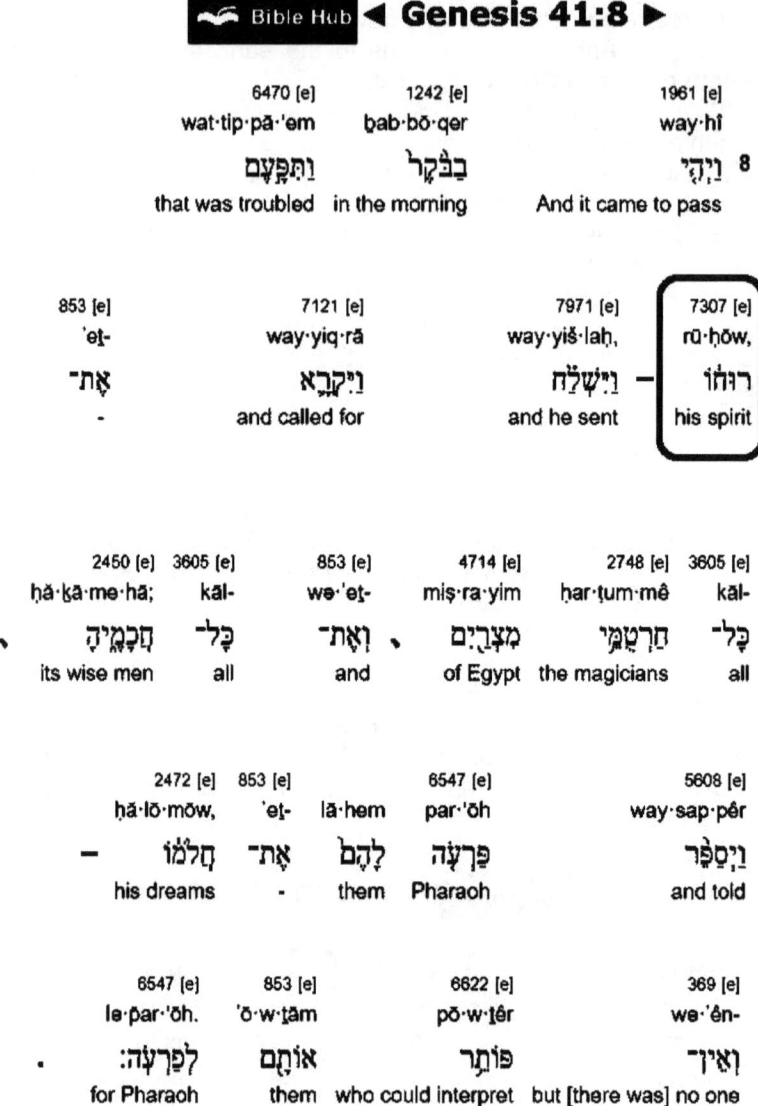

Figure 6.12: Genesis 41:8
[Courtesy of BibleHub.com and Apostolic Bible Polyglot Interlinear.]

The body was created, but it was lifeless, so Yahweh put life into the man's body. There is no mention of an "immortal soul or spirit" in the Bible. For example, see Genesis 7:15.

> *"15 So they came to Noah into the ark, by twos of all flesh in which was the **breath of life**."* (Genesis 7:15 LSB)

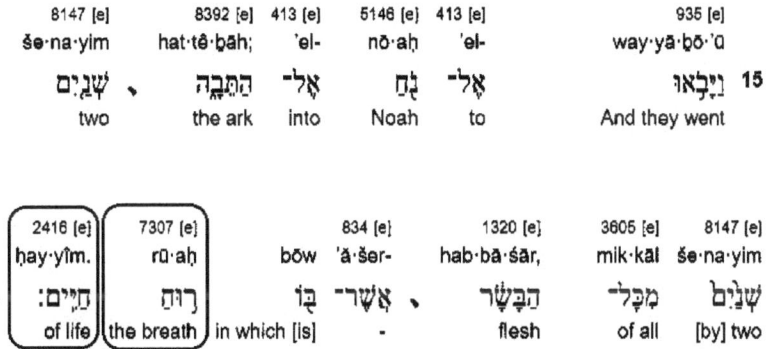

Figure 6.13: Genesis 7:15
[Courtesy of BibleHub.com and Apostolic Bible Polyglot Interlinear.]

This shows that this is exactly the phrase and Hebrew words used for animals' life force. And again, we see this in Genesis 7:21-23.

> "21 Every living thing that moved on land perished—birds, livestock, wild animals, all the creatures that swarm over the earth, and all mankind. 22 Everything on dry land **that had the breath of life in its nostrils** died. 23 Every living thing on the face of the earth was wiped out; people and animals and the creatures that move along the ground and the birds were wiped from the earth. Only Noah was left, and those with him in the ark."
> (Genesis 7:21-23 NIV)

Notice that in the verse above, the word Strong's H2416 "Hayyim" or "Hayyah" we studied in the section above on "soul" is again used here, with the word Strong's H7307 "ruah." Together, they mean "the breath of life."

Also see Psalm 104:25-29 which again uses the word "ruah" which is Strong's H7307, to mean "breath."

> *"25 There is the sea, vast and spacious, teeming with creatures beyond number—living things both large and small. 26 There the ships go to and fro, and Leviathan, which you formed to frolic there. 27 All creatures look to you to give them their food at the proper time. 28 When you give it to them, they gather it up; when you open your hand, they are satisfied with good things. 29 When you hide your face, they are terrified; when **you take away their breath,** they die and return to the dust. "* (Psalm 104:25-29 NKJV)

These and other verses show the **same Hebrew words translated "spirit" in man and animals**, in "things creeping innumerable, both small and great beasts" and in the Leviathan. The point here is that a dozen translators saw it proper in one instance to use "breath," whereas many others chose to use "spirit." How difficult it is to evaluate all these anomalies in Hebrew and Greek translations. I just go with the KJV, but with the realization that there will be discrepancies. We need to be very careful.

Below are the only six Scriptures in the NIV translation and four in the KJV translation with the phrase "the breath of life" in the Bible. The NIV and KJV are the same on the first four.

> *"6 but a mist went up from the earth, and watered the whole surface of the ground. 7 Yahweh God formed man from the dust of the ground, and breathed into his nostrils **the breath of life; and man became a living soul.** 8 Yahweh God planted a garden eastward, in Eden, and there he put the man whom he had formed."* (Genesis 2:6-8 WEB)

> *"16 You shall make a roof in the ship, and you shall finish it to a cubit upward. You shall set the door of the ship in its side. You shall make it with lower, second, and third levels. 17 I, even I, will bring the flood of waters on this earth, to destroy all flesh having **the breath of life** from under the sky. Everything that is in the earth will die. 18 But I will establish my covenant with you. You shall come into the ship, you, your sons, your wife, and your sons' wives with you."* (Genesis 6:16-18 WEB)

> *"14 they, and every animal after its kind, all the livestock after their kind, every creeping thing that creeps on the earth after its kind, and every bird after its kind, every bird of every sort. 15 Pairs from*

> *all flesh **with the breath of life** in them went into the ship to Noah. 16 Those who went in, went in male and female of all flesh, as God commanded him; then Yahweh shut him in."* (Genesis 7:14-16 WEB)

> *"21 Every living thing that moved on land perished—birds, livestock, wild animals, all the creatures that swarm over the earth, and all mankind. 22 Everything on dry land that had **the breath of life** in its nostrils died. 23 Every living thing on the face of the earth was wiped out; people and animals and the creatures that move along the ground and the birds were wiped from the earth. Only Noah was left, and those with him in the ark."* (Genesis 7:21-23 NIV)

Below are two verses, one from the NIV and one from the KJV, where "the breath of life" is used, and the same verse from the KJV is slightly different. It is Strong's 5315 nephesh that is used in both.

> *"30 And to all the beasts of the earth and all the birds in the sky and all the creatures that move along the ground—everything that has **the breath of life** in it—I give every green plant for food." And it was so."* (Genesis 1:30 NIV)

> *"30 And to every beast of the earth, and to every fowl of the air, and to every thing that creepeth upon the earth, **wherein there is life**, I have given every green herb for meat: and it was so."* (Genesis 1:30 KJV)

To finish our search on the phrase "the breath of life," the following Scripture is shown, though it is from the New Testament.

> *"11 But after the three and a half days **the breath of life** from God entered them, and they stood on their feet, and terror struck those who saw them."* (Revelation 11:11 NIV)

> *"11 And after three days and an half **the spirit of life** from God entered into them, and they stood upon their feet; and great fear fell upon them which saw them."* (Revelation 11:11 KJV)

The two verses above are a great example of how translators must make a decision on what word to use. Hopefully, that decision is based solely on linguistic and grammatical considerations, taken in the context of the rest of the writing. Even then, our best scholars disagree. Adding to the problem of creating a perfect translation are the natural inclinations, the inherent biases, and the doctrinal stance of the translator.

Some will say the slight difference in Revelation 11:11 in the NIV compared to the KJV is unimportant. Others use it as a Scripture to base their belief in an immortal spirit in mankind from birth.

Since the same phrase is used for animals and humans, it is obvious that it does not refer to an "immortal soul or spirit." As stated in more detail in the preface above, I debated including more Hebrew and Greek here, but my research found scholars with very erudite, brilliant, and deep-sounding lengthy Hebrew and Greek discussions on the words for soul and spirit **on both sides of the issue**. But the highly educated authors of those intellectual studies couldn't agree on the usage of soul and spirit. So I will trust the two (2) major translations as shown above.

As much as you may hope that man is different from animals and that the natural man, before believing in the Son of God, the Messiah, has some spark of God in him, consider the verses below. Solomon asked God for wisdom, and God gave him great wisdom.

> *"God gave Solomon very great wisdom and understanding, and knowledge as vast as the sands of the seashore."* (1Kings 4:29 NIV)

Below is the writing of the wisest man on Earth, a man of great wisdom, understanding, and knowledge!

> *"17 I said in my heart, "God will judge both the righteous man and the wicked man," for a time for every matter and for every work is there. 18 I said in my heart concerning the sons of men, "God is testing them **in order for them to see that they are but beasts**." 19 For **the fate of the sons of men and the fate of beasts is the same fate for each of them. As one dies so dies the other, and they all have the same breath. So there is no advantage for man over beast**, for all is vanity. 20 **All go to the same place. All came from the dust, and all return to the dust. 21 Who knows that the breath of man ascends upward and the breath of the beast descends downward to the*

> *earth? 22 I have seen that nothing is better than that man should be glad in his works, for that is his portion. For who will bring him to see what will occur after him?"* (Ecclesiastes 3:17-22 LSB)

How clear can Solomon be in the verse above? "**Man has no advantage over a beast,**" and "**as the one dies, so dies the other**."

This makes it very clear that the word spirit is used for both men and animals, and does not necessarily mean an immortal spirit from birth.

The word in the verse below translated as "spirit" is Strong's H7307, rûaḥ רוּחַ, as in all the other verses above.

> "15 "As for me, Daniel, **my spirit was distressed** within me, and the visions of my head kept alarming me." (Daniel 7:15 LSB)

> *"6 So Elihu the son of Barachel the Buzite answered and said, "I am young in years and you are old; Therefore I was shy and afraid to tell you my knowledge. 7 I thought age should speak, And increased years should make wisdom known. 8 But **it is a spirit in man,** And the breath of the Almighty gives them understanding."* (Job 32:6-8 LSB)

The Hebrew word translated "spirit" in Job 32:8 is again Strong's H7307 "ruah," defined as wind, breath, mind, and spirit. This is tied to men understanding things, so it is about a mind of understanding, intellect. It is the same usage as the verses above this section, about skilled artisans, leaders, and warriors. It in no way proves there is an immortal soul or spirit in humankind.

> *"6 Remember Him before the silver cord is snapped and the golden bowl is crushed, the pitcher by the spring is broken and the wheel at the cistern is crushed; 7 then the dust will return to the earth as it was, and **the spirit will return to God who gave it.**"* (Ecclesiastes 12:6-7 LSB)

Above, in verse Ecclesiastes 12:7, "spirit" is Strong's H7307: wind, breath, mind, spirit.

The following verses are part of the great story of the passing of the mantle of Elijah, a prophet of God, to his successor, Elisha.

*"5 Then the sons of the prophets who were at Jericho approached Elisha and said to him, "Do you know that Yahweh will take away your master from over you today?" And he answered, "Yes, I know; be silent." 6 Then Elijah said to him, "Please stay here, for Yahweh has sent me to the Jordan." And he said, "As Yahweh lives and as your soul lives, I will not forsake you." So the two of them went on. 7 Now fifty men of the sons of the prophets went and stood opposite them at a distance, but the two of them stood by the Jordan. 8 And Elijah took his mantle and folded it together and struck the waters, and they were divided here and there, so that the two of them crossed over on dry ground. 9 Now it happened when they crossed over, that Elijah said to Elisha, "Ask what I shall do for you before I am taken from you." And Elisha said, "Please, **let a double portion of your spirit be upon me**." 10 And he said, "You have asked a hard thing. Nevertheless, if you see me when I am taken from you, it shall be so for you; but if not, it shall not be so." 11 As they were going along and talking, behold, there appeared a chariot of fire and horses of fire, and it separated the two of them. And Elijah went up by a whirlwind to heaven. 12 And Elisha was seeing this and he was crying out, "My father, my father, the chariots of Israel and its horsemen!" And he saw Elijah no more. Then he took hold of his own clothes and tore them in two pieces. 13 He also took up the mantle of Elijah that fell from him and returned and stood by the bank of the Jordan. 14 And he took the mantle of Elijah that fell from him and struck the waters and said, "Where is Yahweh, the God of Elijah?" Indeed, he himself also struck the waters, and they were divided here and there! And Elisha crossed over. 15 Then the sons of the prophets who were at Jericho opposite him saw him and said, "**The spirit of Elijah rests on Elisha**." And they came to meet him and bowed themselves to the ground before him." (2 Kings 2:5-15 LSB)*

Again, the word translated "spirit" in 2 Kings 2:9 and 2:15 is Strong's H3707 "ruah." This is in reference to the Spirit of God that was given to Elijah, the great prophet of God, not some immortal soul or spirit that was in Elijah from his birth.

The following is King David telling God that even in his troubled times, he is placing his "spirit" into the hands of God. This is a statement about trusting God and placing your life in His hands. It is not evidence of an immortal soul or spirit in humankind from birth.

> "3 For You are my high rock and my fortress; For Your name's sake You will lead me and guide me. 4 You will bring me out of the net which they have secretly laid for me, For You are my strength. 5 Into Your hand **I commit my spirit;** You have ransomed me, O Yahweh, God of truth. 6 I hate those who regard worthless idols, But I trust in Yahweh.." (Psalm 31:3-6 LSB)

Strong's H7307 "ruah" spirit is used in both verses below. In the first, Psalm 51:10, it is used with an adjective translated as right, steadfast, loyal, faithful, resolute, and more. Remember that this word, ruah, is also translated as "mind." This does not demonstrate the existence of an immortal soul or spirit in humankind. The second usage, in Psalm 51:11, has an adjective to identify it as God's Holy Spirit.

> "10 Create in me a clean heart, O God, And renew a **steadfast spirit within me**. 11 Do not cast me away from Your presence And do **not take Your Holy Spirit from me.**" (Psalm 51:10-11 LSB)

Below are five verses from Proverbs, one from Psalms, and one from Zechariah that have words that have been translated "spirit" in English.

> "2 All the ways of a man are clean in his own eyes; but the Lord weigheth the **spirits**." (Proverbs 16:2)

> "27 He who holds back his words has knowledge, And he who has a cool **spirit** is a man of discernment." (Proverbs 17:27 LSB)

> "14 The **spirit** of a man can endure his sickness, But as for a broken **spirit**, who can bear it?" (Proverbs 18:14 LSB)

> "27 The **spirit** of man is the candle of the Lord, searching all the inward parts of the belly." (Proverbs 20:27)

> "23 A man's lofty pride will bring him low, But a lowly **spirit** will take hold of glory." (Proverbs 29:23 LSB)

> "2 How blessed is the man whose iniquity Yahweh will not take into account, And in whose **spirit** there is no deceit!" (Psalm 32:2 LSB)

> "1 Thus declares Yahweh who stretches out the heavens, lays the foundation of the earth, and **forms the spirit of man** within him," (Zechariah 12:1 LSB)

The word translated "spirit" in the 7 verses above is the same Hebrew word "ruah," which is translated as spirit, wind, breath, and a few other things.

Note the 4 translations of Zechariah 12:1 below, where the translators found good reason to use "breath of life," "breath," or "life." Particularly notice that two are older versions, before Christianity was so beaten and pressed into the "authorized doctrine" of today.

> "1 This is a message from the Lord about Israel: I am the Lord! I stretched out the heavens; I put the earth on its foundations and gave **breath** to humans." (Zechariah 12:1 Contemporary English Version CEV)

> "1 This is a message about Israel from the Lord, the Lord who spread out the skies, created the earth, and gave **life** to man. He says," (Zechariah 12:1 Good News Translation GNT)

> "1 The heauy burthen which the Lorde hath deuised for Israel. Thus saith the Lorde which spread the heauens abrode, layde the foundation of the earth, and gaue man the **breath of lyfe**," (Zechariah 12:1 Bishops' Bible BB1568)

> "1 The heuy burthen which ye LORDE hath deuysed for Israel. Thus saieth the LORDE, which spred the heaues abrode, layde the foundacion of the earth, and geueth man ye **breath of life:**" (Zechariah 12:1 Coverdale Bible CB1535)

While it is true that the majority of the translations today use "spirit" in this verse, you can see some do not.

I do not think there is a need to examine dozens more verses with the word "ruah" to show that the word does not indicate an immortal soul or spirit in man from birth. If you find a Biblical reference to an immortal soul or spirit in humankind from birth, please send me that reference at dan@vigilantvaliant.com.

Chapter 7: New Testament Greek for Soul and Spirit

Of course we want to know what the whole Bible says about an immortal soul or spirit, so we must include the Greek of the New Testament.

Some may say God changed what He did between the Old and New Testaments, but God Himself says He does not change. So let's check out the usage of the words "soul" and "spirit" in the New Testament, like we did in the Old Testament.

The New Testament of the Bible, the books of the Bible written after the resurrection of Yeshua, was written in Greek, to the best of current knowledge. So let's examine the Greek words for soul and spirit to see if any verse proves the existence of an immortal soul or spirit in humankind from their birth.

Greek: Soul

Strong's G5590. Psuché, or psyche
"Definition: breath, the soul
Original Word: ψυχή, ῆς, ἡ
Usage: (a) the vital breath, the breath of life: (b) the human soul: (c) the soul as the seat of affections and will: (d) the self: (e) a human person, an individual."

The first New Testament verse below shows the soul can be destroyed, and therefore the soul of a man does not mean an immortal soul or spirit in mankind from birth.

> *"28 And do not fear those who kill the body but are unable to kill the soul; but rather fear Him who is able to **destroy both soul and body** in hell."* (Matthew 10:28 LSB)

> *"26 For what will it profit a man if he gains the whole world and **forfeits his soul**? Or what will a man give in exchange for his soul?"* (Matthew 16:26 LSB)

Above, if there was an immortal spirit in man from his birth, wouldn't Yeshua be saying "spirit?"

> *"37 And He said to him, '"You shall love the Lord your God with all your heart, and with all your **soul**, and with all your mind."'* (Matthew 22:37 LSB)

Again, if there was an immortal spirit in man from his birth, wouldn't Yeshua be saying "spirit"?

Below, Yeshua uses "soul" in the sense of "heart," or seat of emotions.

*"36 Then Jesus *came with them to a place called Gethsemane, and *said to His disciples, "Sit here while I go over there and pray." 37 And He took with Him Peter and the two sons of Zebedee, and began to be grieved and distressed. 38 Then He *said to them, "My **soul** is deeply grieved, to the point of death; remain here and keep watch with Me.""* (Matthew 26:36-38 LSB)

And yet again, it is the "soul" that God is requiring of the man as he dies, not some immortal soul or spirit.

*"19 And I will say to my **soul**, "Soul, you have many goods laid up for many years to come; take your ease, eat, drink and be merry."' 20 But God said to him, 'You fool! This very night your **soul** is required of you; and now who will own what you prepared?' 21 So is the one who stores up treasure for himself, and is not rich toward God.""* (Luke 12:19-21 LSB)

It is of great importance that Peter used Greek to quote King David's Hebrew use of Strong's H5325 "nephesh" or "napsi." The quote below from Peter is in Greek, but he is quoting King David's Hebrew from the Old Testament.

*"9 Therefore my heart is glad and my glory rejoices; My flesh also will dwell securely. 10 For **You will not forsake my soul to Sheol;** You will not give Your Holy One over to see corruption. 11 You will make known to me the path of life; In Your presence is fullness of joy; In Your right hand there are pleasures forever."* (Psalm 16:9-11 LSB)

*"26 Therefore my heart was glad and my tongue exulted; Moreover my flesh also will live in hope; 27 Because **You will not forsake my soul to Hades**, Nor give Your Holy One over to see corruption. 28 You have made known to me the ways of life; You will make me full of gladness with Your presence.'"* (Acts 2:26-28 LSB)

Figure 7.1: Psalm 16:10
[Courtesy of BibleHub.com and Apostolic Bible Polyglot Interlinear.]

Yeshua Himself says that God can destroy the "soul."

Figure 7.2: Acts 2:27
[Courtesy of BibleHub.com and Apostolic Bible Polyglot Interlinear.]

So we have the equivalency of the Hebrew word Strong's H5325 "nephesh" or "napsi" with the Greek word Strong's G5590 "psuché" by a person not only fluent in both languages at that time but also well trained in the teaching of Yeshua from His own mouth.

> *"28 And do not fear those who kill the body but are unable to **kill the soul;** but rather fear Him who is able to **destroy both soul and body** in hell."* (Matthew 10:28 LSB)

Again, in both occurrences of the word "soul" above, Strong's G5590 "psychen" is used. That makes the soul **mortal**! Strong's G5590 is used again in Revelation 16:3, describing the vials of punishment poured out on the Earth in the End Times.

> "3 And the second angel poured out his vial upon the sea; and it became as the blood of a dead man: and every **living soul died in the sea.**" (Revelation 16:3)

It says "in" the sea, not "on" the sea, so this is not aimed at humans, but all animals and all creatures in the seas and oceans will die. I know it is sad; however, there is no sea on the new earth, created after the current Earth is destroyed.

The point here is to again see that "soul" was used for "living creature" and not an immortal soul in mankind from birth.

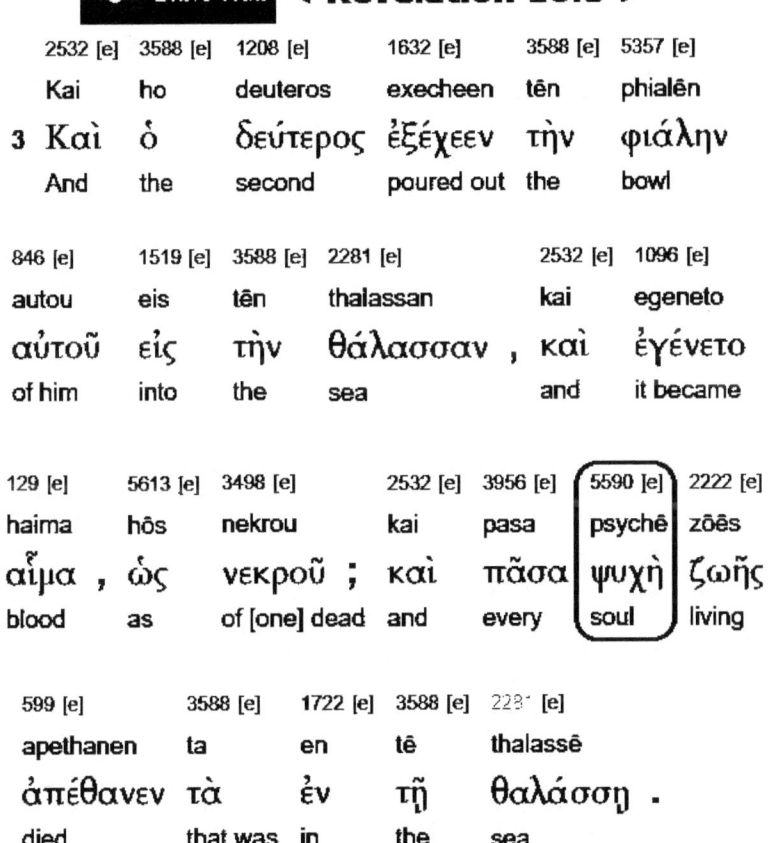

Figure 7.3: Revelation 16:3
[Courtesy of BibleHub.com and Apostolic Bible Polyglot Interlinear.]

What has our glance at the Greek used for "soul" in the New Testament shown us? We have learned that it is talking about exactly what the definition we saw at the start of this section said: the breath of life, or the human soul, the soul as the seat of affections and will, or the self, or a human person, an individual. Nowhere, in any verse, did it prove the existence of an immortal human soul in mankind from birth.

What about the word "spirit?"

Greek: Spirit

Strong's G4151 pneuma
Definition: wind, spirit
Original Word: πνεῦμα, ατος, τό
Usage: wind, breath, spirit

Greek words translated "spirit" occur 287 times in the New Testament of the Bible; therefore, we will not be examining all of them but only those that are of interest. If you find I have overlooked an occurrence that seems to prove humans have an immortal spirit from birth, please let me know at dan@vigilantvaliant.com.

Since the quest here is to see if any verse of Scripture in the New Testament proves the existence of an immortal soul or spirit existing in a human from birth, we will **not be looking** at the uses of the word "spirit" when used of Yahweh, God the Father, or Yeshua, The Son of God, or of angels, either good or evil.

> *"39 And He went a little beyond them, and fell on His face and prayed, saying, "My Father, if it is possible, let this cup pass from Me; yet not as I will, but as You will." 40 And He *came to the disciples and *found them sleeping, and *said to Peter, "So, you men could not keep watch with Me for one hour? 41 Keep watching and praying that you may not enter into temptation; the **spirit is willing**, but the flesh is weak." 42 He went away again a second time and prayed, saying, "My Father, if this cannot pass away unless I drink it, Your will be done." 43 And again He came and found them sleeping, for their eyes were heavy."* (Matthew 26:39-43 LSB)

As seen in our Hebrew study, we will see that the Greek word for "spirit" can also mean the mind or heart of a person, as in the seat of emotions. Matthew 26:41 above has Yeshua using the word "spirit" for the willpower or heartfelt desires of his Apostles. But this is not a doctrinal statement about a man being born with an immortal soul or spirit. This same incident is in Mark 14:38, so that will not be repeated.

Below, it says her spirit came again when Yeshua brought a young girl back to life.

> *"49 While He was still speaking, someone *came from the house of the synagogue official, saying, "Your daughter has died; do not trouble the Teacher anymore." 50 But when Jesus heard this, He answered him, "Do not be afraid any longer; only believe, and she will be saved." 51 So when He came to the house, He did not allow anyone to enter with Him, except Peter and John and James, and the girl's father and mother. 52 Now they were all crying and lamenting for her, but He said, "Stop crying, for she has not died, but is asleep." 53 And*

> *they began laughing at Him, knowing that she had died. 54 He, however, took her by the hand and called, saying, "Child, arise!" 55 And **her spirit returned,** and she stood up immediately. And He gave orders for something to be given her to eat. 56 And her parents were astounded, but He directed them to tell no one what had happened."* (Luke 8:49-56 LSB)

From the verse above, Luke 8:55 shows there is something in a human that keeps them alive. This agrees with James 2:26 below.

> *"26 For as the body without **the spirit** is dead, so faith without works is dead also."* (James 2:26)

Both verse selections above use the English word "spirit" for Strong's G4151 pneuma. Remember Strong's usage of "wind, breath, or spirit" in that order. Translators chose what they liked.

According to the Oxford Dictionary:
"Pneuma (πνεῦμα, Lat. spiritus) is connected etymologically with πνέω, breathe or blow, and has a basic meaning of 'air in motion' or 'breath' as something necessary to life. In Greek tragedy, it is used for the 'breath of life,' and it is the 'spirit' of the New Testament. In early Greek thought, pneuma is often connected with the soul; in Aristotle, it frequently denotes 'warm air', sometimes 'heat', and the term is also used of seismic winds which are trapped within the earth. Its precise meaning, then, must always be determined in its context."

So whether pneuma is translated as wind, breath, blow, or spirit, it all depends on the preconceived notion of the translator.

While we previewed the following verses in the Old Testament Hebrew section, that was for the phrase "the breath of life." Here we see it again to see if it necessarily means an immortal spirit in man from birth.

> *"11 But after the three and a half days **the breath of life** from God entered them, and they stood on their feet, and terror struck those who saw them."* (Revelation 11:11 **NIV**)

> *"11 And after three days and an half **the spirit of life** from God entered into them, and they stood upon their feet; and great fear fell upon them which saw them."* (Revelation 11:11 **KJV**)

Note that above, the NIV says "the breath of life" and the KJV says "the spirit of life." It is not definitive proof of an immortal spirit in man from birth.

> "3 Your adornment must not be merely external—braiding the hair, and wearing gold jewelry, or putting on garments; 4 but let it be the hidden person of the heart, with the incorruptible quality of a **lowly and quiet spirit,** which is precious in the sight of God." (1 Peter 3:3-4 LSB)

While 1 Peter 3:4 above says a spirit is "not corruptible," this would be very weak support for humans having an immortal soul or spirit from birth. However, it is understandable that some may use this verse to state so.

> "5 deliver such a one to Satan for the destruction of his flesh, so that **his spirit may be saved** in the day of the Lord." (1 Corinthians 5:5 LSB)

> "18 For they have **refreshed my spirit** and yours. Therefore recognize such men." (1 Corinthians 16:18 LSB)

> "1 Therefore, having these promises, beloved, let us cleanse ourselves from all **defilement of flesh and spirit,** perfecting holiness in the fear of God." (2 Corinthians 7:1 LSB)

> "26 For just as the **body without the spirit is dead**, so also faith without works is dead." (James 2:26 LSB)

> "59 They went on stoning Stephen as he was calling out and saying, "Lord Jesus, **receive my spirit!**"" (Acts 7:59 LSB)

Remember that Stephen was a saved believer in Yeshua (Jesus). Believers receive the Spirit of God when they are saved. So Stephen did have a spirit at that time; however, he may have just been using this Greek word, "pneuma," in its other meanings.
Remember, Strong's gives this word's usage as "wind, breath, spirit." Revelation 11:11, above, uses "spirit of life" or "breath of life. So this in no way proves that Stephen was referring to an immortal spirit.
So looking at all the Scriptures from the New Testament above on Soul and Spirit, we see that while they do use the word

spirit about men as some non-physical part, none prove definitively that this is an immortal spirit in man from birth.

Old Testament Scriptures with Soul and Spirit

This section studies verses that are of great interest in that they contain both the words for spirit and soul. I have collected only those where both are used of a man, seemingly indicating parts of a man, as in body, soul, and spirit.

It should be noted that there are only 11 of these verses in the KJV Bible. Six of these verses are in the Old Testament, and five are in the New Testament. We will study them below in the order they appear in the Bible.

The first Old Testament Scripture with both the words "soul" and "spirit" is in the book of Leviticus.

> "6 The soul that turns to **mediums** or to soothsayers, prostituting himself with them, **I will set My face against that soul** and will cut him off from among his people." (Leviticus 20:6 TLV)

This is an injunction from God against listening to fortune tellers, witches, wizards, sorcerers, and the like. Mediums work through familiar spirits which are evil spirits or demons. The "soul" is just the person who disobeyed this command. There is no indication of an immortal spirit in mankind in this verse.

The second Scripture we encounter speaks of Hannah, the mother of Samuel, who cried to Yahweh because she was childless. As she was praying to God and moving her lips, Eli the priest saw her and thought she was drunk. When he told her to stop getting drunk, Hannah replied the following to explain that she was not drunk but grieving.

> "15 But Hannah answered and said, "No, my lord, I am a woman **oppressed in spirit;** I have drunk neither wine nor strong drink, but I have **poured out my soul** before Yahweh."" (1 Samuel 1:15 LSB)

The third verse also speaks of the soul and the spirit. Let's check the Hebrew.

> "11 Indeed I will not hold back my mouth; I will speak in the distress of **my spirit;** I will muse on the bitterness of **my soul**." (Job 7:11 LSB)

Once again, from the BibleHub Interlinear Bible:

Figure 7.4: Job 7:11
[Courtesy of BibleHub.com and Apostolic Bible Polyglot Interlinear.]

In Job 7:11 above, the word translated "spirit" is a form of Strong's H7307 ruah, and the word translated "soul" is a form of Strong's H5315 nephesh.

An excellent example of translation being guided by a preexisting mindset is found in Job 12:10, where, in five translations, they are all translated differently.

This is included here, though the KJV does not have "soul" and "spirit," as other translations do.

To prepare for a better understanding, we look at verses 7-9 first from the Legacy Standard Bible (LSB).

> "7 "But now ask the beasts, and let them instruct you; And the birds of the sky, and let them tell you. 8 Or muse to the earth, and let it instruct you; And let the fish of the sea recount it to you. 9 Who among all these does not know That the hand of Yahweh has done this," (Job 12:7-9 LSB)

Now verse 10 from five translations follows.

> "10 In whose hand is the **soul** of every living thing, and the **breath** of all mankind." (Job 12:7-10 KJV)

> "10 In his hand is the **life** of every creature and the **breath** of all mankind." (Job 12:10 NIV)

> "10 Because in his hand are the **souls** of everything that lives and the **spirit** of all flesh and man" (Job 12:10 AMP)

> *"10 In his hand is the **life** of every living thing and the **spirit** of every human being."* (Job 12:10 CJB)

> *"10 In whose hand [is] the **breath** of every living thing, And the **spirit** of all flesh of man."* (Job 12:10 LSV)

Please look those over again. **Note that "soul," "breath," "life," and "spirit" are used interchangeably!** We have to be so careful with translations and seek the closest meaning to the original language.

From the excellent Bible Hub Interlinear Bible, we see the following; Both "nepes" (soul or life) and "ruah" (breath or spirit) are used in one sentence.

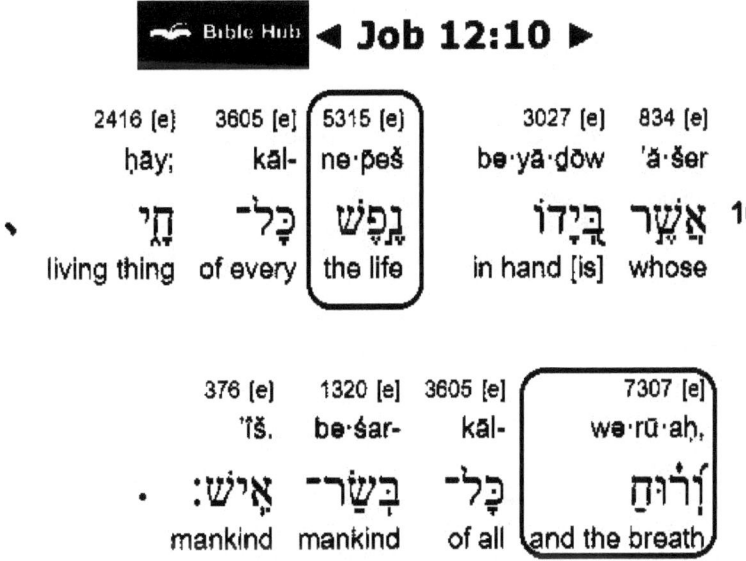

Figure 7.5: Job 12:10
[Courtesy of BibleHub.com and Apostolic Bible Polyglot Interlinear.]

In the fourth verse below, Isaiah is telling God how he desires to worship Him.

> *"8 Indeed, while following the way of Your judgments, O Yahweh, We have hoped for You eagerly; Your name—the memory of You—is the desire of **our souls**. 9 At night **my soul** longs for You, Indeed, **my spirit** within me seeks You earnestly; For when the earth experiences Your*

> *judgments, The inhabitants of the world learn righteousness."* (Isaiah 26:8-9 LSB)

Remember, spirit can also be translated as "breath." In the fifth verse in the Old Testament, with both the words "soul" and "spirit," God is speaking of His Soul and His Spirit.

> *"1 "Behold, My Servant, whom I uphold; My chosen one in whom **My soul** is well-pleased. I have put **My Spirit** upon Him; He will bring forth justice to the nations.""* (Isaiah 42:1 LSB)

Finally, the sixth verse is again from Isaiah.

> *"16 For I will not contend forever, neither will I always be angry; for **the spirit would faint** before me, and **the souls whom I have made**."* (Isaiah 57:16 WEB)

How often in life have we "lost spirit" or had our "spirit fail?" This may well be talking about spirit as emotional energy, like team spirit. Regardless of how you interpret the meaning, it is not proof of an immortal spirit in humans from birth.

These six verses in the Old Testament do mention a soul and a spirit in man as two separate things.

It should be noted that Hannah, Job, and Isaiah, the speakers of the verses above, were all close to God and probably saved, righteous people. Therefore, they are likely to have received the Holy Spirit of God.

Nevertheless, not just dismissing these verses, while they do indicate a spirit of some kind in people, none prove this is an immortal spirit from birth in every human. I am including this verse in this section, though the spirit spoken of is clearly the Holy Spirit of God, for the Bible makes it clear that those who love Yahweh and try their best to obey Yahweh, He puts some of His spirit in them to help them along the way.

> *"13 But the angel said to him, "Do not be afraid, Zechariah, for your prayer has been heard, and your wife Elizabeth will bear you a son, and you will call his name John. 14 And you will have joy and gladness, and many will rejoice at his birth. 15 For he will be great in the sight of the Lord; and he will not drink any wine or strong drink, and **he will be filled with the Holy Spirit** while yet in his mother's womb. 16 And he will turn many of the sons of Israel back to the Lord their God. 17 And he will go*

> *before Him **in the spirit and power of Elijah**, to turn the hearts of the fathers back to the children, and the disobedient to the attitude of the righteous, to make ready a people prepared for the Lord.""* (Luke 1:13-17 LSB)

> *"25 And behold, there was a man in Jerusalem whose name was Simeon, and this man was righteous and devout, waiting for the comfort of Israel, and the **Holy Spirit was upon him**. 26 And it had been revealed to him by the Holy Spirit that he would not see death before he had seen the Lord's Christ."* (Luke 2:25-26 LSB)

God puts some of His spirit in certain people to do certain jobs.

New Testament Scriptures with Soul and Spirit

Now we will look at the five New Testament verses that have both words, soul and spirit, in them. In the first verse of the New Testament, using both "spirit" and "soul," Yahweh is speaking of His Soul and His Spirit.

> *"18 "Behold, My Servant whom I have chosen; My Beloved in whom **My soul is well-pleased**; I will put **My Spirit upon Him**, And He shall proclaim justice to the Gentiles."* (Matthew 12:18 LSB)

The three verses below are not part of our five-verse count because "soul" and "spirit" are in two separate verses. Nevertheless, for thoroughness sake, we include them here, unnumbered. We see Mary's prayer when she learned she would bear the Savior. She mentions both her soul and her spirit, so a person could say it shows a person has a spirit. Note, however, that it also perfectly fits the meaning of her emotional seat, or her mind.

> *"46 And Mary said: "**My soul** magnifies the Lord, 47 And **my spirit** has rejoiced in God my Savior. 48 For He has looked upon the humble state of His slave, For behold, from this time on, all generations will count me blessed."* (Luke 1:46-48 LSB)

The second verse in the New Testament using both "spirit" and "soul" is in 1 Corinthians.

> *"45 So also it is written, "The first man, Adam, became a **living soul.**" The last Adam became a **life-giving spirit.**"* (1 Corinthians 15:45 LSB)

This is contrasting Adam, the first human soul, with Christ, a spirit who could bring life to others.

The third verse is:

> *"23 Now may the God of peace Himself sanctify you entirely, and may your **spirit** (Strong's G5141) **and soul** (Strong's G5590) and body be preserved complete, without blame at the coming of our Lord Jesus Christ."* (1 Thessalonians 5:23 LSB)

Above, G5141 is again "pneuma," and G5590 is "psyche." Some of these verses above speak of Mary, Yeshua's mother, and of Paul's audience, the church, and the saved people in Thessalonica. Therefore, it is talking about those who have received the Holy Spirit of God.

Forms of both Strong's G5590 "psyche" and Strong's G4151 "pneuma" are used in the fourth verse, Hebrews 4:12, below.

> *"12 For the word of God is living and active and sharper than any two-edged sword, and piercing as far as the division of **soul and spirit,** of both joints and marrow, and able to judge the thoughts and intentions of the heart."* (Hebrews 4:12 LSB)

Figure 7.6: Hebrews 4:12
[Courtesy of BibleHub.com and Apostolic Bible Polyglot Interlinear.]

The verse above was written to the Hebrews in the church; therefore it was written to saved, born-again Christians who had received the Holy Spirit of God.

Even if we take this to be a general statement about all humans, it speaks of some kind of spirit, not an immortal spirit, in humans from birth.

The fifth and last New Testament verse using both "spirit" and "soul" speaks of God's Spirit and human souls.

*"22 Since you have purified your **souls** in obeying the truth through the **Spirit** in sincere love of the*

brethren, love one another fervently with a pure heart," (1 Peter 1:22 NKJV)

Remember, in this study, the burden of proof is on those who would say the Bible teaches an immortal soul or spirit in all humankind from birth as an innate part of a human being. You cannot securely believe something on the basis that the Bible does not speak of it. We must believe only what the Bible clearly teaches.

While some verses do have both "soul" and "spirit" in them, they might serve as ancillary support for some stronger verse, some direct and powerfully clear verse, but I can find no such verse.

Have we seen any Scripture in the Bible that proves there is an immortal soul or spirit in all humankind from birth? No!

Chapter 8: Do Humans Have a Soul That Will Live Forever?

What does the Bible say about any part of a human living forever?

> *"15 Everyone who hates his brother is a murderer, and you know that **no murderer has eternal life** abiding in him."* (1 John 3:15 LSB)

Read that carefully. It says the unsaved do not have eternal life. It does not say the murderer's soul or spirit will have eternal life in the Lake of Fire, in hell, in Hades, in Gehenna, or anywhere else. It says the murderer does not have eternal life, either in an immortal soul or an immortal spirit.

In fact, the Bible says that, after they sinned, God threw humans out of the Garden of Eden specifically so they would not eat of the Tree of Life and live forever. **Please read that again!**

> *"22 Then Yahweh God said, "Behold, the man has become like one of Us to know good and evil; and now, **lest he send forth his hand and take also from the tree of life and eat and live forever**"— 23 therefore Yahweh God sent him out from the garden of Eden, to cultivate the ground from which he was taken. 24 So He drove the man out; and at the east of the garden of Eden He stationed the cherubim and the flaming sword which turned every direction to guard the way to the tree of life."* (Genesis 3:22-24 LSB)

If humankind already possessed an immortal soul or spirit, they would not need to eat the fruit of the Tree of Life. It would have been meaningless for God to say the verse above. Do you think God says meaningless things and does meaningless acts, like throwing man out of the Garden of Eden?

The Book of Revelation in the New Testament confirms God's statement in Genesis, the last book reaffirming the first.

> *"7 He who has an ear, let him hear what the Spirit says to the churches. **To him who overcomes, I will grant to eat of the tree of life** which is in the Paradise of God.""* (Revelation 2:7 LSB)

> *"Blessed are **they that do his commandments, that they may have right to the tree of life**, and*

may enter in through the gates into the city." (Revelation 22:14)

Humans must "overcome" to gain the "right to the Tree of Life" by the Throne of God, which now resides in Heaven. They must "do His commandments" to gain the right to the Tree of Life and live forever.

This is a straightforward statement from Yahweh, The Living God, that humans are not born with an immortal soul or spirit, and do not have an innate right to eternal life.

"11 But you, O man of God, flee from these things, and pursue righteousness, godliness, faith, love, perseverance, gentleness. 12 Fight the good fight of faith. **Take hold of the eternal life** *to which you were called, and you made the good confession in the presence of many witnesses. 13 I charge you in the presence of God, who gives life to all things, and of Christ Jesus, who testified the good confession before Pontius Pilate, 14 that you keep the commandment without stain or reproach until the appearing of our Lord Jesus Christ, 15 which He will bring about at the proper time—He who is the blessed and only Sovereign, the King of kings and Lord of lords, 16* **who alone has immortality** *and dwells in unapproachable light, whom no man has seen or can see. To Him be honor and eternal might! Amen."* (1 Timothy 6:11-16 LSB)

How can Bible readers have any doubt that humans are not born with an immortal soul or spirit when Paul states point blank that only God has immortality in Himself as an innate part of His being? It is He and He alone who gives eternal life to those He chooses, to those who properly seek to "take hold of the eternal life." He has given it to the Holy Angels who have obeyed Him and done His will, and to others who believe and obey Him, even His own Son, our Messiah. **If Yahweh gives immortal life as a gift to those who believe and obey, those who do not believe and obey do not receive the gift and do not have eternal life.**

Also, Paul states straight out that man is mortal and corruptible and must be changed to enter the Kingdom of God. That is exactly the opposite of having an immortal soul. If mankind already had immortality, Paul would not say, "This mortal must put on immortality."

"50 Now this I say, brethren, that **flesh and blood cannot inherit the kingdom of God; nor does**

> *corruption inherit incorruption. 51 Behold, I tell you a [mystery: We shall not all sleep, but **we shall all be changed**— 52 in a moment, in the twinkling of an eye, at the last trumpet. For the trumpet will sound, and **the dead will be raised incorruptible, and we shall be changed. 53 For this corruptible must put on incorruption, and this mortal must put on immortality.** 54 So when this corruptible has put on incorruption, and this mortal has put on immortality, then shall be brought to pass the saying that is written: "Death is swallowed up in victory." 55 "O Death, where is your sting? O Hades, where is your victory?"'* (1 Corinthians 15:50-55 WEB)

Only one being, one entity, the Living God, has eternal life inherent as part of who they are.

> *"19 Therefore Jesus answered and was saying to them, "Truly, truly, I say to you, the Son can do nothing from Himself, unless it is something He sees the Father doing; for whatever the Father does, these things the Son also does in the same manner. 20 For the Father loves the Son, and shows Him all things that He Himself is doing; and the Father will show Him greater works than these, so that you will marvel. 21 For just as the Father raises the dead and gives them life, even so the Son also gives life to whom He wishes. 22 For not even the Father judges anyone, but He has given all judgment to the Son, 23 so that all will honor the Son even as they honor the Father. He who does not honor the Son does not honor the Father who sent Him. 24 "Truly, truly, I say to you, **he who hears My word, and believes Him who sent Me, has eternal life,** and does not come into judgment, but has passed out of death into life. 25 Truly, truly, I say to you, an hour is coming and now is, when the dead will hear the voice of the Son of God, and those who hear will live. 26 **For just as the Father has life in Himself, even so He gave to the Son also to have life in Himself;** 27 and He gave Him authority to execute judgment, because He is the Son of Man. 28 Do not marvel at this; for **an hour is coming, in which all who are in the tombs will hear His voice, 29 and will come forth; those who did the good deeds to a resurrection of life,***

those who committed the evil deeds to a resurrection of judgment. 30 "I can do nothing from Myself. As I hear, I judge; and My judgment is righteous, because I do not seek My own will, but the will of Him who sent Me." (John 5:19-30 LSB)

Yeshua Himself confirms what Paul said above, for He tells us both that His Father has life "in himself" and that God the Father has given to the Son of God, Yeshua, to have life "in Himself." He also stresses that Judgment Day is coming and that all will be resurrected—those who have done good to eternal life and those who have done evil to damnation. It doesn't matter if that sounds harsh to some people. It doesn't matter if they don't believe. God's Son, Yeshua Hamashiach (Jesus the Messiah), says it is going to happen.

The devil says to humans, "Ye shall not surely die." (Genesis 3:4) Yahweh says to humans, "Thou shalt surely die." (Genesis 2:17) But then He offers them the **gift** of eternal life **if** they believe and obey.

Who are YOU going to believe?

Does the Bible Say Humans Are Immortal?

The words "immortal" and "immortality" are found only six times in the Bible, all in the New Testament. In two of those instances, it is used in the Epistle 1 Timothy and refers to God.

The other four uses are for those seeking immortality, clearly showing they do not have immortality. Of these, two are found in 1 Corinthians. We have seen this verse before, but let's look at it again.

> *"52 in a moment, in the twinkling of an eye, at the last trumpet. For the trumpet will sound, and the dead will be raised incorruptible, and we will be changed. 53 For this corruptible must put on the incorruptible, and **this mortal must put on immortality**. 54 But when this corruptible puts on the incorruptible, and this mortal puts on immortality, then will come about the word that is written, "Death is swallowed up in victory."* (1 Corinthians 15:52-54 LSB)

Read that again.

First, "we shall be changed" is in future tense, not past or even present, as is "shall have put on." These are future events, showing that even the saved are not born with an immortal soul.

Second, "this mortal must put on immortality." **Paul says point blank, "This mortal."** For those who try to say he is speaking only of the body, prove that! Paul also says, "We shall be changed." In neither case does he say the body.

If mankind already possesses an immortal soul, why would Paul say "this mortal?" If the essence of a man, his soul or spirit, was immortal, would Paul not say we are immortal? If we have an immortal soul, would the body rotting in the grave make us mortal? Or is that disposable, like your hair after being cut off? If they bury your hair, have they killed you?

Do you honestly believe that 1 Corinthians 15:53 above proves all humankind is immortal, but has a mortal body? Paul says "the dead shall be raised" and "we shall be changed." He is saying that after the physical body is dead, this change happens. He says, "For this mortal must put on immortality." When he says "this mortal," of whom is he speaking? He has just said, "We shall be changed."

Some would like to read that as "And we who are an immortal soul must put on an immortal body." Is that what you think it truly means? Could Paul not have written the sentence just as I wrote above to make it very clear?

He could have, but he did not!

The other time immortality is used is in Romans 2:7.

> *"7 to those who by perseverance in doing good **seek for glory and honor and immortality, eternal life;**"* (Romans 2:7 LSB)

Paul is speaking to the church in Rome, believers who have been saved, baptized, and born-again. Despite being saved, Paul says they are seeking immortality! Why would anyone seek what they already have? **This clearly states that these saved, baptized, and born-again Christians are not immortal and do not have an immortal soul or spirit.**

Paul says that eternal life and immortality are brought by Jesus Christ. **If they are brought to mankind, they are not already possessed by mankind.**

> *"9 who has saved us and called us with a holy calling, not according to our works, but according to His own purpose and grace which was given to us in Christ Jesus from all eternity, 10 but now has*

> been manifested by the appearing of our Savior Christ Jesus, who abolished death and **brought life and immortality to light through the gospel:**" (2 Timothy 1:9-10 LSB)

The term 'incorruptible" can mean immortal, and it is used only four times in the Bible.

The use below in 1 Corinthians 9:25 again shows we are seeking an incorruptible crown, or immortality, meaning we do not yet have it.

> "25 Now everyone who competes in the games exercises self-control in all things. They then do it to receive a **corruptible crown, but we an incorruptible.**" (1 Corinthians 9:25 LSB)

> "52 in a moment, in the twinkling of an eye, at the last trumpet. For the trumpet will sound, and the dead will be raised **incorruptible,** and we will be changed." (1 Corinthians 15:52 LSB)

Above, we see the dead shall be raised incorruptible, showing we are not currently incorruptible.

> "3 Blessed be the God and Father of our Lord Jesus Christ, who according to His great mercy has caused us to be born again to a living hope through the resurrection of Jesus Christ from the dead, 4 to obtain an inheritance **incorruptible** and undefiled and unfading, having been kept in heaven for you, 5 who are protected by the power of God through faith for a salvation ready to be revealed in the last time." (1 Peter 1:3-5 LSB)

Again, we hope for the resurrection to an incorruptible inheritance.

> "22 Since you have in obedience to the truth purified your souls for a love of the brothers without hypocrisy, fervently love one another from the heart, 23 for you have been **born again** not of corruptible seed **but incorruptible,** that is, through the living and enduring word of God. 24 For, "All flesh is like grass, And all its glory like the flower of grass. The grass withers, And the flower falls off," (1 Peter 1:22-24 LSB)

Above, the last use of the word "incorruptible" in the Bible is **after being born-again.** Some may argue here that we gain immortality immediately upon being born-again. Debating that is not part of this study, though you should read Romans 2:7 above again. The question being researched is, "Is there an immortal soul or spirit in man from birth?"

None of the verses above prove we do.

Does the Bible Say Humans Are Mortal?

> *"22Then Yahweh God said, "Behold, the man has become like one of Us to know good and evil; and now, **lest he send forth his hand and take also from the tree of life and eat and live forever**"— 23 therefore Yahweh God sent him out from the garden of Eden, to cultivate the ground from which he was taken. 24 So He drove the man out; and at the east of the garden of Eden He stationed the cherubim and the flaming sword which turned every direction to guard the way to the tree of life."* (Genesis 3:22-24 LSB)

This clearly says that if a man eats from the Tree of Life, he will live for ever. Otherwise, he won't, so he is not immortal.

> *"6 And the Lord was sorry that He had made man on the earth, and He was grieved in His heart. 7 So the Lord said, "**I will destroy man** whom I have created from the face of the earth, both man and beast, creeping thing and birds of the air, for I am sorry that I have made them." 8 But Noah found grace in the eyes of the Lord."* (Genesis 6:6-8 NKJV)

> *"13 Then God said to Noah, "The end of all flesh has come before Me; for the earth is filled with violence because of them; and behold, **I am about to destroy them** with the earth."* (Genesis 6:13 LSB)

> *"17 And behold, I Myself am bringing floodwaters on the earth, to destroy from under heaven all flesh in which is the breath of life; **everything that is on the earth shall die**."* (Genesis 6:17 NKJV)

> *"4 For after seven more days I will cause it to rain on the earth forty days and forty nights, and **I will***

> destroy from the face of the earth all living things that I have made.'" *(Genesis 7:4 NKJV)*

> "23 So He destroyed all living things which were on the face of the ground: both man and cattle, creeping thing and bird of the air. **They were destroyed** from the earth. Only Noah and those who were with him in the ark remained alive." (Genesis 7:23 NKJV)

> "23 And Abraham came near and said, **"Would You also destroy the righteous with the wicked?"** (Genesis 18:23 NKJV)

Clearly, the wicked are destroyed, but the righteous are saved from destruction.

> "15 for Yahweh your God in the midst of you is a jealous God—lest the anger of Yahweh your God be kindled against you, and **He destroy you** from the face of the earth." (Deuteronomy 6:15 LSB)

> "16 It stood still, but I could not discern the form thereof: an image was before mine eyes, there was silence, and I heard a voice, saying, 17 **Shall mortal man** be more just than God? Shall a man be more pure than his maker? 18 Behold, he put no trust in his servants; and his angels he charged with folly: 19 How much less in them that dwell in houses of clay, whose foundation is in the dust, which are crushed before the moth? 20 **They are destroyed from morning to evening: they perish for ever without any regarding it. 21 Doth not their excellency which is in them go away? They die, even without wisdom."** (Job 4:16-21)

How clear can the Bible get? It says man is not immortal but is mortal and is destroyed, dies, and perishes for ever.

> "11 My days are past; my plans are torn apart, Even the wishes of my heart. 12 They make night into day, saying, 'The light is near,' in the presence of darkness. 13 If **I hope for Sheol as my home**, I make my bed in the darkness; 14 If I call to the pit, 'You are my father'; To the worm, 'my mother and my sister'; 15 Where now is my hope? And who

> *beholds my hope? 16 **Will it go down with me to Sheol?** Shall we together go down into the dust?"'* (Job 17:11-16 LSB)

> *"But the way of **the ungodly shall perish**"* (Psalm 1:6)

If you believe in an eternal conscious hell, you don't believe the ungodly shall perish.

> *"29 All the prosperous of the earth will eat and worship, All those who go down to the dust will bow before Him, Even **he who cannot keep his soul alive.**"* (Psalm 22:29 LSB)

> *"18 Behold, the eye of Yahweh is on those who fear Him, On those who wait for His lovingkindness, 19 To deliver their soul from death And to keep them alive in famine."* (Psalm 33:18-19 LSB)

> *"**21 Evil shall slay the wicked,** And those who hate the righteous will be condemned."* (Psalm 34:21 LSB)

If you believe in eternal hell, you don't believe that evil brings death.

> *"9 For evildoers will be cut off, But those who hope for Yahweh, they will inherit the land. 10 Yet a little while and **the wicked man will be no more; You will look carefully at his place, and he will not be there.** 11 But the lowly will inherit the land And will delight themselves in abundant peace."* (Psalm 37:9-11 LSB)

Psalm 37:10 says **the wicked "will be no more**." This clearly means he shall not exist.

> *"**20 But the wicked will perish;** And the enemies of Yahweh will be like the glory of the pastures, **They vanish—in smoke they vanish away.**"* (Psalm 37:20 LSB)

> *"**20 But the wicked shall perish.** The enemies of Yahweh shall be like the beauty of the fields. **They will vanish—vanish like smoke.**"* (Psalm 37:20 WEB)

The wicked will "vanish." How much clearer can that be: "vanish away?"

"For the Lord loves the just and will not forsake his faithful ones. **Wrongdoers will be completely destroyed; the offspring of the wicked will perish.**" (Psalm 37:28 in the New International Version NIV is significantly different than the KJV.)

What phrase does the Bible use? The wrongdoers will be **"completely destroyed."**

"For the Lord loveth judgment, and forsaketh not his saints; they are preserved for ever: but **the seed of the wicked shall be cut off.**" (Psalm 37:28 KJV)

"For the Lord loves justice And does not forsake His godly ones; They are preserved forever, But the **descendants of the wicked will be cut off.**" (Psalm 37:28 New American Standard Bible (NASB) Appears to agree with KJV not NIV.)

"37 Mark the perfect man, and behold the upright: for the end of that man is peace. 38 But the **transgressors shall be destroyed together:** the end of the wicked shall be cut off." (Psalm 37:37-38)

"13 **For You have delivered my soul from death.** Have You not kept my feet from falling, That I may walk before God In the light of the living?" (Psalm 56:13 NKJV)

"27 For, behold, those who are far from You **will perish**; You have **destroyed** everyone who is unfaithful to You.." (Psalm 73:27 LSB)

"48 **What man can live and not see death? Can he deliver his life from the power of the grave?**" (Psalm 89:48 LSB)

"7 When the wicked spring up like grass, And when all the workers of iniquity flourish, It is that they may be **destroyed forever.**" (Psalm 92:7 LSB)

If you believe in eternal conscious hell, you don't believe the lost are "destroyed for ever," but that they live forever.

*"The wicked shall see it, and be grieved; he shall **gnash with his teeth, and melt away**: the desire of the **wicked shall perish.**"* (Psalm 112:10)

The wicked shall "melt away," which does not mean to live forever. The desire of the wicked shall "perish," does not mean to live forever.

*"20 The Lord preserveth all them that love him: but all **the wicked will he destroy.**"* (Psalm 145:20)

*"3 Put not your trust in princes, nor in the son of man, in whom there is no help. 4 His breath goeth forth, he returneth to his earth; **in that very day his thoughts perish.**"* (Psalm 146:3-4)

*"28 The **destruction of transgressors and of sinners** shall be together, And **those who forsake the Lord shall be consumed.** 29 For they shall be ashamed of the terebinth trees Which you have desired; And you shall be embarrassed because of the gardens Which you have chosen. 30 For you shall be as a terebinth whose leaf fades, And as a garden that has no water. 31 The strong shall be as tinder, And the work of it as a spark; Both will burn together, And no one shall quench them."* (Isaiah. 1:28–31 NKJV)

*"4 Behold, all souls are mine; as the soul of the father, so also the soul of the son is mine: the **soul that sinneth, it shall die.**"* (Ezekiel 18:4)

*"20 **The soul that sinneth, it shall die.** The son shall not bear the iniquity of the father, neither shall the father bear the iniquity of the son: the righteousness of the righteous shall be upon him, and the wickedness of the wicked shall be upon him."* (Ezekiel 18:20)

Yahweh says it again. **Both Ezekiel 18:4 and 18:20 say the "soul" shall die.** We know it doesn't mean we will keel over dead the minute we sin. But it does mean that someday we will die. **Clearly, a soul that "dies" is not immortal.**

*"23 **Do I have any pleasure at all that the wicked should die?"** says the Lord God, **"and not that he should turn from his ways and live?"*** (Ezekiel 18:23 NKJV)

*"32 For **I have no pleasure in the death of one who dies**," says the Lord God. "Therefore **turn and live!"**"* (Ezekiel 18:32)

"10 "Now as for you, son of man, say to the house of Israel, 'Thus you have spoken, saying, "Surely our transgressions and our sins are upon us, and we are rotting away in them; how then can we live?"' 11 Say to them, 'As I live!' declares Lord Yahweh, 'I take no pleasure in **the death of the wicked**, but rather that the wicked **turn from his way and live**. Turn back, turn back from your evil ways! **Why then will you die**, O house of Israel?' 12 Now as for you, son of man, say to the sons of your people, 'The righteousness of a righteous man will not deliver him in the day of his transgression, and as for the wickedness of the wicked, he will not stumble because of it in the day when he turns from his wickedness; whereas a righteous man will not be able to live by his righteousness on the day when he commits sin.' 13 When I say to the righteous he will surely live, and he so trusts in his righteousness that he does iniquity, none of his righteous deeds will be remembered; but in that same iniquity of his which he has done **he will die**. 14 But when I say to the wicked, '**You will surely die**,' and he turns from his sin and does justice and righteousness, 15 if a wicked man restores a pledge, pays back what he has taken by robbery, walks by the statutes of life without committing iniquity, he shall surely live; he shall not die. 16 None of his sins that he has done will be remembered against him. He has done justice and righteousness; he shall surely live. 17 "Yet the sons of your people say, 'The way of the Lord is not right,' when it is their own way that is not right. 18 When the righteous turns from his righteousness and does iniquity, then **he shall die in it.** 19 But when the wicked turns from his wickedness and does justice and righteousness, he will live by them. 20 Yet you say, 'The way of the Lord is not right.' O house of Israel, I will judge each of you according to his ways."'" (Ezekiel 33:10-20 LSB)

Yahweh says He has no pleasure in the death of the wicked: **"he shall die," "thou shalt surely die."** This is exactly what He told Adam and Eve in the Garden of Eden. Yahweh does not say sinners will be tortured forever and ever.

> "1 For behold, the day is coming, Burning like an oven, And all the proud, yes, all who do wickedly will be stubble. And the day which is coming shall **burn them up**," Says the Lord of hosts, "That will **leave them neither root nor branch."** (Malachi 4:1 NKJV)

Of the wicked, God says He shall "burn them up," and no root or branch is left. They will not burn forever and ever, but will be totally burned up, with nothing left.

> "13 Enter by the narrow gate; for wide is the gate and broad is the way that **leads to destruction**, and there are many who go in by it. 14 Because narrow is the gate and difficult is the way which leads to life, and there are few who find it." (Matthew 7:13-14 NKJV)

> "28 And fear not them which kill the body, but are not able to **kill the soul**: but rather fear him which is able to **destroy both soul and body in hell**." (Matthew 10:28)

This is a strong verse directly from Yeshua's mouth. Think about it deeply. It uses the word destroy for the body in the fire of hell. We know the body burns up to ashes and turns to ash, which itself may be burned up into the elements we were made from. But it also talks about the "soul" in exactly the same way. It clearly says God can "destroy" the soul of man. A second word used is "kill." Other humans can kill our bodies, but they cannot kill our souls. For those who say "destroy" does not mean destroy, now they must also say "kill" does not mean kill. Note that it does not say that man has a spirit; he only has a body and a soul.

> "30 Let both grow together until the harvest: and in the time of harvest I will say to the reapers, **Gather ye together first the tares, and bind them in bundles to burn them**: but gather the wheat into my barn." (Matthew 13:30)

> *"36 Then He left the crowds and went into the house. And His disciples came to Him and said, "Explain to us the parable of the tares of the field." 37 And He answered and said, "The one who sows the good seed is the Son of Man, 38 and the field is the world; and as for the good seed, these are the sons of the kingdom; and the tares are the sons of the evil one; 39 and the enemy who sowed them is the devil, and the harvest is the end of the age; and the reapers are angels. 40 So just as the tares are gathered up and burned with fire, so shall it be at the end of the age. 41 The Son of Man will send forth His angels, and they will gather out of His kingdom all stumbling blocks, and those who commit lawlessness, 42 and **will throw them into the fiery furnace; in that place there will be weeping and gnashing of teeth.** 43 Then the righteous will shine forth as the sun in the kingdom of their Father. He who has ears, let him hear."* (Matthew 13:36-43 LSB)

> *"49 So it will be at the end of the age; the angels will come forth and take out the wicked from among the righteous, 50 and will throw them into the fiery furnace; in that place there will be weeping and gnashing of teeth."* (Matthew 13:49-50 LSB)

Does the Bible Say Humans Have Eternal Life?

The phrase "Eternal Life" is found 26 times in the Bible, all in the New Testament. Every one of these 26 occurrences concerns people asking Yeshua how to gain eternal life (which they know they do not have), or Yeshua telling people how to gain eternal life (which they do not have), or Yeshua giving them eternal life (which they don't have), or eternal life being a **gift** from God (which they do not have yet). There is no verse that says humans have eternal life from birth.

> *"16 And behold, someone came to Him and said, "Teacher, **what good thing shall I do that I may have eternal life?**" 17 And He said to him, "Why are you asking Me about what is good? There is only One who is good; but **if you wish to enter into life, keep the commandments.**""* (Matthew 19:16-17 LSB)

Yeshua Himself says humans must "enter into life" by keeping the commandments. We do not already posses eternal life. Since they are listening to and obeying Yeshua, we know they are saved by faith, but faith and love are shown by obedience.

> *"29 And everyone who has left houses or brothers or sisters or father or mother or children or farms for My name's sake, will receive one hundred times as much, and **will inherit eternal life.**"* (Matthew 19:29 LSB)

Again, from the mouth of Yeshua, **we must "inherit eternal life." We do not already possess it** as an inherent attribute of being human.

> *"17 And as He was setting out on a journey, a man ran up to Him and knelt before Him, and began asking Him, "Good Teacher, what shall I do **to inherit eternal life?**""* (Mark 10:17 LSB)

> *"30 except one who will receive one hundred times as much now in the present age—houses and brothers and sisters and mothers and children and farms, along with persecutions—and **in the age to come, eternal life.**"* (Mark 10:30 LSB)

> *"25 And behold, a scholar of the Law stood up and was putting Him to the test, saying, "Teacher, what shall I do to **inherit eternal life**?""* (Luke 10:25 LSB)

> *"18 And a ruler questioned Him, saying, "Good Teacher, what shall I do to **inherit eternal life**?""* (Luke 18:18 LSB)

> *"15 so that whoever **believes** will in Him **have eternal life.**"* (John 3:15 LSB)

The opposite of "have eternal life" is "perish," not "have eternal life but somewhere else, not in heaven."

> *"39 You search the Scriptures because you think that **in them you have eternal life**; it is these that bear witness about Me;"* (John 5:39 LSB)

> *"54 He who eats My flesh and drinks My blood **has eternal life,** and I will raise him up on the last day."* (John 6:54 LSB)

> *"68 But Simon Peter answered Him, "Lord, to whom shall we go? **You have the words of eternal life**."* (John 6:68 NKJV)

> *"And **I give unto them eternal life;** and they shall never perish, neither shall any man pluck them out of my hand."* (John 10:28)

Again, the opposite of "eternal life" is "perish," not "eternal life" somewhere else.

> *"2 As You have given Him authority over all flesh, that **He should give eternal life** to as many as You have given Him."* (John 17:2 NKJV)

> *"48 And when the Gentiles heard this, they began rejoicing and glorifying the word of the Lord, and **as many as had been appointed to eternal life believed."*** (Acts 13:48 LSB)

> *"7 to those who by perseverance in doing good **seek for glory and honor and immortality, eternal life;**"* (Romans 2:7 LSB)

> *"21 That as sin hath reigned unto death, even so might grace reign through righteousness **unto eternal life by Jesus Christ our Lord**."* (Romans 5:21)

> *"23 For the wages of sin is death; but the gift of God is **eternal life through Jesus Christ our Lord**."* (Romans 6:23)

Does the Bible say the wages of sin is eternal life in torture in Hell? No! It says, **"The wages of sin is death."**

> *"12 **Fight the good fight of faith. Take hold of the eternal life to which you were called,** and you made the good confession in the presence of many witnesses."* (1 Timothy 6:12 LSB)

> *"19 Laying up in store for themselves a good foundation against the time to come, **that they may lay hold on eternal life**."* (1 Timothy 6:19)

> *"**In hope of eternal life,** which God, that cannot lie, promised before the world began;"* (Titus 1:2)

> *"7 That being justified by his grace, we should be made heirs according **to the hope of eternal life**."* (Titus 3:7)

> *"2 and the life was manifested, and we have seen and bear witness **and proclaim to you the eternal life,** which was with the Father and was manifested to us"* (1 John 1:2 LSB)

> *"25 And this is the promise that He has promised us—**eternal life**."* (1 John 2:25 NKJV)

> *"15 Everyone who hates his brother is a murderer, and you know that **no murderer has eternal life abiding in him.**"* (1 John 3:15 LSB)

Read the verse above again. This one verse should end our quest. It is considering a murderer to be an unsaved, not born-again person. Since everyone who hates his brother is a murderer (in their heart), all people who have hated someone **do not have eternal life** in heaven, the Lake of Fire, or anywhere else. If they repent, believe in Yeshua, and obey Him, then they can gain the gift of eternal life.

> *"11 And this is the testimony: that God has given us **eternal life, and this life is in His Son.**"* (1 John 5:11 NKJV)

If God has "given us eternal life, and this life is in His Son," then before we believed in His Son, we did not have eternal life abiding in us.

> *"13 These things I have written to you who believe in the name of the Son of God, **that you may know that you have eternal life,** and that you may continue to believe in the name of the Son of God."* (1 John 5:13 NKJV)

One friend emphasizes the verse above, noting that "You have eternal life" is written to believers. Once a person is born-again by repenting, confessing, and believing in Yeshua Hamashiach (Jesus the Messiah), they have eternal life, IF they don't lose it by going into perdition.

> *"20 And we know that the Son of God has come, and has given us understanding so that we may know Him who is true; and we are in Him who is true, in His Son Jesus Christ. **This is the true God and eternal life.**"* (1 John 5:20 LSB)

As always, these say nothing about an unsaved, not born-again human having eternal life, but about seeking it.

If you find a Bible Scripture clearly saying humans, from birth, possess eternal life, an immortal soul, or an eternal spirit, please share that Scripture with me at Dan@vigilantvaliant.com.

How Do Humans Receive a Spirit?

If humans do not possess an immortal spirit from birth, how can they ever gain immortality in eternal life? Yeshua directly told Nicodemus what it takes for a person to see the Kingdom of God. The phrase "born-again" is found only three times in the Bible, both in the New King James Version (NKJV) and the New International Version (NIV).

> *"3 Jesus answered and said to him, "Most assuredly, I say to you, unless one is **born again**, he cannot see the kingdom of God.""* (John 3:3 NKJV)

> *"7 Do not marvel that I said to you, 'You must be **born again**.'."* (John 3:7 NKJV)

> *"23 Having been **born again**, not of corruptible seed but incorruptible, through the word of God which lives and abides forever,"* (1 Peter 1:23 NKJV)

Let us examine these verses closely, as they are from the very mouth of the Savior, Yeshua Hamashiach, Jesus the Messiah.

The entire story of Nicodemus is found in John 3:1-18.

> *"1 There was a man of the Pharisees named Nicodemus, a ruler of the Jews. 2 This man came to Jesus by night and said to Him, "Rabbi, we know that You are a teacher come from God; for no one can do these signs that You do unless God is with him.""* (John 3:1-2 NKJV)

We see that Nicodemus was a Pharisee, a religious man. He came to Yeshua to ask questions in an honest way, seeking the truth, not trying to trap Him, as the Pharisees and Sadducees had often done.

> "3 Jesus answered and said to him, "Most assuredly, I say to you, unless one is **born again, he cannot see the kingdom of God.**" 4 Nicodemus said to Him, "How can a man be born when he is old? Can he enter a second time into his mother's womb and be born?" 5 Jesus answered, "Most assuredly, I say to you, **unless one is born of water and the Spirit, he cannot enter the kingdom of God.** 6 That which is born of the flesh is flesh, and that which is born of the Spirit is spirit. 7 Do not marvel that I said to you, '**You must be born again.**' 8 The wind blows where it wishes, and you hear the sound of it, but cannot tell where it comes from and where it goes. So is everyone who is born of the Spirit.""* (John 3:3-8 NKJV)

Yeshua is very clear in His statement. The natural man cannot enter the Kingdom of God. Humans must be "born-again." So humans must be "born of water and of the Spirit." There may be some debate about whether being "born of water" means the natural human birth when a woman's water breaks or if that means baptism. But that doesn't matter for our study here. It is the next part that was the crux of salvation, the basis for immortality in eternal life.

> "9 **Nicodemus answered and said to Him, "How can these things be?"** 10 Jesus answered and said to him, "Are you the teacher of Israel, and do not know these things? 11 Most assuredly, I say to you, We speak what We know and testify what We have seen, and you do not receive Our witness. 12 If I have told you earthly things and you do not believe, how will you believe if I tell you heavenly things? 13 No one has ascended to heaven but He who came down from heaven, that is, the Son of Man who is in heaven. 14 And as Moses lifted up the serpent in the wilderness, even so must the Son of Man be lifted up, 15 that **whoever believes in Him should not perish but have eternal life.** 16 For God so loved the world that He gave His only begotten Son, that **whoever believes in Him should not perish but have everlasting life.** 17 For God did not send His Son into the world to

> condemn the world, but that the world through Him might be saved. 18 **"He who believes in Him is not condemned;** but he who does not believe is condemned already, because he has not believed in the name of the only begotten Son of God." (John 3:1-18 NKJV)

Yeshua answers Nicodemus' question on how to be born-again of the Spirit by saying that whoever believes in Him, the only begotten Son of God, will have eternal life. That eternal life means they would have an immortal spirit. So the dozens and dozens of Scriptures above show that man does not have an immortal spirit from birth; their first natural physical birth was by water. Yeshua states that clearly here. Humans must be born-again, born of the Spirit. Then and only then do they have a spirit that can live forever.

Paul explains to the Corinthians that the "natural man" cannot understand spiritual things, but the one who has repented and believes in Yeshua Hamashiach (Jesus the Messiah) has received the Holy Spirit of the Living God. They are born-again of the Spirit. Therefore, they can understand spiritual things.

> "11 For what man knows the things of a man except the spirit of the man which is in him? Even so no one knows the things of God except the Spirit of God. 12 **Now we have received, not the spirit of the world, but the Spirit who is from God,** that we might know the things that have been freely given to us by God. 13 These things we also speak, not in words which man's wisdom teaches but which the Holy Spirit teaches, comparing spiritual things with spiritual. 14 **But the natural man does not receive the things of the Spirit of God, for they are foolishness to him; nor can he know them, because they are spiritually discerned."** (1Corinthians 2:11-14 NKJV)

> "20 I have been crucified with Christ; **it is no longer I who live, but Christ lives in me**; and the life which I now live in the flesh I live by faith in the Son of God, who loved me and gave Himself for me." (Galatians 2:20 NKJV)

Speaking of when this immortal life will begin, Paul says it will be at the return of Yeshua to Earth.

> "20 But now Christ is risen from the dead, and has become the firstfruits of those who have fallen

> *asleep. 21 For since by man came death, by Man also came the resurrection of the dead. 22 For as in Adam all die, even so **in Christ all shall be made alive. 23 But each one in his own order: Christ the firstfruits, afterward those who are Christ's at His coming.** 24 Then comes the end, when He delivers the kingdom to God the Father, when He puts an end to all rule and all authority and power. 25 For He must reign till He has put all enemies under His feet. 26 The last enemy that will be destroyed is death. 27 For "He has put all things under His feet." But when He says "all things are put under Him," it is evident that He who put all things under Him is excepted. 28 Now when all things are made subject to Him, then the Son Himself will also be subject to Him who put all things under Him, that God may be all in all." (1 Corinthians 15:20-28 NKJV)*

Continuing on this theme, Paul tells us exactly when we will receive immortality. At the return of Christ, believers, whether dead and in the grave or alive, will put on immortality. Obviously, if Paul is saying we are mortal, and must "put on immortality" at that time, we did not have an immortal soul or spirit before then.

> *"52 in a moment, in the twinkling of an eye, **at the last trumpet.** For the trumpet will sound, and the dead will be raised incorruptible, and we will be changed. 53 For this corruptible must put on the incorruptible, and **this mortal must put on immortality.** 54 But when this corruptible puts on the incorruptible, and this mortal puts on immortality, then will come about the word that is written, "Death is swallowed up in victory. 55 O death, where is your victory? O death, where is your sting?"" (1 Corinthians 15:52-55 LSB)*

This reinforces what Paul told the Thessalonians earlier: that at the last trumpet call, Yeshua will return to Earth and raise the believing dead, and together with those believers who are still alive, He will give them eternal life.

> *"14 For **if we believe that Jesus died and rose again**, even so God will bring with Him those who have fallen asleep in Jesus. 15 For this we say to you by the word of the Lord, that we who are alive and remain until the coming of the Lord, will not*

*precede those who have fallen asleep. 16 **For the Lord Himself will descend from heaven with a shout, with the voice of the archangel and with the trumpet of God,** and the dead in Christ will rise first. 17 Then we who are alive and remain will be caught up together with them in the clouds to meet the Lord in the air, and so we shall always be with the Lord." (1 Thessalonians 4:14-17 LSB)*

This confirms what Yeshua Himself said about a resurrection of the saved, or the righteous.

*"12 And He also went on to say to the one who had invited Him, "When you give a luncheon or a dinner, do not invite your friends or your brothers or your relatives or rich neighbors, lest they also invite you in return and that will be your repayment. 13 But when you give a reception, invite the poor, the crippled, the lame, the blind, 14 and you will be blessed, since they do not have the means to repay you; for it will be repaid to you **at the resurrection of the righteous.**""* (Luke 14:12-14 LSB)

Yeshua had promised eternal life to those who believed in Him. But it was hard to let that sink in. When His friend Lazarus died, Yeshua had this discussion with Martha, Lazarus' sister. She already knew the just would rise on the last day, at the last trumpet. But Yeshua told her that it is He who gives eternal life and can make us immortal.

*"21 Martha then said to Jesus, "Lord, if You had been here, my brother would not have died. 22 But even now I know that whatever You ask from God, God will give You." 23 Jesus *said to her, **"Your brother will rise again." 24 Martha *said to Him, "I know that he will rise again in the resurrection on the last day."** 25 Jesus said to her, "I am the resurrection and the life; he who believes in Me will live even if he dies, 26 and everyone who lives and believes in Me will never die—ever. Do you believe this?" 27 She *said to Him, "Yes, Lord; I have believed that You are the Christ, the Son of God, the One who comes into the world.""* (John 11:21-27 LSB)

Yeshua never let there be any doubt about when He would give eternal life to those who believed. He repeats here that He will raise them up "at the last day."

> "39 **Now this is the will of Him who sent Me, that of all that He has given Me I lose nothing, but raise it up on the last day.** 40 For this is the will of My Father, that everyone who sees the Son and believes in Him will have eternal life, and **I Myself will raise him up on the last day.**" 41 Therefore the Jews were grumbling about Him, because He said, "I am the bread that came down from heaven." 42 They were saying, "Is not this Jesus, the son of Joseph, whose father and mother we know? How does He now say, 'I have come down from heaven'?" 43 Jesus answered and said to them, "Stop grumbling among yourselves. 44 No one can come to Me unless the Father who sent Me draws him; and **I will raise him up on the last day.**" (John 6:39-44 LSB)

> "47 Most assuredly, I say to you, **he who believes in Me has everlasting life.** 48 I am the bread of life. 49 Your fathers ate the manna in the wilderness, and are dead. 50 This is the bread which comes down from heaven, that one may eat of it and not die. 51 **I am the living bread which came down from heaven. If anyone eats of this bread, he will live forever;** and the bread that I shall give is My flesh, which I shall give for the life of the world." 52 The Jews therefore quarreled among themselves, saying, "How can this Man give us His flesh to eat?" 53 Then Jesus said to them, "Most assuredly, I say to you, **unless you eat the flesh of the Son of Man and drink His blood, you have no life in you. 54 Whoever eats My flesh and drinks My blood has eternal life, and I will raise him up at the last day.** 55 For My flesh is food indeed, and My blood is drink indeed. 56 He who eats My flesh and drinks My blood abides in Me, and I in him. 57 As the living Father sent Me, and I live because of the Father, so he who feeds on Me will live because of Me. 58 This is the bread which came down from heaven—not as your fathers ate the manna, and are dead. **He who eats this bread will live forever.**"" (John 6:47-58 NKJV)

Remember, at Passover, the Passover Lamb was to be roasted and eaten by the believers. Yeshua is talking about accepting His sacrifice of His body and blood on the cross at His crucifixion as our Passover Lamb. At that "last supper" Passover meal, Yeshua commanded us to observe that Passover Feast meal in remembrance of Him by drinking wine and eating bread in the Passover meal, meaning we accept His offer of salvation and make Him our Lord and Savior. That acceptance makes Him our personal Passover Lamb.

Remember that John the Baptist identified Yeshua as the Lamb of God.

*"29 The next day John saw Jesus coming toward him, and said, "**Behold! The Lamb of God** who takes away the sin of the world!"* (John 1:29 NKJV)

Reviewing these last few verses and how Yeshua spoke about the resurrection on the last day, at the last trumpet, there is no way an honest reader can say this is only the empty and rotted body He is speaking of. It is the entire person.

Also, note that Yeshua says He was offering up His body and blood to gain eternal life for believers. He says to those who do not accept Him, Yeshua, as their savior, "Ye have no life in you." See John 6:53, above.

Let that sink in. The unsaved do not have life in them. Obviously, they are walking around with a soul—a nephesh. Like Adam and Eve after they sinned. But they had lost the chance at eternal life—at immortality. These people, who do not accept Jesus as their Lord and Savior, have no life in them (John 6:53). They do not have an immortal soul or spirit.

*"13 If you then, being evil, know how to give good gifts to your children, how much more will **your heavenly Father give the Holy Spirit to those who ask Him?**""* (Luke 11:13 LSB)

*"38 And Peter said to them, "Repent, and each of you be baptized in the name of Jesus Christ for the forgiveness of your sins; and **you will receive the gift of the Holy Spirit.**"* (Acts 2:38 LSB)

*"37 Now on the last day, the great day of the feast, Jesus stood and cried out, saying, "If anyone is thirsty, let him come to Me and drink. 38 He who believes in Me, as the Scripture said, 'From his innermost being will flow rivers of living water.'" 39 **But this He spoke of the Spirit, whom those who***

> *believed in Him were going to receive; for the Spirit was not yet given,* because Jesus was not yet glorified." (John 7:37-39 LSB)

The Holy Spirit is a gift from Yahweh, our God. Eternal life is also a gift from God. Gifts are the giving of something we don't have so that we will have it when the gift is given.

> "22 But now having been set free from sin, and having become slaves of God, you have your fruit to holiness, and the end, everlasting life. 23 For the wages of sin is death, but **the gift of God is eternal life** in Christ Jesus our Lord." (Romans 6:22-23 NKJV)

The two verse selections from above strongly prove that mankind is not born with an immortal soul and is not born with eternal life. Both are gifts from God, the Living God, Yahweh, the God of Abraham, through His Son, and our Savior, Yeshua Hamashiach, Jesus the Messiah.

The following is a great Scripture quote from Paul, who shows that the "natural man" cannot discern the things of the spirit because he doesn't have the spirit of God in him. But to those who believe and are baptized, God has given the "spirit which is of God."

> "9 But as it is written: 'Eye has not seen, nor ear heard, Nor have entered into the heart of man The things which God has prepared for those who love Him.' 10 But God has revealed them to us through His Spirit. For the Spirit searches all things, yes, the deep things of God. 11 **For what man knows the things of a man except the spirit of the man which is in him?** Even so no one knows the things of God except the Spirit of God. 12 **Now we have received, not the spirit of the world, but the Spirit who is from God,** that we might know the things that have been freely given to us by God. 13 These things we also speak, not in words which man's wisdom teaches but which the Holy Spirit teaches, comparing spiritual things with spiritual. 14 **But the natural man does not receive the things of the Spirit of God,** for they are foolishness to him; **nor can he know them, because they are spiritually discerned.**" (1 Corinthians 2:9-14 NKJV)

Above, Paul says believers have not received the "spirit of this world." He seems to say that it is the spirit in the "natural man" that cannot understand spiritual things. Those Scriptures that seem to say there is a spirit in the natural, unsaved man may be speaking of the "spirit of this world," which is clearly not a personal, immortal spirit.

> "1 And I, brothers, was **not able to speak to you as to spiritual men, but as to fleshly men**, as to infants in Christ. 2 I gave you milk to drink, not solid food, for you were not yet able to receive it. Indeed, even now you are still not able," (1 Corinthians 3:1-2 LSB)

> "17 But you, beloved, remember the words which were spoken before by the apostles of our Lord Jesus Christ: 18 how they told you that **there would be mockers** in the last time who would walk according to their own ungodly lusts. 19 These are sensual persons, who cause divisions, **not having the Spirit.**" (Jude 1:17-19 NKJV)

Paul says the carnal mind cannot understand spiritual things. Those who mock Jews and Christians are these sensual, carnal people who do not understand, because they cannot understand, for spiritual things are discerned by the spirit.

> "14 But if you have bitter jealousy and selfish ambition in your heart, do not be arrogant and so lie against the truth. 15 **This wisdom is not coming down from above, but is earthly, natural, demonic.** 16 For where jealousy and selfish ambition exist, there is disorder and every evil practice." (James 3.14-16 LSB)

> "23 But an hour is coming, and now is, when the **true worshipers will worship the Father in spirit** and truth; for such people the Father seeks to be His worshipers. 24 God is spirit, and those who worship Him **must worship in spirit** and truth.'" (John 4.23–24)

Later in the First Epistle to the Corinthians, Paul confirms and emphasizes that when they are baptized in the name of Yeshua (Jesus), believers receive the Spirit of God. Some people believe God is so kind that He will save all people. This Scripture says otherwise.

> *"9 Or do you not know that the unrighteous will not inherit the kingdom of God? Do not be deceived; neither the sexually immoral, nor idolaters, nor adulterers, nor effeminate, nor homosexuals, 10 nor thieves, nor the greedy, nor drunkards, nor revilers, nor swindlers, will inherit the kingdom of God. 11 And such were some of you; but you were washed,* **but you were sanctified, but you were justified in the name of the Lord Jesus Christ and in the Spirit of our God.***"* (1 Corinthians 6:9-11 LSB)

The Holy Spirit of God that believers receive is called "the spirit of adoption."

> *"14 For as many as are being led by the Spirit of God, these are sons of God. 15 For you have not received a spirit of slavery leading to fear again, but* **you have received the Spirit of adoption as sons** *by whom we cry out, "Abba! Father!" 16* **The Spirit Himself testifies with our spirit that we are children of God,***"* (Romans 8:14-16 LSB)

What is the end of those who do not accept Yeshua as their Lord and Savior? Their end is destruction, not eternal life in hell. If you are not sure of that, please see my Bible study, "Will Humans Be Tortured Forever in Hell?"

> *"18 For many walk, of whom I have told you often, and now tell you even weeping, that they are the* **enemies of the cross of Christ:** *19* **Whose end is destruction***, whose God is their belly, and whose glory is in their shame, who mind earthly things."* (Philippians 3:18-19)

Verses Used to Try to Prove an Immortal Soul in All Men from Birth

The following verses are addressed because they are used by Bible studies attempting to prove that humans have an immortal soul from birth that will live eternally either in the Kingdom of Heaven or eternally in hell (by which they mean the Lake of Fire). The word hell is not in the Bible at all, whether in Hebrew or Greek. It is an amalgamation of Hades, Sheol, Gehenna, and Tartarus.

> "**The meek** shall eat and be satisfied: they shall praise the Lord that seek him: **your heart shall live for ever.**" (Psalm 22:26 KJV)

First, note that this says your "heart" shall live forever, and in no translation I could find is it translated as "soul" or "spirit." Second, compare this with what Yeshua said in His Sermon on the Mount.

> "Blessed are the **meek: for they shall inherit the earth.**" (Matthew 5:5)

Does Yeshua mean all humans who are meek will be saved and earn an eternal life of immortality? Does this hold for even meek murderers? I believe almost all will agree that Yeshua means that all who believe in Him and are meek will be raised at the resurrection to live in the new earth, which will be governed by the Kingdom of God.

This does not in any way prove that all humans have an immortal soul from birth.

> "Surely goodness and mercy shall follow me all the days of my life: and **I will dwell in the house of the Lord for ever.**" (Psalm 23:6)

This is a Psalm of King David, whom Yahweh calls a man after His own heart. David is one of the faithful, along with Abraham, Isaac, and Jacob, and one of the saved who receive the Holy Spirit of God.

Neither this verse nor any of the verses above proves in any way that all humans have an immortal soul from birth.

> "7 No one can redeem the life of another or give to God a ransom for them— 8 the ransom for a life is costly, no payment is ever enough— 9 **so that they should live on forever** and not see decay." (Psalm 49:7-9 NIV)

Again, this is about men being "saved," "redeemed," and living forever. This does not in any way prove that all humans have an immortal soul from birth.

> "16 Therefore we do not lose heart, but though our outer man is decaying, yet our **inner man is being renewed day by day.**" (2 Corinthians 4:16 LSB)

The "inner man" being renewed day by day is the weakest attempt I have seen of those trying to prove an immortal soul exists in a man from birth. The following verses tell believers about an eternal house, or body, given upon resurrection.

> *"18 While we look not at the things which are seen, but at the things which are not seen: for the things which are seen are temporal; but the **things which are not seen are eternal.**"* (2 Corinthians 4:18)

> *"1 For we know that if the earthly tent we live in is destroyed, we have a building from God, **an eternal house in heaven**, not built by human hands. 2 Meanwhile we groan, longing to be clothed instead with our heavenly dwelling,"* (2 Corinthians 5:1-2 NIV)

This is again speaking about saved believers and does not in any way prove that all humans have an immortal soul from birth. You may wonder why this verse is even here, but remember the title of the section we are currently in, "Verses Used to Try to Prove an Immortal Soul in All Men from Birth." I can only guess that they use it because "everlasting consolation" was the point here, though that is so off-point as to be useless as proof. It is included only for thoroughness, and in any case, it is talking to believers.

> *"16 Now may our Lord Jesus Christ Himself, and our God and Father, who has loved us and given us **everlasting consolation** and good hope by grace,"* (2 Thessalonians 2:16 NKJV)

> "1 In the same way, you wives, be subject to your own husbands so that even if any of them are disobedient to the word, they may be won without a word by the conduct of their wives, 2 as they observe your pure conduct with fear. 3 Your adornment must not be merely external—braiding the hair, and wearing gold jewelry, or putting on garments; 4 but let it be the hidden person of the heart, with the **incorruptible** quality of a lowly and quiet spirit, which is precious in the sight of God. 5 For in this way in former times the holy women also, who hoped in God, used to adorn themselves, being subject to their own husbands, 6 just as Sarah obeyed Abraham, calling him lord. You have become her children if you do good, not fearing any intimidation." (1 Peter 3:1-6 LSB)

Does this seem to say the spirit in a man is incorruptible? Of whom is it speaking? It is speaking of saved wives who are born-again and have received the Holy Spirit of God. This does not in any way prove that all humans have an immortal soul from birth.

Another verse people use to try to prove humans have an immortal soul from birth is Mark 12:27.

> *"26 But concerning the dead, that they rise, have you not read in the book of Moses, in the burning bush passage, how God spoke to him, saying, 'I am the God of Abraham, the God of Isaac, and the God of Jacob'? 27 He is not the God of the dead, but the **God of the living**. You are therefore greatly mistaken.""* (Mark 12:26-27 NKJV)

Because Yeshua says Yahweh is the God of the living, some say this proves these people have an immortal soul. However, He is talking about the saved faithful who have received the Holy Spirit of God by faith.

> *"21 And another of the disciples said to Him, "Lord, permit me first to go and bury my father." 22 But Jesus *said to him, "Follow Me, and **allow the dead to bury their own dead**.""* (Matthew 8:21-22 LSB)

As for the non-believers who are physically alive, Yeshua called these walking, talking people "dead." These walking, talking dead can bury the physically dead. It was more important for this disciple to follow Jesus. The clear implication here is that this believer, a disciple, was not dead spiritually. When did he become non-dead, unlike the rest of his walking, talking dead family? He became spiritually alive when he believed and received the Holy Spirit of God.

> *"12 having been buried with him in baptism, in which you were also raised with him through your faith in the working of God, who raised him from the dead. 13 When you **were dead in your sins** and in the uncircumcision of your flesh, God made you alive with Christ. He forgave us all our sins,"* (Colossians 2:12-13 NIV)

> *"1 And **you were dead in your transgressions and sins,** 2 in which you formerly walked according to the course of this world, according to the ruler of the power of the air, the spirit that is now working in*

> *the sons of disobedience, 3 among whom we all also formerly conducted ourselves in the lusts of our flesh, doing the desires of the flesh and of the mind, and were by nature children of wrath, even as the rest. 4 But God, being rich in mercy because of His great love with which He loved us, 5* **even when we were dead in our transgressions,** *made us alive together with Christ—by grace you have been saved—"* (Ephesians 2:1-5 LSB)

Paul says that **before** being saved, they were "dead in their sins," but that upon believing in Yeshua, He quickened them and brought them to life, in that they would now live forever. This harkens back to Adam and Eve in the Garden of Eden, when God said, "For in the day that thou eatest thereof, thou shalt surely die." Just as Yeshua says walking, talking non-believers are dead, and Paul says they are brought to life (quickened) upon believing. Adam and Eve were still walking and talking after their sin, but they were "dead" in their sin.

The Slam Dunk: The Mic Drop

Yes, we have read this before, but please read the following Scripture section carefully from beginning to end. Yahweh, the living God, the eternal God, is speaking to His people, which includes believing Christians. **Please pray to God, our Father, to guide you in understanding what He is saying to you through Ezekiel.**

> *"20* **The soul who sins shall die.** *The son shall not bear the guilt of the father, nor the father bear the guilt of the son. The righteousness of the righteous shall be upon himself, and the wickedness of the wicked shall be upon himself."*
>
> *21 "But if a wicked man turns from all his sins which he has committed, keeps all My statutes, and does what is lawful and right, he shall surely live; he shall not die. 22 None of the transgressions which he has committed shall be remembered against him; because of the righteousness which he has done, he shall live. 23 Do I have any pleasure at all that the wicked should* **die***?" says the Lord God, "and not that he should turn from his ways and live?"*
>
> *24 "But when a righteous man turns away from his righteousness and commits iniquity, and does according to all the abominations that the wicked*

*man does, shall he live? All the righteousness which he has done shall not be remembered; because of the unfaithfulness of which he is guilty and the sin which he has committed, because of them he shall **die**".*

*25 "Yet you say, 'The way of the Lord is not fair.' Hear now, O house of Israel, is it not My way which is fair, and your ways which are not fair? 26 When a righteous man turns away from his righteousness, commits iniquity, and **dies** in it, it is because of the iniquity which he has done that he **dies**. 27 Again, when a wicked man turns away from the wickedness which he committed, and does what is lawful and right, he preserves himself alive. 28 Because he considers and turns away from all the transgressions which he committed, he shall surely live; he shall not **die**. 29 Yet the house of Israel says, 'The way of the Lord is not fair.' O house of Israel, is it not My ways which are fair, and your ways which are not fair?"*

*30 "Therefore I will judge you, O house of Israel, every one according to his ways," says the Lord God. "Repent, and turn from all your transgressions, so that iniquity will not be your ruin. 31 Cast away from you all the transgressions which you have committed, and get yourselves a new heart and a new spirit. For **why should you die**, O house of Israel? 32 For I have no pleasure in the **death** of one who **dies**," says the Lord God. "Therefore turn and live!"* (Ezekiel 18:20-32 NKJV)

Do you think the Almighty God cannot make Himself understood? Don't you think the Creator God is capable of choosing the right words to convey what He meant? Do you trust a minister's or leader's interpretation, however good-hearted, over the actual words of God? Does it make any sense at all when someone tells you the word "die" doesn't mean "die" but "live forever?" Does it make sense that this only means the body, not the soul or spirit?

If God was simply telling unrepentant sinners their physical bodies would die, how is that any different from those whose sins are forgiven but who still die a physical death? I believe it is impossible that the physical body is what God is talking about in these verses. We have all heard of lifelong thieves, murderers, and other sinners who never repented.

Did their bodies die any earlier in life than everybody else's? If not, then you are making God a liar by believing He meant body here. Adam and Eve are proof of this. Their bodies lived full lives after sinning by eating the forbidden fruit. God was not talking about physical bodies in Genesis, and He is not talking about physical bodies in the passage above from Ezekiel.

Is it really feasible to believe that God actually meant "will live forever in torture" instead of "**die**?"

> *"14 Then death and Hades **were thrown into the lake of fire. This is the second death**, the lake of fire. 15 And if anyone's name was **not found written in the book of life, he was thrown into the lake of fire.**"* (Revelation 20:14-15 LSB)

Why is the Lake of Fire called "**The Second Death**?" People die once, are resurrected for judgment, and if they are not found in the Book of Life, are thrown into the Lake of Fire. What is the clear and straightforward meaning of the Bible? Does "Second **Death**" mean they die, or that they live forever in torture?

Verse 30 above shows God meant the opposite of "die" was "live." The opposite of "living forever" in the Kingdom of Heaven is **not** "living forever" in hell. The opposite of "to live" is "to die." One Hebrew word used in the verses above is Strong's H4191, "muth." It has one meaning: to die. Another Hebrew word used is Strong's H4194, "maveth." It has only one meaning: death.

Look up any English translation of the Bible, and they all say die! Using BibleGateway.com's "All English Translations" link at the bottom of search results for Ezekiel 18:20 shows that **fifty-two (52) English translations all say die!**

We have seen from the Scriptures that "soul" and "spirit" are often used interchangeably. We have examined the Hebrew words for "soul" and "spirit" in the Old Testament and the Greek words for "soul" and "spirit" in the New Testament.

We have read every verse in the Bible about being immortal or having immortality.

We have read every verse in the Bible about being incorruptible.

We have read every verse in the Bible about "eternal life."

If I have missed any verses, please let me know.

We have seen in the Old Testament that Yahweh God stresses, "*The soul that sinneth, it shall **die**.*"

We have seen in the New Testament Paul stressing, "*For the wages of sin is **death**.*"

Do we find any support in the Bible for the idea that all humans are born with an immortal soul or spirit? Or have we found just the opposite? Have we seen that the Bible says humans are mortal and every part of them will die unless they repent, are saved, are born-again, and are given the gift of eternal life? To learn more about being born-again, please see my Bible study, "How Jesus and His 12 Apostles Say We Are Saved."

How many times do we have to hear it before we turn from the customs and teachings of men to the clear word from God Himself?

If you think I have missed any important, pertinent Scriptures, please let me know at dan@vigilantvaliant.com.

This is why I think that the first deception we are under is the belief that the condemned will not die but live as immortals, in eternal torture forever and ever.

This belief is not only directly against what God says over and over throughout the entire Bible, but it is also in agreement with the devil's lie to Adam and Eve, in direct contradiction to God, that they would not surely die.

So if people dying in their sins die and believers can gain eternal life, just how does that work?
Let's see what the Bible and Yahweh, the Living God, really say about what happens after the death of a human.

Chapter 9: What Does the Bible Say Happens After Death?

So some are saved, and some are condemned. What details does the Bible give about what happens after we die?

The Bible says some of mankind will be saved to live eternally with Yahweh, the Almighty God. How can we be saved? For a more thorough understanding, please see my Bible study, "How Jesus and His 12 Apostles Say We Are Saved." The main points follow.

1. Have faith in Yahweh the Father.
2. Have faith in Yeshua, the Son.
3. Repent of our sins.
4. Be baptized (in obedience to Yeshua, not required to be saved).
5. Be obedient, Keep the commandments, and do good works.
6. Endure to the end of our lives (Essential).

We have seen that those who reject Yahweh and His Son, our Savior, the Christ, Yeshua Hamashiach, Jesus the Messiah, will die. They will not be given immortality in order to be tortured forever and ever.

So how does the Bible say this will happen? How does this work? We all know for an absolute fact, from our own life experiences, that all people die physically. Death is a surety.

> "27 And as **it is appointed unto men once to die, but after this the judgment**:" (Hebrews 9:27)

> *"7 And the LORD God formed man of the dust of the ground, **and breathed into his nostrils the breath of life; and man became a living soul.**"* (Genesis 2:7)

> *"19 In the sweat of thy face shalt thou eat bread, **till thou return unto the ground; for out of it wast thou taken: for dust thou art, and unto dust shalt thou return.**"* (Genesis 3:19)

> *"6 The silver chain will snap, and the golden lamp will fall and break; the rope at the well will break, and the water jar will be shattered. **7 Our bodies will return to the dust of the earth, and the breath of life will go back to God, who gave it to us**."* (Ecclesiastes 12:6-7 GNT Good News Translation)

Together, the above verses say that when all people die, the breath of life separates from their body, the body decomposes, and the breath of life is returned to Yahweh.

To get to the Kingdom of Heaven or to be condemned, once we are dead, we must be resurrected. There are two resurrections spoken of in the Bible and two deaths.

The First Death

There is no Scripture I can find that uses the phrase "first death." The phrase is here because there are four Scriptures (below) that talk of the "second death," therefore there must be a first death. I would guess that no one would argue that the physical death talked about in dozens and dozens of Scriptures above is the "First Death." Every human alive knows they will die unless they are raptured.

> *"11 For He pays a man according to his work, And makes him find it according to his way. 12 Truly, God will not act wickedly, And the Almighty will not pervert justice. 13 Who appointed Him with authority over the earth? And who has laid on Him the whole world? 14 If He should set His heart on it,* **If He should gather to Himself His spirit and His breath, 15 All flesh would breathe its last together, And man would return to dust."** (Job 34:11-15 LSB)

Job talks of God gathering to Himself His spirit and His breath, and saying that all men would die.

After death, we sleep until The Resurrection

> *"16 Yahweh said to Moses, "Behold,* **you shall sleep with your fathers.** *This people will rise up and play the prostitute after the strange gods of the land where they go to be among them, and will forsake me and break my covenant which I have made with them."* (Deuteronomy 31:16 WEB)

> *"10 Then Saul swore to her by Yahweh, saying, "As Yahweh lives, no punishment shall come upon you for this thing." 11 Then the woman said, "Whom shall I bring up for you?" And he said, "Bring up Samuel for me." 12 And the woman saw Samuel and cried out with a loud voice; and the woman*

> spoke to Saul, saying, "Why have you deceived me? For you are Saul." 13 And the king said to her, "Do not be afraid; but what do you see?" And the woman said to Saul, "**I see a divine being coming up out of the earth.**" 14 And he said to her, "What is his form?" And she said, "An old man is coming up, and he is wrapped with a robe." And Saul knew that it was Samuel, and he bowed with his face to the ground and prostrated himself. 15 Then Samuel said to Saul, "**Why have you disturbed me by bringing me up**?" And Saul answered, "I am greatly distressed, for the Philistines are waging war against me, and God has turned away from me and no longer answers me, either by the hand of the prophets or by dreams; therefore I have called you, that you may make known to me what I should do." 16 And Samuel said, "Why then do you ask me, since **Yahweh has turned away from you and has become your adversary**? 17 So Yahweh has done accordingly as He spoke by my hand, for Yahweh has torn the kingdom out of your hand and given it to your neighbor, to David. 18 As you did not listen to the voice of Yahweh and did not execute His burning anger on Amalek, so Yahweh has done this thing to you this day. 19 Moreover Yahweh will also give over Israel along with you into the hands of the Philistines, therefore **tomorrow you and your sons will be with me.** Indeed Yahweh will give over the camp of Israel into the hands of the Philistines!"" (1 Samuel 28:10-19 LSB)

Samuel says he was disturbed and brought up from the earth, not down from heaven. Also note that Samuel, the saved prophet, says Saul the king, who was now God's enemy, will be "with me." This could not be in heaven for an enemy of God, but in the land of the dead.

> "12 When your days are fulfilled, and **you sleep with your fathers**, I will set up your offspring after you, who will proceed out of your body, and I will establish his kingdom." (2 Samuel 7:12 WEB)

> "7 Now the rest of the acts of Abijam and all that he did, are they not written in the Book of the Chronicles of the Kings of Judah? And there was war between Abijam and Jeroboam. 8 **And Abijam slept with his fathers,** and they buried him in the

city of David; and Asa his son became king in his place." (1 Kings 15:7-8 LSB)

*"20 Have I sinned? What have I done to You, O watcher of men? Why have You set me as Your target, So that I am a burden to myself?
21 Why then do You not forgive my transgression And take away my iniquity? For now I will lie down in the dust; And **You will seek me earnestly, but I will not be**.""* (Job 7:20-21 LSB)

*"10 But man dies and lies prostrate. Man breathes his last, and where is he? 11 As water evaporates from the sea, And a river becomes parched and dried up, 12 **So man lies down and does not rise. Until the heavens are no longer, He will not awake nor be aroused out of his sleep.** 13 "Oh that You would conceal me in Sheol, That You would hide me until Your anger returns to You, That You would set a limit for me and remember me! 14 If a man dies, will he live again? All the days of my labor I will wait Until my change comes."* (Job 14:10-14 LSB)

The resurrections spoken of in the Bible take place very close to the time when the heavens and Earth are done away with and a new heaven and new earth are created. So Job knew that men would not rise until the time when the heavens were to be done away with.

*"5 For **there is no remembrance of You in death;** In Sheol who will give You thanks?"* (Psalm 6:5 LSB)

*"13 Look and answer me, O Yahweh my God; Give light to my eyes, **lest I sleep the sleep of death**,"* (Psalm 13:3 LSB)

*"17 The **dead praise not the Lord**, neither any that go down **into silence**."* (Psalm 115:17)

This says people go into silence in death, not wailing, and if the saved ones are awake and in heaven, why are they not praising Yahweh. Job 14:12 above says that men will not rise until the heavens are no longer. Yahweh says He will destroy the old heavens and earth and create a new heaven and a new earth. That is at the time of the resurrection and the Day of Judgment.

"3 Put not your trust in princes, in a son of man, in whom there is no salvation. 4 When his breath departs, he returns to the earth; **on that very day his plans perish.***"* (Psalms 146:3-4 ESV)

When we die, all our thinking stops; our thoughts perish.

"3 This is an evil in all that is done under the sun, that there is one fate for all. Furthermore, the hearts of the sons of men are full of evil, and madness is in their hearts throughout their lives. Afterwards they go to the dead. 4 For whoever is joined with all the living, there is confidence; surely a live dog is better than a dead lion. 5 For the living know they will die; **but the dead do not know anything, nor have they any longer a reward, for the memory of them is forgotten. 6 Indeed their love, their hate, and their zeal have already perished, and they will never again have a portion in all that is done under the sun.** *7 Go then, eat your bread in gladness and drink your wine with a merry heart; for God has already accepted your works. 8 Let your clothes be white all the time, and let not oil be lacking on your head. 9 See life with the woman whom you love all the days of your vain life, which He has given to you under the sun—all the days of your vanity; for this is your portion in life and in your labor in which you have labored under the sun. 10 Whatever your hand finds to do, do it with all your might; for* **there is no working or explaining or knowledge or wisdom in Sheol** *where you are going."* (Ecclesiastes 9:3-10 LSB)

"38 They will roar together like young lions; They will growl like lions' cubs. 39 When they become heated up, I will set before them their feast And make them drunk, that they may exult And **may sleep a perpetual sleep And not wake up,"** *declares Yahweh. 40 "***I will bring them down like lambs to the slaughter,** *Like rams together with male goats."* (Jeremiah 51:38-40 LSB)

"1 "Now at that time, Michael, the great prince who stands guard over the sons of your people, will stand. And there will be a time of distress such as never happened since there was a nation until that

*time; and at that time your people, everyone who is found written in the book, will be rescued. 2 And many of those **who sleep in the dust of the ground will awake, these to everlasting life, but the others to reproach and everlasting contempt.**"* (Daniel 12:1-2 LSB)

Three translations explain the following verse more thoroughly.

*"13 But go thou thy way till the end be: for **thou shalt rest,** and stand in thy lot **at the end of the days**."* (Daniel 12:13 KJV)

*"13 As for you, go your way **till the end**. You will **rest**, and then **at the end of the days you will rise** to **receive your allotted inheritance**." (Daniel 12:13 NIV)*

*"13 But as for you, go on your way **until the end. You will rest, and will arise** to your inheritance **at the end of the days**."* (Daniel 12:13 BSB)

In this one verse, Daniel 12:13, an angel says it all. The unnamed angel told Daniel to continue doing what he was doing until the end of his life, when he dies. He says Daniel will then rest. But at the end of the days, Daniel shall be raised from the dead, from his rest, and will receive a reward.

*"22 And one of the synagogue officials named Jairus *came up, and on seeing Him, *fell at His feet 23 and *pleaded with Him earnestly, saying, **"My little daughter is at the point of death;** please come, that by coming, You may lay Your hands on her, so that she will be saved and live." 24 And He went off with him; and a large crowd was following Him and pressing in on Him. 25 And a woman—who had a hemorrhage for twelve years 26 and had endured much at the hands of many physicians, and had spent all that she had and was not helped at all, but rather had grown worse— 27 after hearing about Jesus, she came up in the crowd behind Him and touched His garment. 28 For she was saying, "If I just touch His garments, I will be saved from this." 29 And immediately the flow of her blood was dried up; and she knew within her body that she had been healed of her affliction. 30*

And immediately Jesus, perceiving in Himself that the power proceeding from Him had gone forth, turned around in the crowd and was saying, "Who touched My garments?" 31 And His disciples were saying to Him, "You see the crowd pressing in on You, and You say, 'Who touched Me?'" 32 And He was looking around to see the woman who had done this. 33 But the woman fearing and trembling, aware of what had happened to her, came and fell down before Him and told Him the whole truth. 34 And He said to her, "Daughter, your faith has saved you; go in peace and be healed of your affliction." 35 While He was still speaking, they *came from the house of the synagogue official, saying, **"Your daughter has died;** *why trouble the Teacher anymore?" 36 But Jesus, overhearing what had been spoken, *said to the synagogue official, "Do not be afraid, only [e]believe." 37 And He allowed no one to accompany Him, except Peter and James and John the brother of James. 38 And they *came to the house of the synagogue official; and He *saw a commotion, and people loudly crying and wailing. 39 And entering in, He *said to them, "Why are you making a commotion and crying?* **The child has not died, but is asleep."** *40 And they began laughing at Him. But putting them all out, He *took along the child's father and mother and His own companions, and *entered the room where the child was. 41 And taking the child by the hand, He *said to her, "Talitha kum!" (Which translated means, "Little girl, I say to you, arise!"). 42 And immediately* **the little girl stood up** *and began to walk, for she was twelve years old. And immediately they were completely astounded."* (Mark 5:22-42 LSB)

"49 *While He was still speaking, someone *came from the house of the synagogue official, saying,* **"Your daughter has died;** *do not trouble the Teacher anymore." 50 But when Jesus heard this, He answered him, "Do not be afraid any longer; only believe, and she will be saved." 51 So when He came to the house, He did not allow anyone to enter with Him, except Peter and John and James, and the girl's father and mother. 52 Now they were all crying and lamenting for her, but He said, "Stop crying, for* **she has not died, but is asleep."** *53 And they began laughing at Him,* **knowing that she**

had died. *54 He, however, took her by the hand and called, saying, "Child, arise!" 55 And her spirit returned, and she stood up immediately. And He gave orders for something to be given her to eat. 56 And her parents were astounded, but He directed them to tell no one what had happened." (Luke 8:49-56 LSB)*

*"13 And **no one has ascended into heaven**, but He who descended from heaven, the Son of Man.." (John 3:13 LSB)*

Yeshua says clearly, "No one has ascended into heaven." They are sleeping until the resurrection on the Last Day.

"26 For just as the Father has life in Himself, even so He gave to the Son also to have life in Himself; *27 and He gave Him authority to execute judgment, because He is the Son of Man. 28 Do not marvel at this; for an hour is coming, in which **all who are in the tombs will hear His voice, 29 and will come forth;** those who did the good deeds **to a resurrection of life,** those who committed the evil deeds **to a resurrection of judgment.**" (John 5:26-29 LSB)*

The Bible says, "all" that are in the tombs shall come forth in resurrection, some to the resurrection of life, clearly meaning eternal life in heaven. These saved Christians and those who have done good were in their graves until they were resurrected.

*"54 He who eats My flesh and drinks My blood has eternal life, and **I will raise him up on the last day.**" (John 6:54 LSB)*

How much more clearly can Yeshua say it? He Himself said He will raise them up on the last day, not before. According to Yeshua, no man has ascended up to heaven!

*"60 And he kneeled down, and cried with a loud voice, Lord, lay not this sin to their charge. And when he had said this, **he fell asleep**." (Acts 7:60)*

*"36 For David, after he had served the purpose of God in his own generation, **fell asleep** and was laid among his fathers **and saw corruptio**n;" (Acts 13:36 LSB)*

*"28 But let a man examine himself, and so let him eat of the bread and drink of the cup. 29 For he who eats and drinks in an unworthy manner eats and drinks judgment to himself, not discerning the Lord's body. 30 For this reason many are weak and sick among you, **and many sleep.**"* (1 Corinthians 11:28-30 NKJV)

*"12 Now if Christ is preached, that He has been raised from the dead, how do some among you say that there is no resurrection of the dead? 13 But if there is no **resurrection of the dead**, not even Christ has been raised. 14 And if Christ has not been raised, then our preaching is vain, your faith also is vain. 15 Moreover we are even found to be false witnesses of God, because we bore witness against God that He raised Christ, whom He did not raise, if in fact the dead are not raised. 16 For if the dead are not raised, not even Christ has been raised. 17 And if Christ has not been raised, your faith is worthless; you are still in your sins. 18 Then those also **who have fallen asleep in Christ have perished.** 19 If we have hoped in Christ in this life only, we are of all men most to be pitied. 20 But now **Christ has been raised from the dead,** the first fruits of **those who have fallen asleep.** 21 For since by a man came death, by a man also came the resurrection of the dead. 22 For as in Adam all die, so also in Christ all will be made alive. 23 **But each in his own order: Christ the first fruits, after that those who are Christ's at His coming.** 24 Then comes the end, when He hands over the kingdom to the God and Father, when He has abolished all rule and all authority and power. 25 For He must reign until He has put all His enemies under His feet. 26 The last enemy to be abolished is death."* (1 Corinthians 15:12-26 LSB)

*"50 Now I say this, brothers, that flesh and blood cannot inherit the kingdom of God, nor does the corruptible inherit the incorruptible. 51 Behold, I tell you a mystery: **we will not all sleep, but we will all be changed, 52 in a moment, in the twinkling of an eye, at the last trumpet.** For the trumpet will sound, and **the dead will be raised incorruptible, and we will be changed. 53 For this corruptible*

> *must put on the incorruptible, and this mortal must put on immortality. 54 But when this corruptible puts on the incorruptible, and this mortal puts on immortality, then will come about the word that is written, "Death is swallowed up in victory. 55 O death, where is your victory? O death, where is your sting?" 56 Now the sting of death is sin, and the power of sin is the law; 57 but thanks be to God, who gives us the victory through our Lord Jesus Christ!"* (1 Corinthians 15:50-57 LSB)

This is a very powerful verse. Think this through: **"This mortal must put on immortality."** Paul clearly says humans are mortal. They must "put on" immortality.

> *"13 But all things become visible when they are exposed by the light, for everything that becomes visible is light. 14 For this reason it says,* ***"Awake, sleeper, And arise from the dead,*** *And Christ will shine on you." 15 Therefore look carefully how you walk, not as unwise but as wise, 16 redeeming the time, because the days are evil."* (Ephesians 5:13-16 LSB)

> *"13 But we do not want you to be uninformed, brothers, about those who* ***are asleep,*** *so that you will not grieve as do the rest who have no hope. 14 For if we believe that Jesus died and rose again, even so God will bring with Him those who have fallen asleep in Jesus. 15 For this we say to you by the word of the Lord, that we who are alive and remain until the coming of the Lord,* ***will not precede those who have fallen asleep.*** *16 For the Lord Himself will descend from heaven with a shout, with the voice of the archangel and with the trumpet of God,* ***and the dead in Christ will rise first.*** *17 Then we who are alive and remain will be caught up together with them in the clouds to meet the Lord in the air, and so we shall always be with the Lord."* (1 Thessalonians 4:13-17 LSB)

Every preacher I have ever heard and every article on this I have ever read agree that "prevent" here means "to go before." What does Paul say is the condition of those who have physically died, believing and accepting Yeshua as their savior? In 1 Thessalonians 4:13, he calls them "them which are **asleep**." Paul says that twice! It is at the trumpet blast of God signaling the return of Christ that they "shall rise." They are dead, but "dead in Christ."

The verses below are about when Lazarus, the brother of Mary and Martha, died, and Yeshua went to the family three days after Lazarus died. There is an important reason Yeshua waited for three days. The Jews of that day knew that some people appear dead through certain diseases or conditions but do revive after a couple of days. But by the third day, you know for sure, for the body is by then visibly rotting and stinking. That means they are really dead. Jesus waited until everyone knew for certain that Lazarus was truly dead.

> *"5 Now Jesus loved Martha and her sister and Lazarus. 6 So when He heard that he was sick, He then stayed two days in the place where He was. 7 Then after this He *said to the disciples, "Let us go to Judea again." 8 The disciples *said to Him, "Rabbi, the Jews were just now seeking to stone You, and are You going there again?" 9 Jesus answered, "Are there not twelve hours in the day? If anyone walks in the day, he does not stumble, because he sees the light of this world. 10 But if anyone walks in the night, he stumbles, because the light is not in him." 11 He said these things, and after that He *said to them, **"Our friend Lazarus has fallen asleep; but I go, so that I may awaken him."** 12 The disciples then said to Him, "Lord, **if he has fallen asleep, he will be saved from his sickness.**" 13 Now Jesus had spoken of his death, but they thought that He was speaking of actual sleep. 14 So **Jesus then said to them plainly, "Lazarus is dead,** 15 and I am glad for your sakes that I was not there, so that you may believe; but let us go to him." 16 Therefore Thomas, who is called Didymus, said to his fellow disciples, "Let us also go, so that we may die with Him.""* (John 11:5-16 LSB)

> *"21 Martha then said to Jesus, "Lord, if You had been here, my brother would not have died. 22 But even now I know that whatever You ask from God, God will give You." 23 **Jesus *said to her, "Your brother will rise again."** 24 Martha *said to Him, "I know that he will rise again in the resurrection on the last day." 25 Jesus said to her, **"I am the resurrection and the life; he who believes in Me will live even if he dies, 26 and everyone who***

> *lives and believes in Me will never die*—ever. Do you believe this? 27 She *said to Him, "Yes, Lord; I have believed that You are the Christ, the Son of God, the One who comes into the world.""* (John 11:21-27 LSB)

Yeshua plainly told His own Apostles that the dead "sleep." Martha knew the dead will be raised in a resurrection "at the last day," the day the trumpet of God will sound. Yeshua teaches her a very important doctrine. Those who believe in Yeshua as their Savior but physically die shall live again, and those who live and believe in Him shall never die. Now the whole world knows that all people die physically. No one listening thought He meant His believers would not physically die. They knew that by saying "shall never die," He meant they would be raised at the resurrection to eternal life. **Until then, they sleep**, like Lazarus, His friend.

> *"10 Who died for us, that, **whether we wake or sleep**, we should live together with him." (1 Thessalonians 5:10)*

> *"24 For Christ did not enter holy places made with hands, mere copies of the true ones, but into heaven itself, now to appear in the presence of God for us; 25 nor was it that He would offer Himself often, as the high priest enters the holy places year by year with blood that is not his own. 26 Otherwise, He would have needed to suffer often since the foundation of the world; but now once at the consummation of the ages He has been manifested to put away sin by the sacrifice of Himself. 27 And inasmuch as **it is appointed for men to die once and after this comes judgment**, 28 so Christ also, having been offered once to bear the sins of many, will appear a second time for salvation without reference to sin, to those who eagerly await Him."* (Hebrews 9:24-28 LSB)

The verse above, Hebrews 9:27, says that after death comes judgment. Since all judgments happen at the end times, what do men do between death and judgment? We sleep the sleep of death, whether for one year or one thousand years, and are at judgment when we wake. Judgment comes as the first thing after death. The sleeper does not know how long he slept.

The Resurrections

If we are dead, asleep in the grave, we must be awakened, resurrected, to stand trial.

> *"1 Now at that time, Michael, the great prince who stands guard over the sons of your people, will stand. And there will be a time of distress such as never happened since there was a nation until that time; and at that time your people, **everyone who is found written in the book, will be rescued. 2 And many of those who sleep in the dust of the ground will awake, these to everlasting life, but the others to reproach and everlasting contempt.**"* (Daniel 12:1-2 LSB)

> *"24 "Truly, truly, I say to you, he who hears My word, and believes Him who sent Me, has eternal life, and does not come into judgment, **but has passed out of death into life.** 25 Truly, truly, I say to you, an hour is coming and now is, when the dead will hear the voice of the Son of God, and those who hear will live. 26 For just as the Father has life in Himself, even so He gave to the Son also to have life in Himself; 27 and He gave Him authority to execute judgment, because He is [a]the Son of Man. 28 Do not marvel at this; for an hour is coming, **in which all who are in the tombs will hear His voice, 29 and will come forth; those who did the good deeds to a resurrection of life, those who committed the evil deeds to a resurrection of judgment.**"* (John 5:24-29 LSB)

Above, Yeshua explains the two resurrections: the Resurrection of Life and the Resurrection of Damnation.
Remember, as we saw in a section above, that the word "damned" as used in the Bible means to be judged (with a negative outcome) or to be condemned. It does not mean eternal torture.

The First Resurrection

Again, remember that there are two resurrections spoken of in the Bible. The "first" resurrection is clearly labeled in Revelation 20:5, but there is another called the second resurrection.

Yeshua says this First Resurrection is for the "blessed and holy" and that they will not suffer the Second Death but have eternal life. We should pray, love God, and work to be part of this resurrection.

> "23 "Oh, that my words were written! Oh, that they were inscribed in a book! 24 That they were engraved on a rock With an iron pen and lead, forever! 25 **For I know that my redeemer lives, And He shall stand at last on the earth; 26 And after my skin is destroyed, this I know, That in my flesh I shall see God,** 27 Whom I shall see for myself, And my eyes shall behold, and not another. How my heart yearns within me!" (Job 19:23-27 NKJV)

Job, who wrote possibly the oldest book of the Bible, knew very much about God. He knew God would stand on the Earth in the latter days, and as for himself, he would die, be buried, and rot. But somehow God would bring him back in a body to see Him.

> "12 And He also went on to say to the one who had invited Him, "When you give a luncheon or a dinner, do not invite your friends or your brothers or your relatives or rich neighbors, lest they also invite you in return and that will be your repayment. 13 But when you give a reception, invite the poor, the crippled, the lame, the blind, 14 and you will be blessed, since they do not have the means to repay you; for it will be repaid to you **at the resurrection of the righteous.**"" (Luke 14:12-14 LSB)

> "28 Do not marvel at this; for an hour is coming, in which all who are in the tombs will hear His voice, 29 and will come forth; **those who did the good deeds to a resurrection of life,** those who committed the evil deeds to a resurrection of judgment." (John 5:28-29 LSB)

> "40 And this is the will of Him who sent Me, that everyone who sees the Son and believes in Him may have everlasting life; and **I will raise him up at the last day.**" (John 6:40 NKJV)

> "44 No one can come to Me unless the Father who sent Me draws him; and **I will raise him up at the last day.**" (John 6:44)

Yeshua promises He will raise up faithful believers "at the last day." This is the resurrection of the just, the resurrection of life, and the first resurrection.

*"42 So also is the **resurrection of the dead.** It is sown a corruptible body, it is raised an incorruptible body; 43 it is sown in dishonor, it is raised in glory; it is sown in weakness, it is raised in power; 44 it is sown a natural body, it is raised a spiritual body. If there is a natural body, there is also a spiritual body. 45 So also it is written, **"The first man, Adam, became a living soul."** The last Adam became a life-giving spirit. 46 However, the spiritual is not first, but the natural; then the spiritual. 47 The first man is from the earth, earthy; the second man is from heaven. 48 As is the earthy, so also are those who are earthy; and as is the heavenly, so also are those who are heavenly. 49 And just as we have borne the image of the earthy, we will also bear the image of the heavenly. 50 Now I say this, brothers, that flesh and blood cannot inherit the kingdom of God, nor does the corruptible inherit the incorruptible. 51 **Behold, I tell you a mystery: we will not all sleep,** but we will all be changed, 52 in a moment, in the twinkling of an eye, at the last trumpet. For the trumpet will sound, and the dead will be raised incorruptible, and we will be changed. 53 For this corruptible must put on the incorruptible, and **this mortal must put on immortality.** 54 But when this corruptible puts on the incorruptible, and this mortal puts on immortality, then will come about the word that is written, "Death is swallowed up in victory. 55 O death, where is your victory? O death, where is your sting?" 56 Now the sting of death is sin, and the power of sin is the law; 57 but thanks be to God, who gives us the victory through our Lord Jesus Christ!"* (1 Corinthians 15:42-57 LSB)

*"8 More than that, I count all things to be loss because of the surpassing value of knowing Christ Jesus my Lord, for whom I have suffered the loss of all things, and count them but rubbish so that I may gain Christ 9 and be found in Him, not having a righteousness of my own which is from the Law, but that which is through faith in Christ, the righteousness which is from God upon faith, 10 that I may know Him and the power of His resurrection and the fellowship of His sufferings, being conformed to His death, 11 **in order that I may attain to the resurrection from the dead. Pressing On Toward the Goal***

12 Not that I have already obtained it or have already become perfect, but I press on so that I may lay hold of that for which also I was laid hold of by Christ Jesus. 13 **Brothers, I do not consider myself as having laid hold of it yet,** but one thing I do: forgetting what lies behind and reaching forward to what lies ahead, 14 I press on toward the goal for the prize of the upward call of God in Christ Jesus. 15 Let us therefore, as many as are perfect, think this way; and if in anything you think differently, God will reveal that also to you. 16 However, let us keep walking in step with the same standard to which we have attained. 17 Brothers, join in following my example, and look for those who walk according to the pattern you have in us. 18 For many walk—of whom I often told you, and now tell you even crying—**as enemies of the cross of Christ, 19 whose end is destruction,** whose god is their stomach and glory is in their shame, who set their thoughts on earthly things. 20 For our citizenship is in heaven, from which also we eagerly wait for a Savior, the Lord Jesus Christ, 21 **who will transform the body of our humble state into conformity with the body of His glory,** by His working through which He is able to even subject all things to Himself." (Philippians 3:8-21 LSB)

"13 But we do not want you to be uninformed, brothers, **about those who are asleep,** so that you will not grieve as do the rest who have no hope. 14 For if we believe that Jesus died and rose again, **even so God will bring with Him those who have fallen asleep in Jesus. 15 For this we say to you by the word of the Lord, that we who are alive and remain until the coming of the Lord, will not precede those who have fallen asleep.** 16 For the Lord Himself will descend from heaven with a shout, with the voice of the archangel and with the trumpet of God, **and the dead in Christ will rise first.** 17 Then we who are alive and remain will be caught up together with them in the clouds to meet the Lord in the air, and so we shall always be with the Lord." (1 Thessalonians 4:13-17 LSB)

"4 Then I saw thrones, and they sat on them, and judgment was given to them. And I saw the souls of those who had been beheaded because of their *witness of Jesus and because of the word of God, and who also had not worshiped the beast or his image, and had not received the mark on their forehead and on their hand. And they came to life and reigned with Christ for a thousand years. 5 The rest of the dead did not come to life until the thousand years were finished.* **This is the first resurrection. 6 Blessed and holy is the one who has a part in the first resurrection. Over these the second death has no authority,** *but they will be priests of God and of Christ and will reign with Him for a thousand years."* (Revelation 20:4-6 LSB)

Twice above, Yeshua says He will raise the saved up on the "Last Day." This is the First Resurrection, the Resurrection of the Just, and the Resurrection of Life.

The Rapture of the Saved

Yes we saw this verse selection before, but there we were focusing on the resurrection. Now we are focusing on the rapture.

"13 But we do not want you to be uninformed, brothers, about **those who are asleep,** *so that you will not grieve as do the rest who have no hope. 14 For if we believe that Jesus died and rose again,* **even so God will bring with Him those who have fallen asleep in Jesus. 15 For this we say to you by the word of the Lord, that we who are alive and remain until the coming of the Lord, will not precede those who have fallen asleep.** *16 For the Lord Himself will descend from heaven with a shout, with the voice of the archangel and with the trumpet of God,* **and the dead in Christ will rise first. 17 Then we who are alive and remain will be caught up together with them in the clouds to meet the Lord in the air, and so we shall always be with the Lord."* (1 Thessalonians 4:13-17 LSB)

"42 So also is the **resurrection of the dead. It is sown a corruptible body, it is raised an incorruptible body;** *43 it is sown in dishonor, it is raised in glory; it is sown in weakness, it is raised in power; 44 it is sown a natural body, it is raised a spiritual body.* **If there is a natural body, there is**

*also a spiritual body. 45 So also it is written, "The first man, Adam, became a living soul." The last Adam became a life-giving spirit. 46 However, the spiritual is not first, but the natural; then the spiritual. 47 The first man is from the earth, earthy; the second man is from heaven. 48 As is the earthy, so also are those who are earthy; and as is the heavenly, so also are those who are heavenly. 49 And just as we have borne the image of the earthy, we will also bear the image of the heavenly. 50 Now I say this, brothers, that flesh and blood cannot inherit the kingdom of God, nor does the corruptible inherit the incorruptible. 51 **Behold, I tell you a mystery: we will not all sleep, but we will all be changed, 52 in a moment, in the twinkling of an eye, at the last trumpet. For the trumpet will sound, and the dead will be raised incorruptible, and we will be changed. 53 For this corruptible must put on the incorruptible, and this mortal must put on immortality.** 54 But when this corruptible puts on the incorruptible, and this mortal puts on immortality, then will come about the word that is written, "Death is swallowed up in victory. 55 O death, where is your victory? O death, where is your sting?" 56 Now the sting of death is sin, and the power of sin is the law; 57 but thanks be to God, who gives us the victory through our Lord Jesus Christ!"* (1 Corinthians 15:42-57 LSB)

So the last trumpet will sound, and the Resurrection of the Saved comes first, with the Rapture of still living Saved happening immediately thereafter, joining them in the clouds with Yeshua.

The Second Resurrection

There is no phrase in the Bible saying "The Second Resurrection." Nevertheless, the Scriptures above do talk of the "first resurrection," differentiating it from the one or more that follow. So we know there are at least two resurrections.

Those who died while being faithful to Christ will live and reign with Him for one thousand years. Others are raised after the one thousand years. **This is the Second Resurrection,** as it is the only one we know of after the first.

The verses below are so full of important points that a large selection is quoted. Please read it all, but note the bolded sections. The note that follows speaks to each point.

*"26 Jesus answered them and said, "Truly, truly, I say to you, you seek Me, not because you saw signs, but because you ate of the loaves and were filled. 27 Do not work for the food which perishes, **but for the food which endures to eternal life, which the Son of Man will give to you,** for on Him the Father, God, set His seal." 28 Therefore they said to Him, "What should we do, so that we may work the works of God?" 29 Jesus answered and said to them, "This is the work of God, that you believe in Him whom He has sent." 30 So they said to Him, "What then do You do for a sign so that we may see, and believe You? What work do You perform? 31 Our fathers ate the manna in the wilderness; as it is written, 'He gave them bread from heaven to eat.'" 32 Jesus then said to them, "Truly, truly, I say to you, Moses has not given you the bread from heaven, but My Father gives you the true bread from heaven. 33 For the bread of God is that which comes down from heaven and gives life to the world." 34 Then they said to Him, "Lord, always give us this bread." 35 **Jesus said to them, "I am the bread of life.** He who comes to Me will never hunger, and he who believes in Me will never thirst. 36 But I said to you that you have seen Me, and yet do not believe. 37 All that the Father gives Me will come to Me, and the one who comes to Me I will never cast out. 38 For I have come down from heaven, not to do My own will, but the will of Him who sent Me. 39 **Now this is the will of Him who sent Me, that of all that He has given Me I lose nothing, but raise it up on the last day.** 40 **For this is the will of My Father, that everyone who sees the Son and believes in Him will have eternal life, and I Myself will raise him up on the last day.**" 41 Therefore the Jews were grumbling about Him, because He said, "I am the bread that came down from heaven." 42 They were saying, "Is not this Jesus, the son of Joseph, whose father and mother we know? How does He now say, 'I have come down from heaven'?" 43 Jesus answered and said to them, "Stop grumbling among yourselves. 44 No one can come to Me unless the Father who sent Me draws him; and **I will raise him up on the last day.** 45 It is written in the prophets, 'And they shall all be taught by God.' Everyone who has heard and learned from the Father comes to Me. 46*

Not that anyone has seen the Father, except the One who is from God; He has seen the Father. 47 **Truly, truly, I say to you, he who believes has eternal life. 48 I am the bread of life.** *49 Your fathers ate the manna in the wilderness, and they died. 50 This is the bread which comes down from heaven, so that one may eat of it and not die. 51* **I am the living bread that came down from heaven; if anyone eats of this bread, he will live forever;** *and also the bread which I will give for the life of the world is My flesh." 52 Then the Jews began to argue with one another, saying, "How can this man give us His flesh to eat?" 53 So Jesus said to them, "Truly, truly, I say to you, unless you eat the flesh of the Son of Man and drink His blood, you have no life in yourselves. 54 He who eats My flesh and drinks My blood has eternal life, and I will raise him up on the last day. 55 For My flesh is true food, and My blood is true drink. 56 He who eats My flesh and drinks My blood abides in Me, and I in him. 57 As the living Father sent Me, and I live because of the Father, so he who eats Me, he also will live because of Me."* (John 6:26-57 LSB)

Examining the verses above, please note the following: John 6:27 says **man must "endure" unto "everlasting life,"** which the Son of Man (Yeshua) "gives" him. He does not have it. It is given if he endures faithfully until his death. Yeshua will "raise it up" "at the last day." Man does not go to heaven upon death. Anyone who "believeth on Him," Yeshua, "may have," not "does have," "everlasting life." When? "At the last day." The Bible is very clear about this, if we can break through our delusions or the "traditions of men" Yeshua warned about. John 6:51 says if a man eats, consumes, and brings into his being, his heart, "the Bread of Life," he will not **"die."** Can you find any verse at all where Yeshua says you will be tortured forever? Why do Yeshua and Yahweh Himself use the word **"die"** if that is not what they mean? Do you really believe They could not have gotten the message across to us clearly if they meant "tortured forever?" Do you really believe that They, the Godhead, all-knowing, knowing the future and past, would not have said "tortured forever" clearly instead of saying dozens and dozens of times words like die, destroyed, destruction? Also, verse John 6:51 above says that if a man receives Yeshua, he shall live for ever. What do you think "IF" means there? **Would not almost all people reading that without prejudice, bias, tradition, or delusion say that it means that IF you do believe, you will live for ever, and IF you don't, you won't?**

"14 But this I confess to you, that according to the Way, which they call a sect, I do serve the God of our fathers, believing everything that is in accordance with the Law and that is written in the Prophets; 15 having a hope in God, for which these men are waiting, that **there shall certainly be a resurrection of both the righteous and the unrighteous.***"* (Acts 24:14-15 LSB)

"4 Then I saw thrones, and they sat on them, and judgment was given to them. And I saw the souls of those who had been beheaded because of their witness of Jesus and because of the word of God, and who also had not worshiped the beast or his image, and had not received the mark on their forehead and on their hand. **And they came to life and reigned with Christ for a thousand years. 5 The rest of the dead did not come to life until the thousand years were finished.** *This is the first resurrection. 6 Blessed and holy is the one who has a part in the first resurrection. Over these the second death has no authority, but they will be priests of God and of Christ and will reign with Him for a thousand years."* (Revelation 20:4-6 LSB)

"7 **And when the thousand years are finished,** *Satan will be released from his prison, 8 and will come out to deceive the nations which are in the four corners of the earth, Gog and Magog, to gather them together for the war; the number of them is like the sand of the seashore. 9 And they came up on the broad plain of the earth and surrounded the camp of the saints and the beloved city, and fire came down from heaven and devoured them. 10 And the devil who deceived them was thrown into the lake of fire and brimstone, where the beast and the false prophet are also, and they will be tormented day and night forever and ever."* (Revelation 20:7-10 LSB)

"28 Do not marvel at this; for an hour is coming, in which all who are in the tombs will hear His voice, 29 and will come forth; those who did the good deeds to a resurrection of life, those who committed the evil deeds **to a resurrection of judgment.***"* (John 5:28-29 LSB)

In looking at 59 English translations, John 5:29 is translated 41 times as judgment, 13 times as condemnation, and only 5 times as damnation. As we shall see next, this is the Judgment Resurrection.

So one thousand years have passed since the First Resurrection. This is the Second Resurrection, the Resurrection of Judgment, the Resurrection of the Unjust, sometimes called the General Resurrection.

The Great White Throne Judgment

There are a few different words used for the judgments to come. Let us examine the Scriptures to try to understand these judgments in an orderly fashion.

In Revelation 4 - 7 we see the throne of God the Father.

> "1 After these things I looked, and behold, a door standing open in heaven, and the first voice which I had heard, like the sound of a trumpet speaking with me, said, "Come up here, and I will show you what must take place after these things." 2 Immediately I was in the Spirit, and behold, **a throne was standing in heaven, and One sitting on the throne.** 3 And He who was sitting was like a jasper stone and a sardius in appearance; and there was a rainbow around the throne, like an emerald in appearance. 4 Around the throne were twenty-four thrones, and upon those thrones I saw twenty-four elders sitting, clothed in white garments, and golden crowns on their heads. 5 And out from the throne come flashes of lightning and sounds and peals of thunder. And there were seven lamps of fire burning before the throne, which are the seven Spirits of God. 6 And before the throne there was something like a sea of glass, like crystal. And in the center and around the throne, four living creatures full of eyes in front and behind. 7 And the first creature was like a lion, and the second creature like a calf, and the third creature had a face like that of a man, and the fourth creature was like a flying eagle. 8 And the four living creatures, each one of them having six wings, are full of eyes around and within, and day and night they do not cease to say, "Holy, holy, holy is the Lord God, the Almighty, who was and who is and who is to come." 9 And when the living creatures give glory and

honor and thanks to Him who sits on the throne, to Him who lives forever and ever, 10 the twenty-four elders will fall down before Him who sits on the throne, and will worship Him who lives forever and ever, **and will cast their crowns before the throne, saying, 11 "Worthy are You, our Lord and our God, to receive glory and honor and power, for You created all things, and because of Your will they existed, and were created.""**
(Revelation 4:1-11 LSB)

"5 And one of the elders *said to me, "Stop crying! Behold, **the Lion that is from the tribe of Judah, the Root of David, has overcome so as to open the scroll and its seven seals."** *6 Then I saw in the midst of the throne and the four living creatures and* **in the midst of the elders a Lamb standing, as if slain,** *having seven horns and seven eyes, which are the seven Spirits of God, sent out into all the earth. 7 And* **He came and took the scroll out of the right hand of Him who sits on the throne.** *8 And when He had taken the scroll, the four living creatures and the twenty-four elders fell down before the Lamb, each one having a harp and golden bowls full of incense, which are the prayers of the saints. 9 And they *sang a new song, saying,* **"Worthy are You to take the scroll and to open its seals, because You were slain and purchased for God with Your blood people from every tribe and tongue and people and nation. 10 And You made them to be a kingdom and priests to our God, and they will reign upon the earth."** *11 Then I looked, and I heard the voice of many angels around the throne and the living creatures and the elders; and the number of them was myriads of myriads, and thousands of thousands, 12 saying with a loud voice, "Worthy is the Lamb that was slain to receive power and riches and wisdom and strength and honor and glory and blessing." 13 And every created thing which is in heaven and on the earth and under the earth and on the sea, and all things in them, I heard saying, "To Him who sits on the throne, and to the Lamb, be the blessing and the honor and the glory and the might forever and ever.""* (Revelation 5:5-13 LSB)

> "15 Then the kings of the earth and the great men and the commanders and the rich and the strong and every slave and free man hid themselves in the caves and among the rocks of the mountains; 16 and they *said to the mountains and to the rocks, "Fall on us and **hide us from the presence of Him who sits on the throne, and from the wrath of the Lamb,** 17 for the great day of their wrath has come, and who is able to stand?"" (Revelation 6:15-17 LSB)

> "9 After these things I looked, and behold, a great multitude which no one could count, from every nation and all tribes and peoples and tongues, standing before the throne and before the Lamb, clothed in white robes, and palm branches were in their hands; 10 and they cry out with a loud voice, saying, **"Salvation belongs to our God who sits on the throne, and to the Lamb.""** (Revelation 7:9-10 LSB)

This throne is clearly the **throne of God,** the Father, because Yeshua approached the **throne of God,** and the Father gave Yeshua the book. Also because the kings of the Earth want to hide from "Him that sitteth on the throne, and from the . . . Lamb." Also, the "great multitude" says "salvation" to "God which sitteth upon the throne" and "unto the Lamb."

This is not the throne of any judgment, for we shall see next that Yahweh, the Almighty Father, has assigned all judgment to Yeshua, His Son.

All men will stand before God the Son in judgment.

It appears there will be at least two different times people will stand before Yeshua for judgment. Yeshua says God the Father has assigned "all judgment" to Yeshua, Jesus, the Son of God.

> "19 Therefore Jesus answered and was saying to them, "Truly, truly, I say to you, the Son can do nothing from Himself, unless it is something He sees the Father doing; for whatever the Father does, these things the Son also does in the same manner. 20 For the Father loves the Son, and shows Him all things that He Himself is doing; and the Father will show Him greater works than these, so that you will marvel. 21 For just as the Father raises the dead and gives them life, even so the

> Son also gives life to whom He wishes. 22 **For not even the Father judges anyone, but He has given all judgment to the Son,** 23 so that all will honor the Son even as they honor the Father. He who does not honor the Son does not honor the Father who sent Him. 24 "Truly, truly, I say to you, **he who hears My word, and believes Him who sent Me, has eternal life, and does not come into judgment, but has passed out of death into life."** (John 5:19-24 LSB)

Yeshua says true believers will "not come into judgment."

> "24 "Most assuredly, I say to you, he who hears My word and believes in Him who sent Me has everlasting life, and **shall not come into judgment,** but has passed from death into life." (John 5:24 NKJV)

> "1 Therefore there is now **no condemnation for those who are in Christ Jesus."** (Romans 8:1 LSB)

Note that the last verse, John 5:24, is shown in four English versions below to show that a better word for condemnation is judgment.

> "24 Yes, indeed! I tell you that whoever hears what I am saying and **trusts the One who sent me** has eternal life — that is, **he will not come up for judgment** but has already crossed over from death to life!" (John 5:24 Complete Jewish Bible, CJB)

> "24 Truly, truly, I say to you, whoever hears my word and believes him who sent me has eternal life. **He does not come into judgment,** but has passed from death to life." (John 5:24 English Standard, ESV)

> "24 Very truly I tell you, whoever hears my word and believes him who sent me has eternal life and **will not be judge**d but has crossed over from death to life." (John 5:24 New International Version, NIV)

> "24 Verily, verily, I say to you -- He who is hearing my word, and is believing Him who sent me, hath

*life age-during, **and to judgment he doth not come**, but hath passed out of the death to the life." (John 5:24 Young's Literal Translation, YLT)*

Every Man Will Give an Account of Himself to God.

*"36 But I tell you that every careless word that people speak, **they shall give an accounting for it in the day of judgment.**" (Matthew 12:36 LSB)*

*"27 And as it is appointed for men **to die once, but after this the judgment,**" (Hebrews 9:27 NKJV)*

*"25 Most assuredly, I say to you, the hour is coming, and now is, when the dead will hear the voice of the Son of God; and those who hear will live. 26 For as the Father has life in Himself, so He has granted the Son to have life in Himself, 27 **and has given Him authority to execute judgment** also, because He is the Son of Man. 28 Do not marvel at this; for the hour is coming in which all who are in the graves will hear His voice 29 and come forth—those who have done good, to the resurrection of life, and those who have done evil, to the resurrection of condemnation. 30 I can of Myself do nothing. As I hear, I judge; and **My judgment is righteous,** because I do not seek My own will but the will of the Father who sent Me." (John 5:25-30 NKJV)*

The Judgment Seat of Christ

*"10 But you, **why do you judge your brother?** Or you again, why do you view your brother with contempt? **For we will all stand before the judgment seat of God.** 11 For it is written, "As I live, says the Lord, to Me every knee shall bow, And every tongue shall confess to God." 12 So then **each one of us will give an account of himself to God.** 13 Therefore let us not judge one another anymore, but rather judge this—not to put a stumbling block or offense before a brother." (Romans 14:10-13 LSB)*

From the wonderful bible study tool at www.BibleHub.com, their Interlinear Bible shows the following about the Greek word used to name this judgment seat:

Strong's Concordance G968 "bema"
"béma: a step, raised place, by impl. a tribunal
Original Word: βῆμα, ατος, τό
Part of Speech: Noun, Neuter
Transliteration: béma
Definition: a step, a raised place, and by implication, a tribunal
Usage: an elevated place ascended by steps, a throne, a tribunal."

◄ **Bible Hub** ◄ **Romans 14:10** ►

4771 [e]	1161 [e]	5101 [e]	2919 [e]	3588 [e]	80 [e]	4771 [e]	2228 [e]
Sy	de	ti	krineis	ton	adelphon	sou	ē
Σὺ	δὲ,	τί	κρίνεις	τὸν	ἀδελφόν	σου,	ἢ
You	however	why	judge you	the	brother	or you	or

2532 [e]	4771 [e]	5101 [e]	1848 [e]	3588 [e]	80 [e]	4771 [e]	3956 [e]
kai	sy	ti	exoutheneis	ton	adelphon	sou	pantes
καὶ	σὺ	τί	ἐξουθενεῖς	τὸν	ἀδελφόν	σου ?	πάντες
also	you	why	do despise	the	brother	of you	All

1063 [e]	3936 [e]		3588 [e]	968 [e]	3588 [e]	2316 [e]
gar	parastēsometha		tō	bēmati	tou	Theou
γὰρ	παραστησόμεθα	τῷ		βήματι	τοῦ	Θεοῦ.
for	we will stand before		the	judgment seat	of	God

Figure 9.1 : Romans 14:10
[Courtesy of BibleHub.com and Apostolic Bible Polyglot Interlinear.]

"9 Therefore we also have as our ambition, whether at home or absent, to be pleasing to Him. 10 For we must all appear before **the judgment seat of Christ,** *so that each one may be recompensed for his deeds in the body, according to what he has done, whether good or bad." (2 Corinthians 5:9-10 LSB)*

◄ 2 Corinthians 5:10 ►

3588 [e]	1063 [e]	3956 [e]	1473 [e]	5319 [e]	1163 [e]
tous	gar	pantas	hēmas	phanerōthēnai	dei
τοὺς	γὰρ	πάντας	ἡμᾶς	φανερωθῆναι	δεῖ
-	For	all	of us	to be revealed	it behooves

1715 [e]	3588 [e]	968 [e]	3588 [e]	5547 [e]	2443 [e]
emprosthen	tou	bēmatos	tou	Christou	hina
ἔμπροσθεν	τοῦ	βήματος	τοῦ	Χριστοῦ ,	ἵνα
before	the	judgment seat	-	of Christ	that

2865 [e]	1538 [e]	3588 [e]	1223 [e]	3588 [e]	4983 [e]
komisētai	hekastos	ta	dia	tou	sōmatos
κομίσηται	ἕκαστος	τὰ	διὰ	τοῦ	σώματος ,
may receive back	each	the things [done]	in	the	body

4314 [e]	3739 [e]	4238 [e]	1535 [e]	18 [e]	1535 [e]	5337 [e]
pros	ha	epraxen	eite	agathon	eite	phaulon
πρὸς	ἃ	ἔπραξεν ,	εἴτε	ἀγαθὸν	εἴτε	φαῦλον
according to	what	he did	whether	good	or	evil

Figure 9.2 : 2 Corinthians 5:10
[Courtesy of BibleHub.com and Apostolic Bible Polyglot Interlinear.]

  Again, Strong's G968 "bema" is used, so people call this the Bema Seat of Christ. Since everyone will stand before God in some judgment, but true believers will not be judged, this is thought to be more like an awards banquet, where sports or academic awards are given out. There is a type of judging here, as some gain more of a prize, some gain lesser prizes, and some may gain no prize at all or an attendance prize, which in this case is not to be scoffed at, for that is eternal life! But there will be no condemnation here, at the Bema Seat, the Judgment Seat of Christ.

*"3 Suffer hardship with me, as a good soldier of Christ Jesus. 4 No soldier in active service entangles himself in the affairs of everyday life, so that he may please the one who enlisted him as a soldier. 5 And also if anyone competes as an athlete, **he is not crowned unless he competes according to the rules**." (2 Timothy 2:3-5 LSB)*

*"7 I have fought the good fight, I have finished the course, I have kept the faith. 8 **In the future there is laid up for me the crown of righteousness,** which the Lord, the righteous Judge, will award to me on that day, **and not only to me, but also to all who have loved His appearing.** (2 Timothy 4:7-8 LSB)*

*"12 Blessed is a man who perseveres under trial; **for once he has been approved, he will receive the crown of life** which the Lord has promised to those who love Him." (James 1:12 LSB)*

*"1 Therefore, I exhort the elders among you, as your fellow elder and witness of the sufferings of Christ, and a partaker also of the glory that is to be revealed, 2 shepherd the flock of God among you, overseeing not under compulsion, but willingly, according to God; and not for dishonest gain, but with eagerness; 3 nor yet as lording it over those allotted to you, but being examples to the flock. 4 And when the Chief Shepherd appears, **you will receive the unfading crown of glory."** (1 Peter 5:1-4 LSB)*

*"10 Do not fear what you are about to suffer. Behold, the devil is about to cast some of you into prison, so that you will be tested, and you will have tribulation for ten days. **Be faithful until death, and I will give you the crown of life.**" (Revelation 2:10 LSB)*

So this throne of Yeshua is the reward ceremony.

The Throne of His Glory

The "throne of His glory" appears to me to be "the Great White Throne." as it speaks of the judgment of the condemned. This is sometimes referred to as the "Sheep from the Goats" judgment.

There will be some true believers there who will be saved and gain eternal life, but these will come to that faith after the First Resurrection of the Just, during the thousand-year period called the millennium.

> "31 "But when the Son of Man comes in His glory, and all the angels with Him, then **He will sit on His glorious throne.** 32 And all the nations will be gathered before Him; and **He will separate them from one another, as the shepherd separates the sheep from the goats;** 33 and He will put the sheep on His right, and the goats on the left. 34 "Then the King will say to those on His right, 'Come, you who are blessed of My Father, inherit the kingdom, which has been prepared for you from the foundation of the world. 35 For I was hungry, and you gave Me something to eat; I was thirsty, and you gave Me something to drink; I was a stranger, and you invited Me in; 36 naked, and you clothed Me; I was sick, and you visited Me; I was in prison, and you came to Me.' 37 Then the righteous will answer Him, saying, 'Lord, when did we see You hungry, and feed You, or thirsty, and give You something to drink? 38 And when did we see You a stranger, and invite You in, or naked, and clothe You? 39 And when did we see You sick, or in prison, and come to You?' 40 And the King will answer and say to them, 'Truly I say to you, to the extent that you did it to one of these brothers of Mine, even the least of them, you did it to Me.' 41 "Then He will also say to those on His left, 'Depart from Me, accursed ones, into the eternal fire which has been prepared for the devil and his angels; 42 for I was hungry, and you gave Me nothing to eat; I was thirsty, and you gave Me nothing to drink; 43 I was a stranger, and you did not invite Me in; naked, and you did not clothe Me; sick, and in prison, and you did not visit Me.' 44 Then they themselves also will answer, saying, 'Lord, when did we see You hungry, or thirsty, or a stranger, or naked, or sick, or in prison, and did not take care of You?' 45 Then He will answer them, saying, 'Truly I say to you, to the extent that you did not do it to one of the least of these, you did not do it to Me.' 46 And these will go away into eternal punishment, but the righteous into eternal life."" (Matthew 25:31-46 LSB)

"29 Being then the offspring of God, we ought not to suppose that the Divine Nature is like gold or silver or stone, an image formed by the craft and thought of man. 30 Therefore having overlooked the times of ignorance, God is now commanding men that everyone everywhere should repent, 31 **because He has fixed a day in which He will judge the world in righteousness through a Man whom He determined, having furnished proof to all by raising Him from the dead.""** *(Acts 17:29-31 LSB)*

The verse above shows that it is Yeshua, Jesus, who is sitting on the Great White Throne.

"11 Then I saw a **great white throne** *and Him who sits upon it, from whose presence earth and heaven fled away, and no place was found for them. 12 Then I saw the dead, the great and the small, standing before the throne, and books were opened; and another book was opened, which is the book of life. And the dead were judged from the things which were written in the books, according to their deeds. 13 And the sea gave up the dead which were in it, and death and Hades gave up the dead which were in them, and they were judged, every one of them according to their deeds. 14 Then death and Hades were thrown into the lake of fire. This is the second death, the lake of fire. 15 And if anyone's name was not found written in the book of life, he was thrown into the lake of fire. (Revelation 20:11-15)*

Who Will Be at the Great White Throne Judgment?

"11 Then I saw a great white throne and Him who sits upon it, from whose presence earth and heaven fled away, and no place was found for them. 12 Then **I saw the dead, the great and the small, standing before the throne,** *and books were opened; and another book was opened, which is the book of life.* **And the dead were judged from the things which were written in the books, according to their deeds.** *13 And the sea gave up the dead which were in it, and death and Hades gave up the dead which were in them, and they were judged, every one of them according to their deeds.* **14 Then death and Hades were thrown**

> *into the lake of fire. This is the second death, the lake of fire. 15 And **if anyone's name was not found written in the book of life, he was thrown into the lake of fire.***" *(Revelation 20:11-15 LSB)*

All the saved, born-again, true Christians of all history who had died before the First Resurrection, and those alive who are raptured then, were in the First Resurrection. Everyone who was not in the First Resurrection will be at this general resurrection and the Great White Throne judgment. That will be all those who did not believe in God or in His Messiah and died after the First Resurrection, as well as those who were born after or came to believe after the First Resurrection. So there will be some here who gain eternal life.

The Book of Life

The phrase "Book of Life" is found eleven times in the KJV Bible but is referenced seven more times. We look at these verses about this book here since it is talked about in the Second Resurrection and the Great White Throne Judgment that follows. Some verses talk about "my book" or "your book," but I think all will agree that this is the same book referred to in the verses below. It is Yahweh's record of our lives, under our name. The Scriptures below clearly show that those names written in the book will live an eternal life, and the others will die by being cast into the Lake of Fire. Scripture also shows that names can be blotted out. Hence the Scriptures about enduring to the end!

> "*30 Now it happened on the next day, that Moses said to the people, "You yourselves have committed a great sin; but now I am going up to Yahweh, perhaps I can make atonement for your sin." 31 Then Moses returned to Yahweh and said, "Alas, this people has committed a great sin, and they have made gods of gold for themselves. 32 But now, if You will forgive their sin—but if not, please **blot me out from Your book which You have written!**" 33 And Yahweh said to Moses, "**Whoever has sinned against Me, I will blot him out of My book.**"* (Exodus 32:30-33 LSB)

> "*8 You have taken account of my wanderings; Put my tears in Your bottle. **Are they not in Your book?**"* (Psalm 56:8 LSB)

> *"27 Add iniquity to their iniquity, And may they not come into Your righteousness. 28 **May they be blotted out of the book of life** And may they not be recorded with the righteous."* (Psalm 69:27-28 LSB)

> *"16 Your eyes have seen my unshaped substance; And **in Your book all of them were written** The days that were formed for me, When as yet there was not one of them."* (Psalm 139:16 LSB)

> *"1 "Now at that time, Michael, the great prince who stands guard over the sons of your people, will stand. And there will be a time of distress such as never happened since there was a nation until that time; and at that time your people, **everyone who is found written in the book, will be rescued**. 2 And many of those who sleep in the dust of the ground will awake, these to everlasting life, but the others to reproach and everlasting contempt."* (Daniel 12:1-2 LSB)

The verse below seems to be a reference to the very time Yahweh had the Book of Life written.

> *"16 Then those who feared Yahweh spoke to one another, and Yahweh gave heed and heard it, and **a book of remembrance was written before Him for those who fear Yahweh and who think upon His name.** 17 "**And they will be Mine,**" says Yahweh of hosts, "**on the day that I prepare My own treasured possession, and I will spare them as a man spares his own son who serves him.**" 18 So you will return and see the distinction between the righteous and the wicked, between one who serves God and one who does not serve Him."* (Malachi 3:16-18 LSB)

Malachi says those who serve Yahweh are the righteous, and those who do not are the wicked.

> *"20 Nevertheless do not rejoice in this, that the spirits are subject to you, but **rejoice that your names are recorded in heaven.**"'* (Luke 10:20 LSB)

*"3 Indeed, I ask you also, genuine companion, help these women who have contended together alongside of me in the gospel, with also Clement and the rest of my fellow workers, **whose names are in the book of life**."* (Philippians 4:3 LSB)

*"5 He who overcomes will thus be clothed in white garments, and **I will never erase his name from the book of life**, and I will confess his name before My Father and before His angels."* (Revelation 3:5 LSB)

*"8 All inhabitants of the earth will worship the beast—all whose names have not been written **in the Lamb's book of life**, the Lamb who was slain from the creation of the world."* (Revelation 13:8 NIV)

*"8 "The beast that you saw was, and is not, and is about to come up out of the abyss and go to destruction. And those who dwell on the earth, whose name has not been written in **the book of life** from the foundation of the world, will wonder when they see the beast, that he was and is not and will come."* (Revelation 17:8 LSB)

*"12 Then I saw the dead, the great and the small, standing before the throne, and books were opened; and another book was opened, **which is the book of life**. And the **dead were judged from the things which were written in the books, according to their deeds.**"* (Revelation 20:12 LSB)

This is an important note. Study the Scriptures above well. Books were opened. We don't know how many, but the word books is plural. **Now the dead were judged by the things in these books, plural.** This is our "works," as the Bible is clear: we shall be judged by our works. **But while all are judged out of those books, those whose names are also in the "book of life" will be saved anyway, saved by faith, not works, lest any man boast.**

*"15 And whosoever was not found written in the **book of life** was cast into the lake of fire."* (Revelation 20:15)

> *"27 And nothing defiled, and no one who practices abomination and lying, shall ever come into it, but only those whose names are written in the **Lamb's book of life.**"* (Revelation 21:27 LSB)

> *"And if any man shall take away from the words of the book of this prophecy, God shall take away his part out of the **book of life**, and out of the holy city, and from the things which are written in this book."* (Revelation 22:19)

It is interesting to note that the verse above is a debated one, with some versions having the "Tree of Life" instead of the "Book of Life.""

> *"19 And if anyone takes words away from this scroll of prophecy, God will take away from that person any share in the **tree of life** and in the Holy City, which are described in this scroll."* (Revelation 22:19 NIV)

This anomaly makes no difference in our study and is just included in the spirit of having a thorough Bible study.

The Second Death

Only four Scriptures could be found that use the phrase "Second Death." They are listed below, and all clearly agree that the second death is being thrown into the lake of fire. Please note that it is called **"The Second Death,"** not the "Eternal Torture."

> *"8 "And to the angel of the church in Smyrna write: This is what the first and the last, who was dead, and has come to life, says: 9 'I know your tribulation and your poverty (but you are rich), and the blasphemy by those who say they are Jews and are not, but are a synagogue of Satan. 10 Do not fear what you are about to suffer. Behold, the devil is about to cast some of you into prison, so that you will be tested, and you will have tribulation for ten days. Be faithful until death, and I will give you the crown of life. 11 He who has an ear, let him hear what the Spirit says to the churches. **He who overcomes will never be hurt by the second death.**'"* (Revelation 2:8-11 LSB)

"4 Then I saw thrones, and they sat on them, and judgment was given to them. And I saw the souls of those who had been beheaded because of their witness of Jesus and because of the word of God, and who also had not worshiped the beast or his image, and had not received the mark on their forehead and on their hand. And they came to life and reigned with Christ for a thousand years. 5 The rest of the dead did not come to life until the thousand years were finished. This is the first resurrection. 6 Blessed and holy is the one who has a part in the first resurrection. **Over these the second death has no authority,** but they will be priests of God and of Christ and will reign with Him for a thousand years." (Revelation 20:4-6 LSB)

"11 Then I saw a great white throne and Him who sits upon it, from whose presence earth and heaven fled away, and no place was found for them. 12 **Then I saw the dead, the great and the small, standing before the throne,** and books were opened; and another book was opened, **which is the book of life.** And the dead were judged from the things which were written in the books, according to their deeds. 13 And the sea gave up the dead which were in it, and death and Hades gave up the dead which were in them, and they were judged, every one of them according to their deeds. 14 **Then death and Hades were thrown into the lake of fire. This is the second death, the lake of fire. 15 And if anyone's name was not found written in the book of life, he was thrown into the lake of fire."** (Revelation 20:11-15 LSB)

"1 Then I saw a new heaven and a new earth; for the first heaven and the first earth passed away, and there is no longer any sea. 2 And I saw the holy city, new Jerusalem, coming down out of heaven from God, made ready as a bride adorned for her husband. 3 And I heard a loud voice from the throne, saying, "Behold, the tabernacle of God is among men, and He will dwell among them, and they shall be His people, and God Himself will be among them, 4 and He will wipe away every tear from their eyes; and there will no longer be any death; there will no longer be any mourning, or *crying, or pain. The first things passed away." 5 And He who sits on the throne said, "Behold, I am making all things new." And He *said, "Write, for these words are faithful and true." 6 Then He said to me, "They are done. I am the Alpha and the Omega, the beginning and the end. I will give to the one who thirsts from the spring of the water of life without cost. 7 He who overcomes will inherit these things, and I will be his God and he will be My son. 8 But for the cowardly and unbelieving and abominable and murderers and sexually immoral persons and sorcerers and idolaters and all liars,* **their part will be in the lake that burns with fire and brimstone, which is the second death.""** (Revelation 21:1-8 LSB)

How clear can the Scriptures be? All men suffer the first death, the death of the physical body. Then comes judgment. After judgment, those whose names are not written in the Book of Life will be thrown into the Lake of Fire. And the Bible says this "is the second death."

Verses That Say Souls Will Die in the Lake of Fire

"23 **For the wages of sin is death***, but the gift of God is eternal life in Christ Jesus our Lord."* (Romans 6:23)

First, from Romans 6:23 above, let's remember how humans lose salvation and eternal life. Sin! **And what is the penalty for sin? It is death, not eternal torture.**

The whole chapter of Romans 5 is below. It has 21 verses. Paul, the apostle, wrote this letter to the Christians in Rome. It explains how we are saved. Notes are interspersed.

"1 Therefore, having been justified by faith, we have peace with God through our Lord Jesus Christ, 2 through whom also we have obtained our introduction by faith into this grace in which we stand; and we boast in hope of the glory of God. 3 And not only this, but we also boast in our afflictions, knowing that affliction brings about perseverance; 4 and perseverance, proven character; and proven character, hope; 5 and hope does not put to shame, because the love of God has been poured out within our hearts through the Holy Spirit who was given to us. 6 For while we

> *were still weak, at the right time **Christ died for the ungodly.** 7 For one will hardly die for a righteous man, though perhaps for the good man someone would dare even to die. 8 But God demonstrates His own love toward us, in that while we were yet sinners, **Christ died for us.** 9 Much more then, having now been justified by His blood, we shall be saved from the wrath of God through Him. 10 For if while we were enemies we were reconciled to God through the death of His Son, much more, having been reconciled, we shall be saved by His life. 11 And not only this, but we also boast in God through our Lord Jesus Christ, through whom we have now received the reconciliation."* (Romans 5:1-11 LSB)

Romans 5:6b says Christ died for us. It does not say He was eternally tortured. Romans 5:8b says that Christ died for us and that we are justified by His blood, which saved us from the wrath of Yahweh. If the wages of sin are eternal torture, how could death pay that price? It continues to say that what reconciled us to Yahweh was Yeshua's death, not His eternal torture. It was through Yeshua's death that we received atonement for our sins.

> *"12 Therefore, just as through one man sin entered into the world, **and death through sin,** and so **death spread to all men, because all sinned**— 13 for until the Law sin was in the world, but sin is not imputed when there is no law. 14 Nevertheless **death reigned from Adam until Moses,** even over those who had not sinned in the likeness of the trespass of Adam, who is a type of Him who was to come. 15 But the gracious gift is not like the transgression. For if by the transgression of the one the many died, much more did the grace of God and the gift by the grace of the one Man, Jesus Christ, abound to the many. 16 And the gift is not like that which came through the one who sinned; for on the one hand the judgment arose from one transgression resulting in condemnation, but on the other hand the gracious gift arose from many transgressions resulting in justification."* (Romans 5:12-16 LSB)

When sin entered the world, it did not bring with it eternal torture. Through sin, death entered the world. It was not eternal torture that reigned from Adam to Moses, but death.

> *"17 For if by the transgression of the one, death reigned through the one, much more those who receive the abundance of grace and of the gift of righteousness will reign in life through the One, Jesus Christ. 18 So then as through one transgression there resulted condemnation to all men, **even so through one act of righteousness there resulted justification of life to all men.** 19 For as through the one man's disobedience the many were appointed sinners, even so through the obedience of the One the many will be appointed righteous. 20 Now the Law came in so that the transgression would increase, but where sin increased, grace abounded all the more, 21 **so that, as sin reigned in death,** even so grace would reign through righteousness **to eternal life** through Jesus Christ our Lord."* (Romans 5:17-21 LSB)

We are justified to life, and saved to eternal life. Think this through. The opposite of life is not eternal torture, but death.

> *"15 See, I have set before thee this day **life and good, and death and evil;**"* (Deuteronomy 30:15 KJV)

> *"15 See, **I set before you today life and prosperity, death and destruction.** 16 For I command you today to love the Lord your God, to walk in obedience to him, and to keep his commands, decrees and laws; then you will live and increase, and the Lord your God will bless you in the land you are entering to possess. 17 But if your heart turns away and you are not obedient, and if you are drawn away to bow down to other gods and worship them, 18 I declare to you this day that you will certainly be destroyed. You will not live long in the land you are crossing the Jordan to enter and possess. 19 This day I call the heavens and the earth as witnesses against you that **I have set before you life and death, blessings and curses.** Now choose life, so that you and your children may live."* (Deuteronomy 30:15-19 NIV)

In Deuteronomy 20:15, the NIV (New International Version) may have chosen the better translation word, "destruction," than the KJV. The choice Moses laid before the people that day was not between life in the Kingdom of Heaven or life in a burning pit, but between "life and prosperity" or "**death and destruction**." How clear can Moses and Yahweh be?

> *"10 For yet a little while, and the wicked **shall not be**: yea, thou shalt diligently consider his place, and it shall not be."* (Psalms 37:10 **KJV**)

"The wicked "shall not be." How much more clear can God be?

> *"10 A little while, and the **wicked will be no more**; though you look for them, they will not be found."* (Psalms 37:10 **NIV**)

> *"20 **But the wicked shall perish,** and the enemies of the Lord shall be as the fat of lambs: **they shall consume; into smoke shall they consume away**."* (Psalm 37:20)

> *"7 That when the wicked flourished like grass And all the workers of iniquity blossomed, It was only that they might be **destroyed forevermore**."* (Psalm 92:7 LSB)

> *"10 The wicked shall see it, and be grieved; he shall **gnash with his teeth, and melt away**: the desire of the **wicked shall perish**."* (Psalm 112:10)

> *"12 There is a way which seems right to a man, But **its end is the way of death**."* (Proverbs 14:12 LSB)

> *"28 But rebels and sinners **shall be destroyed together**, and those who forsake the Lord **shall be consumed**."* (Isaiah. 1:28 RSV)

> *"4 Behold, all souls are mine; as the soul of the father, so also the soul of the son is mine: the **soul that sinneth, it shall die**."* (Ezekiel 18:4)

> *"20 **The soul who sins will die.** The son will not bear the iniquity of the father, nor will the father bear the iniquity of the son; the righteousness of the righteous will be upon himself, and the wickedness of the wicked will be upon himself."* (Ezekiel 18:20 LSB)

> *"1 For behold, the day is coming, Burning like an oven, And all the proud, yes, all who do wickedly will be stubble. And the day which is coming shall **burn them up**," Says the Lord of hosts, "That will **leave them neither root nor branch**."* (Malachi 4:1 NKJV)

Yahweh says the evildoers are destroyed, and no root or branch is left.

> "13 Enter through the narrow gate; **for the gate is wide and the way is broad that leads to destruction,** and there are many who enter through it." (Matthew 7:13 LSB)

> *"28 And do not fear those who kill the body but are unable to kill the soul; but rather fear Him who is able to **destroy both soul and body in hell**."* (Matthew 10:28 LSB)

> *"22 For not even the Father judges anyone, but He has given all judgment to the Son, 23 so that all will honor the Son even as they honor the Father. He who does not honor the Son does not honor the Father who sent Him. 24 "Truly, truly, I say to you, he who hears My word, and believes Him who sent Me, has eternal life, and does not come into judgment, **but has passed out of death into life."*** (John 5:22-24 LSB)

Yeshua did not say the saved have passed from eternal torture to life, but from "death" to life. Yahweh will **destroy** the soul in Gehenna—not just the body, but all parts of the unsaved person.

> "29 having been filled with all unrighteousness, wickedness, greed, evil; full of envy, murder, strife, deceit, malice; they are gossips, 30 slanderers, haters of God, violent, arrogant, boastful, inventors of evil, disobedient to parents, 31 without understanding, untrustworthy, unloving, unmerciful; 32 and although **they know the righteous requirement of God, that those who practice such things are worthy of death,** they not only do the same, but also give hearty approval to those who practice them." (Romans 1:29-32 LSB)

Above, Paul says the "judgment of God" is that sinners are worthy of death, not eternal torture.

*"17 If any man destroys the sanctuary of God, **God will destroy him,** for the sanctuary of God is holy, and that is what you are."* (1 Corinthians 3:17 LSB)

*"15 For we are to God the pleasing aroma of Christ among those who are being saved and **those who are perishing**. 16 To the one we are an aroma that brings death; to the other, an aroma that brings life. And who is equal to such a task?"* (2 Corinthians 2:15-16 NIV)

*"8 Whoever sows to please their flesh, from the flesh **will reap destruction**; whoever sows to please the Spirit, from the Spirit **will reap eternal life.**"* (Galatians 6:8 NIV)

*"27 Whatever happens, conduct yourselves in a manner worthy of the gospel of Christ. Then, whether I come and see you or only hear about you in my absence, I will know that you stand firm in the one Spirit, striving together as one for the faith of the gospel 28 without being frightened in any way by those who oppose you. This is a sign to them that **they will be destroyed**, but that you will be saved—and that by God."* (Philippians 1:27-28 NIV)

*"18 (For many walk, of whom I have told you often, and now tell you even weeping, that they are the enemies of the cross of Christ: 19 **Whose end is destruction**, whose God is their belly, and whose glory is in their shame, who mind earthly things.)"* (Philippians 3:18-19)

*"8 In flaming fire taking vengeance on them that know not God, and that obey not the gospel of our Lord Jesus Christ: 9 Who shall be **punished with everlasting destruction** from the presence of the Lord, and from the glory of his power;"* (2 Thessalonians 1:8-9)

*"15 Then when lust has conceived, it gives birth to sin, and **when sin is fully matured, it brings forth death.**"* (James 1:15 LSB)

> *"12 There is one lawgiver, who is able to save and to **destroy**."* (James 4:12)

> *"19 My brothers, if any among you strays from the truth and one turns him back, 20 let him know that he who turns a sinner from the error of his way will **save his soul from death** and will cover a multitude of sins."* (James 5:19-20 LSB)

This is obviously not talking about physical death, as all people die. **This says that the soul dies**. From the verses above and from all the verses in this book so far, what have we learned about the fate of those who die in their sins?

Please put together the dozens of verses above and see what the sum total is—what do all these verses agree on?

Can you come to any other conclusion at all other than what Yahweh, God the Father, the Almighty God, said in His very first command to mankind?

> *"17 but from the tree of the knowledge of good and evil, **you shall not eat from it;** for in the day that you eat from it **you will surely die**."* (Genesis 2:17 LSB)

It was the devil himself who said God lied!

> *"4 And the serpent said to the woman, '**You surely will not die!** 5 For God knows that in the day you eat from it your eyes will be opened, and you will be like God, knowing good and evil.' "* (Genesis 3:4-5 LSB)

Please do your best to put aside the programming that has led you to believe that the Living, loving God would torture people forever and ever in a place of such evil that only the devils and the minds of men can create. Put aside what misled people have taught you, however kindly or sincerely, and use your own brain!

Chapter 10: But What About Hell?

If mankind does not have an immortal spirit or immortal soul to live forever in torture, then what about all we heard and were taught about that place where torture was to happen, Hell?

For a Bible study of "Hell," we shall see every time the word "Hell" or any equivalent is used in the entire Bible, Old Testament, New Testament, in Hebrew, and in Greek.

Let's examine what the Bible really says about Hell.

What Is Hell?

To break the first deception we are under, that God would eternally torture people in burning flames forever and ever; we must have an understanding of what the Bible really says about "hell."

It is very revealing to do a Bible study on the Hebrew and Greek words for "Hell." We will find that there are a number of different words meaning different things that are amalgamated into the one word "Hell."

https://en.wikipedia.org/wiki/Hell
Etymology:
"The modern English word hell is derived from Old English hel, helle (first attested around 725 AD to refer to a nether world of the dead), reaching into the Anglo-Saxon pagan period."

So the word "Hell" in English did not exist until 725 A.D. That is about 700 years after the last Bible scripture was written.
This should be an eye-opener about all the English words we use in the Bible. They are **interpreted** and **translated** by men and women with different educational levels, different social mores, different skills at translating, and different religious beliefs.

We have to be very careful because even commas can totally change the meaning of a sentence.

The two sentences below are totally changed by two punctuation marks. The Hebrew and Greek of Yeshua's day had no punctuation at all.

A woman, without her man, is nothing.
A woman: without her, man is nothing.

These two sentences above have totally different meanings, depending on only two punctuation marks!
All punctuation was **added** to Scripture by translators. In the very best scenario, a well intentioned translator of great skill and knowledge added the English punctuation to make the English meaning identical to the Hebrew or Greek meaning, in the very best

situation, we hope! So let us examine the Scriptures and see what they really say about "hell."

Because the Old Testament was originally written in Hebrew and the New Testament was originally written in Greek, we will examine the two Testaments separately.

Hell in the Old Testament

In the King James Version (KJV) Old Testament, one word is translated from Hebrew to English as "Hell": "She'ol." But another Hebrew word from the Old Testament is used in the New Testament as "Hell," so we will look at that word, "Gehenna," in its Old Testament usage also.

She'Ol in the Hebrew Old Testament

In the Old Testament, the Hebrew word "sheol" is translated into the English words "hell" and "grave."
From www.biblehub.com, the following excerpt is from Strong's Exhaustive Concordance.
Strong's "H7585 Original Word: שְׁאוֹל" she'ol: underworld (place to which people descend at death)"

This is another word where the Hebrew and Greek may be helpful. www.biblegateway.com is a very helpful Bible study site, as is https://biblehub.com/. A search of the KJV Bible by biblegateway.com for the word "hell" says it is used 54 times, 31 times in the Old Testament, and 23 times in the New Testament.

A search for "Hell" in the Hebrew Study Bible (HSB) also finds 31 uses, all being translations of "She'ol" or a derivative thereof. So the KJV and HSB agree that the Hebrew "she'ol" is translated into English "Hell" 31 times in the Old Testament.

A search for "grave" in the Hebrew Study Bible (HSB) finds 60 uses in 57 verses. One word translated "grave" is the Hebrew word Strong's H6900, Qe'ver, or Quburah.

Strong's H6900
"קְבוּרָה קְבֻרָה"
qebûrâh qebûrâh
keb-oo-raw', keb-oo-raw'
Feminine passive participle of H6912; sepulture; (concretely) a sepulchre: burial, burying place, grave, sepulchre.
Total KJV occurrences: 14."

One example is:

> *"20 And Jacob set a pillar upon her **grave**: that is the pillar of Rachel's **grave** unto this day."* (Genesis 35:20)

So of the 60 uses of grave, 14 are the Hebrew word Qe'ver. That leaves 46 other times "grave" is translated. The very fact that this word **"sheol" is translated "grave" about half the time and "hell" the other half** shows we need to be very careful.

While many of us believe in the inerrancy of the Bible, no rational person can help but admit that with approximately 683 translations of the Bible from Hebrew and Greek into English and significant variations in the meanings of passages, not all can be correct; hence, some must be just plain wrong. Though we believe the original writings to be inspired, that does not ensure every copyist and translator was inspired or used the best ancient writings.

The bottom line for me is that I believe by faith that Yahweh is able. He is able to have the main translation(s) accurate enough to guide us to a saving faith in Yeshua, the Christ.

Forms of the Hebrew Word She'Ol

All permutations of "She'OL" are used **79** times in the Old Testament (without "ol").

The Hebrew word "ol" is found 130 times in the Hebrew Study Bible (HSB).

For the other forms:

The Hebrew word "she'ol" is found 42 times in 41 verses in the Hebrew Study Bible (HSB): pit=1; hell=24; grave=17.
The Hebrew word "She·'O·lah" is found nine times in the Hebrew Study Bible (HSB): pit=2; hell=2; grave=5.
The Hebrew word "Mish·she·'ol" is found four times in the Hebrew Study Bible (HSB): hell=4.
The Hebrew word "bish'ol" is found three times in the Hebrew Study Bible (HSB): grave=3.
The Hebrew word "kish'ol" is found two times in the Hebrew Study Bible (HSB): grave=1.
The Hebrew word "chish'ol" is found one time in the Hebrew Study Bible (HSB): grave=1.
The Hebrew word "vish'ol" is found one time in the Hebrew Study Bible (HSB): hell=1.
The Hebrew word "lish'olah" is found one time in the Hebrew Study Bible (HSB: hell=1.
The Hebrew word "she'Alah" is found one time in the Hebrew Study Bible (HSB): Sheol=1.

The Hebrew word "lish'ol" is found 19 times in the Hebrew Study Bible (HSB): ask=9; inquire=1; enquire=4; require=1; hell=1; grave=3.

Note that every time the word is translated as "hell" above, the NASB transliterates it as "sheol."
Note that every time the word is translated as "hell" above, the NIV translates it to "realm of the dead" or "depths."
These two translations, among many others, do not have the word "hell" in the Old Testament!
There are 64 verses with the Hebrew word "sheol" in the Old Testament. As you read through these, see if any of them definitively mean a place of eternal torture for humans who die in their sins.

> *"35 Then all his sons and all his daughters got up to comfort him, but he refused to be comforted. And he said, "Surely I will go down to **Sheol** in mourning for my son." So his father wept for him."* (Genesis 37:35 NASB)

Jacob, whose name Yahweh later changed to Israel, speaks the verse above when his other sons, jealous of Joseph, sold Jacob's son Joseph into slavery. This is the "coat of many colors" story. Can you imagine any way that Jacob, the father of the Israelites, thought he was going down into Hell to be tortured forever and ever? Do you think he thought his favorite son would be sent there?

The only sensible answer is no. Sheol in the verse above is clearly the grave or the land of all the dead, good and bad, not a continuous eternal torture in fire in Hell.

> *"38 But Jacob said, "My son shall not go down with you; for his brother is dead, and he alone is left. If harm should happen to him on the journey you are taking, then you will bring my gray hair down to **Sheol** in sorrow."* (Genesis 42:38 NASB)

> *"29 If you also take this one from me, and harm happens to him, you will bring my gray hair down to **Sheol** in sorrow.""* (Genesis 44:29 NASB)

> *"31 When he sees that the boy is not with us, he will die. So your servants will bring the gray hair of your servant, our father, down to **Sheol** in sorrow."* (Genesis 44:31 NASB)

> "30 But if the Lord brings about an entirely new thing and the ground opens its mouth and swallows them with everything that is theirs, and they descend alive into **Sheol,** then you will know that these men have been disrespectful to the Lord.""
> (Numbers 16:30 NASB)

> "33 So they and all that belonged to them went down alive to **Sheol;** and the earth closed over them, and they perished from the midst of the assembly." (Numbers 16:33 NASB)

> "22 For a fire has flared in My anger, And it burns to the lowest part of **Sheol,** And devours the earth with its yield, And sets on fire the foundations of the mountains." (Deuteronomy 32:22 NASB)

The verse above does mention fire, but note that it is God's anger that burns to the lowest part of She'ol. Also note that Hebrew does not have capital letters. Therefore, the capital "S" in she'ol was added by translators who had been taught it was a proper place, needing a capital first letter. The capital "M" in "My" is used to honor God, who is the speaker. The context shows that it is God who is speaking, so we can agree with the capital M in "My." But would we capitalize the word "grave?" Not usually. We can be misled and deceived, even by one capital letter. There were none in the original, inspired writing. One capital letter can change the meaning.

> "6 The Lord puts to death and makes alive; He brings down to **Sheol** and brings up." (1 Samuel 2:6 NASB)

> "6 The ropes of **Sheol** surrounded me; The snares of death confronted me." (2 Samuel 22:6 NASB)

> "6 So act as your wisdom dictates, and do not let his gray hair go down to **Sheol** in peace." (1 Kings 2:6 NASB)

If She'ol was a Hell of eternal torture, how could anyone go to it in peace?

> "9 But now do not leave him unpunished, for you are a wise man; and you will know what to do to him, and you will bring his gray hair down to **Sheol** with blood."" (1 Kings 2:9 NASB)

>"9 When a cloud vanishes, it is gone; In the same way one who goes down to **Sheol** does not come up." (Job 7:9 NASB)

>"8 They are as high as the heavens; what can you do? Deeper than **Sheol**; what can you know?" (Job 11:8 NASB)

>"13 Oh that You would hide me in **Sheol**, That You would conceal me until Your wrath returns to You, That You would set a limit for me and remember me!" (Job 14:13 NASB)

Is Job asking to be hidden from God's wrath in a place of eternal torture, or in the grave, to rest in peace?

>"13 If I hope for **Sheol** as my home, I make my bed in the darkness;" (Job 17:13 NASB)

>"16 Will it go down with me to **Sheol**? Shall we together go down into the dust?" (Job 17:16 NASB)

>"13 They spend their days in prosperity, and suddenly they go down to **Sheol**." (Job 21:13 NASB)

>"19 Dryness and heat snatch away the snow waters, as **Sheol** snatches those who have sinned." (Job 24:19 NASB)

>"6 **Sheol** is naked before Him, And Abaddon has no covering." (Job 26:6 NASB)

>"5 For there is no mention of You in death; In **Sheol**, who will praise You?" (Psalm 6:5 NASB)

>"17 The wicked will return to **Sheol**, All the nations who forget God." (Psalm 9:17 NASB)

>"10 For You will not abandon my soul to **Sheol**; You will not allow Your Holy One to undergo decay." (Psalm 16:10 NASB)

You do not "undergo decay" in a place of eternal torture, but in the grave.

*"5 The ropes of **Sheol** surrounded me; The snares of death confronted me."* (Psalm 18:5 NASB)

*"3 Lord, You have brought up my soul from **Sheol**; You have kept me alive, that I would not go down to the pit."* (Psalm 30:3 NASB)

*"17 Let me not be put to shame, Lord, for I call upon You; Let the wicked be put to shame, let them be silent in **Sheol**."* (Psalm 31:17 NASB)

*"14 Like sheep they sink down to **Sheol**; Death will be their shepherd; And the upright will rule over them in the morning, And their form shall be for Sheol to consume So that they have no lofty home."* (Psalm 49:14 NASB)

*"15 But God will redeem my soul from the power of **Sheol**, For He will receive me. Selah"* (Psalm 49:15 NASB)

*"15 May death come deceitfully upon them; May they go down alive to **Sheol**, For evil is in their dwelling, in their midst."* (Psalm 55:15 NASB)

*"13 For Your graciousness toward me is great, And You have saved my soul from the depths of **Sheol**."* (Psalm 86:13 NASB)

*"3 For my soul has had enough troubles, And my life has approached **Sheol**."* (Psalm 88:3 NASB)

*"48 What man can live and not see death? Can he save his soul from the power of **Sheol**? Selah"* (Psalm 89:48 NASB)

*"3 The snares of death encompassed me And the terrors of **Sheol** came upon me; I found distress and sorrow."* (Psalm 116:3 NASB)

*"8 If I ascend to heaven, You are there; If I make my bed in **Sheol**, behold, You are there."* (Psalm 139:8 NASB)

*"7 As when one plows and breaks open the earth, Our bones have been scattered at the mouth of **Sheol**."* (Psalm 141:7 NASB)

*"12 Let's swallow them alive like **Sheol**, Even whole, like those who go down to the pit;"* (Proverbs 1:12 NASB)

*"5 Her feet go down to death, Her steps take hold of **Sheol**."* (Proverbs 5:5 NASB)

*"27 Her house is the way to **Sheol**, Descending to the chambers of death."* (Proverbs 7:27 NASB)

*"18 But he does not know that the dead are there, That her guests are in the depths of **Sheol**."* (Proverbs 9:18 NASB)

*"11 **Sheol** and Abaddon lie open before the Lord, How much more the hearts of mankind!"* (Proverbs 15:11 NASB)

*"24 The path of life leads upward for the wise, So that he may keep away from **Sheol** below."* (Proverbs 15:24 NASB)

*"14 You shall strike him with the rod And rescue his soul from **Sheol**."* (Proverbs 23:14 NASB)

***"20 Sheol** and Abaddon are never satisfied, Nor are the eyes of a person ever satisfied."* (Proverbs 27:20 NASB)

*"16 **Sheol**, the infertile womb, Earth that is never satisfied with water, And fire that never says, "Enough.""* (Proverbs 30:16 NASB)

*"10 Whatever your hand finds to do, do it with all your might; for there is no activity, planning, knowledge, or wisdom in **Sheol** where you are going."* (Ecclesiastes 9:10 NASB)

*"6 Put me like a seal over your heart, Like a seal on your arm. For love is as strong as death, Jealousy is as severe as **Sheol**; Its flames are flames of fire, The flame of the Lord."* (Song of Solomon 8:6 NASB)

*"14 Therefore **Sheol** has enlarged its throat and opened its mouth beyond measure; And

Jerusalem's splendor, her multitude, her noise of revelry, and the jubilant within her, descend into it." (Isaiah 5:14 NASB)

"11 Ask for a sign for yourself from the Lord your God; make it deep as **Sheol** or high as heaven.""" (Isaiah 7:11 NASB)

"9 **Sheol** below is excited about you, to meet you when you come; It stirs the spirits of the dead for you, all the leaders of the earth; It raises all the kings of the nations from their thrones." (Isaiah 14:9 NASB)

"11 Your pride and the music of your harps Have been brought down to **Sheol;** Maggots are spread out as your bed beneath you And worms are your covering.'" (Isaiah 14:11 NASB)

"15 Nevertheless you will be brought down to **Sheol,** To the recesses of the pit." (Isaiah 14:15 NASB)

"15 Because you have said, "We have made a covenant with death, And with **Sheol** we have made a pact. The gushing flood will not reach us when it passes by, Because we have made falsehood our refuge and we have concealed ourselves with deception."" (Isaiah 28:15 NASB)

"18 Your covenant with death will be canceled, And your pact with **Sheol** will not stand; When the gushing flood passes through, Then you will become its trampling ground." (Isaiah 28:18 NASB)

"10 I said, "In the middle of my life I am to enter the gates of **Sheol;** I have been deprived of the rest of my years.""" (Isaiah 38:10 NASB)

"18 For **Sheol** cannot thank You, Death cannot praise You; Those who go down to the pit cannot hope for Your faithfulness." (Isaiah 38:18 NASB)

"9 You have journeyed to the king with oil and increased your perfumes; You have sent your messengers a great distance And made them go down to **Sheol.**" (Isaiah 57:9 NASB)

*"15 'This is what the Lord God says: "On the day when it went down to **Sheol** I caused mourning; I closed the deep over it and held back its rivers. And its many waters were stopped up, and I made Lebanon mourn for it, and all the trees of the field wilted away on account of it."* (Ezekiel 31:15 NASB)

*"16 I made the nations quake from the sound of its fall when I made it go down to **Sheol** with those who go down to the pit; and all the well-watered trees of Eden, the choicest and best of Lebanon, were comforted in the earth beneath."* (Ezekiel 31:16 NASB)

*"17 They also went down with it to **Sheol** to those who were slain by the sword; and those who were its strength lived in its shade among the nations."* (Ezekiel 31:17 NASB)

*"21 The strong among the mighty ones shall speak of him and his helpers from the midst of **Sheol**: 'They have gone down, they lie still, the uncircumcised, killed by the sword.'"* (Ezekiel 32:21 NASB)

*"27 Nor do they lie beside the fallen heroes of the uncircumcised, who went down to **Sheol** with their weapons of war and whose swords were placed under their heads; but the punishment for their wrongdoing rested on their bones, though the terror of these heroes was once in the land of the living."* (Ezekiel 32:27 NASB)

*"14 Shall I ransom them from the power of **Sheol**? Shall I redeem them from death? Death, where are your thorns? Sheol, where is your sting? Compassion will be hidden from My sight."* (Hosea 13:14 NASB)

This verse above equates "Sheol" with "death," not an eternal torture in fire in a place called hell.

*"2 Though they dig into **Sheol**, From there My hand will take them; And though they ascend to heaven, From there I will bring them down."* (Amos 9:2 NASB)

> "1 Then Jonah prayed to Yahweh his God **from the stomach of the fish**, 2 and he said, "I called out of my distress to Yahweh, And He answered me. I cried for help **from the belly of Sheol;** You heard my voice."* (Jonah 2:1-2 NASB)

Jonah was in the belly of a great fish. He may have felt like he was in hell, though he was not burning in fire. Is the clear intent of this usage not something like this: "I called for help from the living hellish place I was in?" In the belly of a great fish, his skin was being attacked by stomach acid. Think of that splashing into your lungs every time you got your head above the acid to fight for a breath. Think of the burning of your skin. Think of the horrid stench. Think of the acid burning your eyes. In today's common usage, most of us would say we were in hell. We don't mean an eternally burning fire, but rather that we are in a very bad place.

> "Furthermore, wine betrays an arrogant man, So that he does not achieve his objective. He enlarges his appetite like **Sheol,** And **he is like death**, never satisfied. He also gathers to himself all the nations And collects to himself all the peoples." (Habakkuk 2:5 NASB)

This verse above again equates "sheol" with "death." All people die, and death will consume humans until God intervenes on the Last Day. Did any verse above with she'ol, or a derivative, prove the Bible teaches the eternal torture of the lost in a place named Hell? Make up your own mind.

If not, you have just proved that the Old Testament in no way teaches the eternal torture of those who die in their sins. Why did I include so many verses on Sheol? To make it abundantly clear to you, to have you consider it, and to have you realize that you have been deceived!

Gehenna in the Hebrew Old Testament

The word "Gehenna" in the New Testament is a Greek version or transliteration of the Hebrew word "Hinnom."

"Strong's H2011
הִנֹּם
Hinnôm hin-nome'
Probably of foreign origin, Hinnom was apparently a Jebusite: - Hinnom.
Total KJV occurrences: 13"

The King James Version (KJV), the New American Standard Bible (NASB), the New King James Version (NKJV), and the New International Version (NIV) all agree and have the Hebrew word "Hinnom" 13 times in 11 verses in the Old Testament and none in the New Testament.

We see from Strong's that Hinnom was a man's name.

*"8 And the border went up by the **Valley of the Son of Hinnom** to the southern slope of the Jebusite city (which is Jerusalem). The border went up to the top of the mountain that lies before the Valley of Hinnom westward, which is at the end of the Valley of Rephaim northward."* (Joshua 15:8 NKJV)

BibleHub.com's Interlinear Bible shows us the following: Remember that Hebrew is read from right to left, so start on the right side of the line.

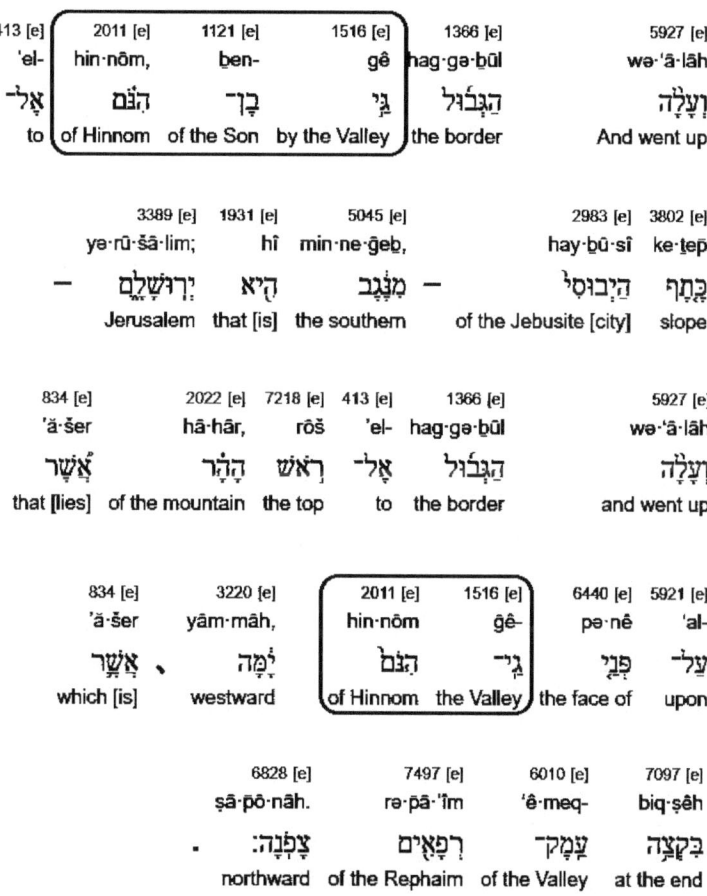

Figure 10.1: Joshua 15:8
[Courtesy of BibleHub.com and Apostolic Bible Polyglot Interlinear.]

So the valley became known as the "Valley of the Sons of Hinnom." In Hebrew, that is ge-ben-Hinnom.

> "16 Then the border came down to the end of the mountain that lies before the **Valley of the Son of Hinnom**, which is in the Valley of the Rephaim on the north, descended to the **Valley of Hinnom**, to the side of the Jebusite city on the south, and descended to En Rogel." (Joshua 18:16 NKJV)

> "10 And he defiled Topheth, which is in **the Valley of the Son of Hinnom**, that no man might make his

son or his daughter pass through the fire to Molech." (2 Kings 23:10 NKJV)

*"3 He burned incense in the **Valley of the Son of Hinnom,** and burned his children in the fire, according to the abominations of the nations whom the Lord had cast out before the children of Israel."* (2 Chronicles 28:3 NKJV)

*"6 Also he caused his sons to pass through the fire in the **Valley of the Son of Hinnom**; he practiced soothsaying, used witchcraft and sorcery, and consulted mediums and spiritists. He did much evil in the sight of the Lord, to provoke Him to anger."* (2 Chronicles 33:6 NKJV)

*"31 And they have built the high places of Tophet, which is in the **Valley of the Son of Hinnom**, to burn their sons and their daughters in the fire, which I did not command, nor did it come into My heart."* (Jeremiah 7:31 NKJV)

From the Bible Dictionary at https://www.biblestudytools.com/dictionary/tophet/:
"Tophet [N] =Topheth, from Heb. toph "a drum," because the cries of children here sacrificed by the priests of Moloch were drowned by the noise of such an instrument; or from taph or toph, meaning "to burn," and hence a place of burning, the name of a particular part in the valley of Hinnom."

*"32 "Therefore behold, the days are coming," says the Lord, "when it will no more be called Tophet, or the **Valley of the Son of Hinnom**, but the Valley of Slaughter; for they will bury in Tophet until there is no room."* (Jeremiah 7:32 NKJV)

*"2 And go out to the **Valley of the Son of Hinnom**, which is by the entry of the Potsherd Gate; and proclaim there the words that I will tell you,"* (Jeremiah 19:2 NKJV)

*"6 therefore behold, the days are coming," says the Lord, "that this place shall no more be called Tophet or the **Valley of the Son of Hinnom**, but the Valley of Slaughter."* (Jeremiah 19:6 NKJV)

"35 And they built the high places of Baal which are in the **Valley of the Son of Hinnom**, to cause their sons and their daughters to pass through the fire to Molech, which I did not command them, nor did it come into My mind that they should do this abomination, to cause Judah to sin.'" (Jeremiah 32:35 NKJV)

"30 Zanoah, Adullam, and their villages; in Lachish and its fields; in Azekah and its villages. They dwelt from Beersheba to the **Valley of Hinnom**." (Nehemiah 11:30 NKJV)

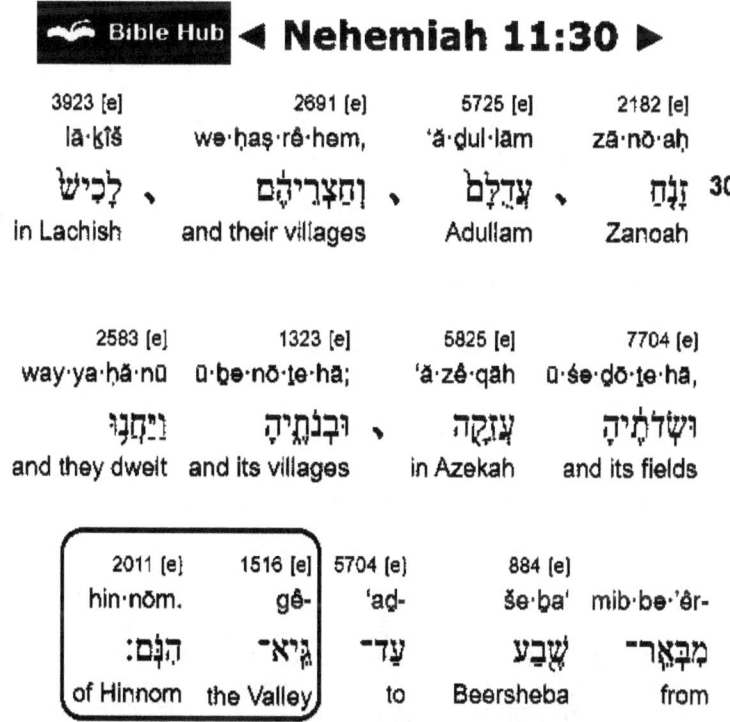

Figure 10.2: Nehemiah 11:30
[Courtesy of BibleHub.com and Apostolic Bible Polyglot Interlinear.]

Note that the word "ben," meaning "son," is not used here. It is just "Hinnom ge," or in English, Left to Right, "Ge Hinnom." This is a very natural growth of the name of any place, even today. If Tom Smith owns a valley, people around the area will call it The Valley of Tom Smith. But when Tom Smith dies and it is inherited by his sons, younger people will start calling it The Valley of the Sons of Smith. But after many years, people will be calling it The Valley of Smith, or

Smith's Valley. And even long after all the Smiths have died or moved away, the valley now has a name: Smith's Valley. For the New Testament Greek, "Ge Hinnom" was transliterated as "Gehenna."

So we see that in the Old Testament, "Ge Hinnom" means only "the Valley of Hinnom." We see that horrible pagan evil went on there, including the burning to death of their children for sacrifice to idols. While it is an example of burning to death, it is a real physical valley in Israel.

Gehenna was known as one thing, a place where dead bodies and garbage were thrown to be burned up, destroyed, turned to ashes, and then gone. While, like some modern city dumps that still have controlled burns, the fire never went out because it had a steady supply of fuel. The smoke of the dump, Gehenna, was always rising, to be seen by those in the area. **But no one in the Old Testament gave any hint that the people thrown into Gehenna would live in torture for ever and ever.**

Nothing in the Old Testament gives even a hint that the Jews used this word to mean some mystical place of eternal torture. And we saw that She'ol was just the grave or the place of the dead, good and bad, so no torture.

We see no hint of eternal torture for unrepentant sinners in the Old Testament.

Hell in the New Testament

Three different words are translated as "Hell" in the New Testament: Gehenna, Hades, and Tartarus.

Gehenna in the Greek New Testament

The Greek word γέεννα (geenna), Strong's G1067, transliterated as "gehenna" in the New Testament, comes from the Hebrew "Ge Hinnom." This means the Valley of Hinnom. We saw that in the Old Testament, it came to mean a horrible place where people were burned to death, but not some real place called "Hell." We examined "ge Hinnom" in the Hebrew Old Testament exactly for this purpose because it is used in the New Testament and often translated as "Hell."

So let us examine its usage in the New Testament to see the meaning there. Sadly, the King James Version (KJV) of the Bible translates all kinds of words into "Hell." For this study of New Testament hell, I will use a more literal translation that does not change the meaning of the Hebrew or Greek words as much.

Young's Literal Translation (YLT) will be used as indicated. "Gehenna" is used 12 times in the Bible (YLT), all in the New

Testament. "Gehenna" is not used **at all** in the King James Version (KJV), but is translated in all these 12 verses as "hell."

> "22 But I -- I say to you, that every one who is angry at his brother without cause, shall be in danger of the judgment, and whoever may say to his brother, Empty fellow! shall be in danger of the sanhedrim, and whoever may say, Rebel! Shall be in danger of the **gehenna** of the fire." (Matthew 5:22 YLT)

> "29 But, if thy right eye doth cause thee to stumble, pluck it out and cast from thee, for it is good to thee that one of thy members may perish, and not thy whole body be cast to **gehenna**." (Matthew 5:29 YLT)

> "30 And, if thy right hand doth cause thee to stumble, cut it off, and cast from thee, for it is good to thee that one of thy members may perish, and not thy whole body be cast to **gehenna**." (Matthew 5:30 YLT)

> "28 And be not afraid of those killing the body, and are not able to kill the soul, but fear rather Him who is able both soul and body to destroy in **gehenna**." (Matthew 10:28 YLT)

> "9 And if thine eye doth cause thee to stumble, pluck it out and cast from thee; it is good for thee one-eyed to enter into the life, rather than having two eyes to be cast to the **gehenna** of the fire." (Matthew 18:9 YLT)

> "15 Wo to you, Scribes and Pharisees, hypocrites! Because ye go round the sea and the dry land to make one proselyte, and whenever it may happen -- ye make him a **son of gehenna** twofold more than yourselves." (Matthew 23:15 YLT)

> "33 Serpents! Brood of vipers! How may ye escape from the judgment of the **gehenna**?" (Matthew 23:33 YLT)

> "43 And if thy hand may cause thee to stumble, cut it off; it is better for thee maimed to enter into the life, than having the two hands, to go away to the

***gehenna**, to the fire -- the unquenchable --" (Mark 9:43 YLT)*

*"45 And if thy foot may cause thee to stumble, cut it off; it is better for thee to enter into the life lame, than having the two feet to be cast to the **gehenna**, to the fire -- the unquenchable --" (Mark 9:45 YLT)*

*"47 And if thine eye may cause thee to stumble, cast it out; it is better for thee one-eyed to enter into the reign of God, than having two eyes, to be cast to the **gehenna** of the fire --" (Mark 9:47 YLT)*

*"5 but I will show to you, whom ye may fear; Fear him who, after the killing, is having authority to cast to the **gehenna**; yes, I say to you, Fear ye Him." (Luke 12:5 YLT)*

*"6 and the tongue [is] a fire, the world of the unrighteousness, so the tongue is set in our members, which is spotting our whole body, and is setting on fire the course of nature, and is set on fire by the **gehenna**." (James 3:6 YLT)*

While the word Gehenna was used as a depiction of the punishment of unrepentant sinners, we have seen that it is the name of the trash dump outside of the city of Jerusalem. It was used to burn dead bodies and trash. Nothing about it lasted "for ever." People did not live forever while burning. The flame was constantly fed, so it constantly burned. No one quenched it. The constantly burning flame made constantly rising smoke, which no one expected to go out because they were constantly throwing in trash and bodies.

Hades in the Greek New Testament

Again, using Young's Literal Translation, we see the word Hades is used 11 times. It is a transliteration of the Greek word Strong's G86, "hades."

Strong's Concordance G86 hadés
"hadés: Hades, the abode of departed spirits.
Transliteration: hadés
Definition: Hades is the abode of departed spirits.
Usage: Hades, the unseen world."

We see that even for this word, which many people equate with hell, there is no indication it is torture forever.

> *"23 And thou, Capernaum, which unto the heaven wast exalted, **unto hades shalt be brought down**, because if in Sodom had been done the mighty works that were done in thee, it had remained unto this day;"* (Matthew 11:23 YLT)

> *"18 And I also say to thee, that thou art a rock, and upon this rock I will build my assembly, and gates of **Hades** shall not prevail against it;"* (Matthew 16:18 YLT)

> *"15 And thou, Capernaum, which unto the heaven wast exalted, unto **hades** thou shalt be brought down."* (Luke 10:15 YLT)

> *"23 and in the **hades** having lifted up his eyes, being in torments, he doth see Abraham afar off, and Lazarus in his bosom,"* (Luke 16:23 YLT)

> *"27 because Thou wilt not leave my soul to **hades**, nor wilt Thou give Thy Kind One to see corruption;"* (Acts 2:27 YLT)

> *"31 having foreseen, he did speak concerning the rising again of the Christ, that his soul was not left to **hades**, nor did his flesh see corruption."* (Acts 2:31)

> *"55 where, O Death, thy sting? where, O **Hades**, thy victory?"* (1 Corinthians 15:55 YLT)

> *"18 and he who is living, and I did become dead, and, lo, I am living to the ages of the ages. Amen! and I have the keys of the **hades** and of the death."* (Revelation 1:18 YLT)

> *"8 and I saw, and lo, a pale horse, and he who is sitting upon him -- his name is Death, and **Hades** doth follow with him, and there was given to them authority to kill, (over the fourth part of the land,) with sword, and with hunger, and with death, and by the beasts of the land."* (Revelation 6:8 YLT)

> *"13 and the sea did give up those dead in it, and the death and the **hades** did give up the dead in them, and they were judged, each one according to their works;"* (Revelation 20:13 YLT)

> *"14 and the death and the **hades** were cast to the lake of the fire -- this [is] the second death;"* (Revelation 20:14 YLT)

Nothing in these verses on Hades above says people will be tortured there forever and ever. The most that can surely be said about it is that it was a generic term for the land of the dead.

Tartarus in the Greek New Testament

The word Tartarus appears in the Bible once. It is the English transliteration of the Greek word "tartarosas."
It is Strong's word G5020.
5020. tartaroó
"tartaroó: to cast into hell
Original Word: ταρταρόω
Part of Speech: Verb
Transliteration: tartaroó
Definition: to cast into hell
Usage: I thrust down to Tartarus or Gehenna."

> *"4 For if God messengers who sinned did not spare, but with chains of thick gloom, having cast [them] **down to Tartarus,** did deliver [them] to judgment, having been reserved,"* (2 Peter 2:4 YLT)

Nothing in this single use says anything about being tortured forever and ever.

Chapter 11: Will Humans Be Tortured for Ever?

Eternal Torture Proof Texts Are Out of Context

Remember that **"A text taken out of context is a pretext for a prooftext."** (Many internet sites attribute the quote to Dr. D.A. Carson, who ascribed it to his father, Tom Carson.)

One thing I have noticed about "prooftexts" is that they are very often used alone. It seems wise to consider the total of all Scriptures on a topic and not cherry-pick one verse out of the entire Bible that seems to support our current opinion. We are studying the Word of God, the Bible, to learn and shape our opinion, not to try to conform it to support our preconceived notions. If there is a verse we cannot explain, but that seems to go against dozens of other verses that have a clear meaning, we can set it aside and ask Yeshua about it later. Remember, God is not the author of confusion. **Any confusion we have about the Bible comes from our lack of knowledge or our refusal to believe.**

So, in the context of searching for Biblical proofs of what the fate of the unrepentant sinner is when they die, let us consider a number of the "prooftexts" of those who say God will torture the unrepentant sinner for ever and ever in fire.

Remember, we have seen above over 35 verses that clearly say the unrepentant sinner will **die**, suffer **death**, and be **destroyed**.

When a person believes in the Messiah of God, Yeshua, and accepts Him as their savior, they are saved, born-again, and given the **gift** of eternal life. They will live forever.

However, some use the verses below about the lost, the unsaved, and the damned that talk about "contempt" or "punishment" being everlasting or for ever and ever. They say this must mean that all men have eternal life from birth, either in the Kingdom of Heaven or in hell. So let us examine what "for ever" means in the entire Bible.

> "2 And many of those who sleep in the dust of the ground will awake, these to everlasting life, but the others to reproach and **everlasting contempt**. 3 And those who have insight will shine brightly like the brightness of the expanse of heaven, and those who lead the many to righteousness, like the stars forever and ever." (Daniel 12:2-3 LSB)

> "46 And these will go away into **eternal punishment**, but the righteous into eternal life.'" (Matthew 25:46 LSB)

> *"11 And the **smoke of their torment goes up forever and ever**; they have no rest day and night, those who worship the beast and his image, and whoever receives the mark of his name.""*
> (Revelation 14:11 LSB)

Do these verses prove that lost humans burn in punishment forever and ever? First, please read those verses again carefully. Do not assume anything. They say the punishment and the contempt are everlasting.

Adolph Hitler is the man who caused the deaths of about six million Jews in the Holocaust. He died 78 years prior to the writing of this book. But even after that many years, people worldwide still have contempt for Adolph Hitler. As stories about the Holocaust are told from survivors' families to children and grandchildren, and as students of history learn of the Holocaust through the next centuries, there will still be contempt for Adolph Hitler centuries from now.

None of this means Hitler is still alive and being shamed and held in contempt daily. Hitler is dead and gone! Contempt for him is not. The contempt for Hitler could be described as everlasting contempt.

Some horrible serial murderers are given consecutive sentences. https://www.law.cornell.edu/wex/consecutive_sentence
"A consecutive sentence, or cumulative sentence, does not begin to run until the expiration of a prior sentence. Unlike concurrent sentences, which are served simultaneously, consecutive sentences follow one another and add (as opposed to combine) to the duration of one's sentence."
"Life without possibility of parole: This is a prison sentence given to a convicted defendant in which they will remain in prison for their entire life and will not have the ability to obtain a conditional release before they complete this sentence."

Some of these people who have committed horrific crimes have been given multiple consecutive life sentences without the possibility of parole.

These are not just the punishment of a life sentence, but "everlasting punishment." The courts clearly mean this person will be punished forever, with no hope of escape or it being reversed, rescinded, or served out. This person's punishment is forever—an everlasting punishment. It does not mean the courts expect this person to live forever. It does mean this person's entire future life will be spent in punishment. This everlasting punishment lasts until they die.

A hundred years from now, some history students may come across a newspaper article on this person's legal case. They may read, "He was thrown in prison forever." They know exactly what it means. He was punished until the day he died.

The terms everlasting contempt and everlasting punishment do not prove this person is immortal or is given everlasting life, eternal life, so they can be punished longer.

The Bible was written from about 1600 B.C. to about 95 A.D. Its first writings were written about 3,620 years ago. Unless we know ancient Hebrew or ancient Greek, we read a translation. The American Bible Society says, in their article at https://news.americanbible.org/article/number-of-english-translations-of-the-bible, "Number of English Translations of the Bible," that roughly 900 English translations have been made. 900!

So we need to carefully examine what the original words of the Bible, in their original languages, really meant. Thank God, most of the main English translations mostly agree on most words most of the time, so it is not critical to learn ancient Hebrew or ancient Greek to read the Bible. But it may be wise to examine a word now and then in Hebrew or Greek.

That said, let us see what Bible support there might be for unrepentant sinners being tortured forever in hell.

What Does For Ever Mean in the Bible?

As 21st-century Americans, what does "forever" mean to us? Different dictionaries define forever as for all future time, for always, for a limitless time, continuously, and lasting or permanent. Yet even for us, we use that term figuratively to make a point. For example, "The drive to St. Louis took forever" and "He was forever talking about his first car." The question is: how did ancient Hebrews or Greeks use the term as it ended up in the Bible? Following are examples of "forever" not meaning what we might think at first glance. In the King James Version, the word "forever" does not appear. The phrase "for ever" appears 381 times in the Old Testament (Hebrew) and 72 times in the New Testament (Greek). We cannot examine all 453 of those times here, so we will use the ones that show that "for ever" does not always mean "without end."

> *"29 And if a man sell a dwelling house in a walled city, then he may redeem it within a whole year after it is sold; within a full year may he redeem it. 30 And if it be not redeemed within the space of a full year, then the house that is in the walled city shall be established **for ever** to him that bought it throughout his generations: it shall not go out in the jubilee. 31 But the houses of the villages which have no wall round about them shall be counted as the fields of the country: they may be redeemed, and they shall go out in the jubilee. 32 Notwithstanding the cities of the Levites, and the*

> *houses of the cities of their possession, may the Levites redeem at any time."* (Leviticus 25:29-32)

Leviticus 25:30 above clearly does not mean through eternity, for Yahweh said He will destroy the Earth and create a new earth. It clearly means a shorter time.

> *"45 You may also buy the children of foreigners living with you and members of their families born in your land; you may own these. 46 You may also bequeath them to your children to own; from these groups you may take your slaves **forever**. But as far as your brothers the people of Israel are concerned, you are not to treat each other harshly."* (Leviticus 25:45-46 CJB)

> *"16 But if he says to you, 'I don't want to leave you,' because he loves you and your household, and because his life with you is a good one; 17 then take an awl, and pierce his ear through, right into the door; and he will be your slave **forever**. Do the same with your female slave."* (Deuteronomy 15:16-17 CJB)

And you thought pierced ears were some modern fad! In the two verses above, obviously, a servant or bondman can only be a bondman until he dies. Therefore, the word forever, when applied to a human, can mean **until their death**.

> *"20 And when he looked on Amalek, he took up his parable, and said, Amalek was the first of the nations; but his latter end shall be that he **perish for ever**."* (Numbers 24:20)

> *"24 And ships shall come from the coast of Chittim, and shall afflict Asshur, and shall afflict Eber, and **he also shall perish for ever**."* (Numbers 24:24)

We think of perishing as the end, so we easily interpret this as meaning he will die and never live again. But in the two verses above, no one would interpret this to mean he will be **in the act of perishing for ever, never dying, but to be in a state of perishing for eternity.** If a city perishes forever, it is not rebuilt. If a race of people, like the Amaleks, perishes forever, there are not even two left alive to repopulate that race. That race is exterminated, and there is no one to continue the bloodline. They perished, and they will never be brought back.

> *"3 An Ammonite or Moabite shall not enter the assembly of the Lord; even to the tenth generation none of his descendants shall enter the assembly of the Lord **forever**,"* (Deuteronomy 23:3 NKJV)

This verse above limits for ever to ten generations. That may be about 400 years, but it is not for eternity, as we are used to the phrase "for ever" meaning. Remember that Ruth was a Moabite, and she is in the genealogy of Yeshua.

> *"11 Then she made a vow and said, "O Lord of hosts, if You will indeed look on the affliction of Your maidservant and remember me, and not forget Your maidservant, but will give Your maidservant a male child, then I will give him to the Lord **all the days of his life,** and no razor shall come upon his head.""* (1 Samuel 1:11)

> *"20 So it came to pass in the process of time that Hannah conceived and bore a son, and called his name Samuel, saying, "Because I have asked for him from the Lord." 21 Now the man Elkanah and all his house went up to offer to the Lord the yearly sacrifice and his vow. 22 But Hannah did not go up, for she said to her husband, "Not until the child is weaned; then I will take him, that he may appear before the Lord and remain there **forever.**""* (1 Samuel 1:20-22 NKJV)

It is obvious that Hannah equated "all the days of his life" with "for ever." Again, these verses show that in dealing with humans, for ever usually means until the end of their lives.

> *"12 So Achish believed David, saying, "He has made his people Israel utterly abhor him; therefore he will be my servant **forever.**""* (1 Samuel 27:12 NKJV)

> *"1 Now it happened in those days that the Philistines gathered their armies together for war, to fight with Israel. And Achish said to David, "You assuredly know that you will go out with me to battle, you and your men." 2 So David said to Achish, "Surely you know what your servant can do." And Achish said to David, "Therefore I will*

> *make you one of my chief guardians **forever.**""* (1 Samuel 28:1-2 NKJV)

A commentary says the phrase "chief guardians" in verse 2 above means Achish made David his bodyguard, or head of his armed forces. So in the two verses above, "**for ever**" obviously means until David's death. And when King David was dying, making Solomon the new king, Bathsheba wished him a long life.

> *"20 And as for you, my lord, O king, the eyes of all Israel are on you, that you should tell them who will sit on the throne of my lord the king after him. 21 Otherwise it will happen, **when my lord the king rests with his fathers,** that I and my son Solomon will be counted as offenders." 22 And just then, while she was still talking with the king, Nathan the prophet also came in"* (1 Kings 1:20-22 NKJV)

> *"31 Then Bathsheba bowed with her face to the earth, and paid homage to the king, and said, "Let my lord King David live **forever!**""* (1 Kings 1:31 NKJV)

Here, Bathsheba was obviously wishing David a long life until he died, not an eternal, everlasting life.

> *"12 Then Solomon spoke: "The Lord said He would dwell in the dark cloud. 13 I have surely built You an exalted house, And a place for You to dwell in **forever.**""* (1 Kings 8:12-13 NKJV)

No matter how sturdy the temple was, Solomon knew it would not last for eternity. In this verse, for ever clearly means a long, long time—perhaps thousands of years.

> *"3 **And the Lord said to him:** "I have heard your prayer and your supplication that you have made before Me; I have consecrated this house which you have built to put My name there **forever**, and My eyes and My heart will be there perpetually. 4 Now if you walk before Me as your father David walked, in integrity of heart and in uprightness, to do according to all that I have commanded you, and if you keep My statutes and My judgments, 5 then I will establish the throne of your kingdom over Israel forever, as I promised David your father, saying, 'You shall not fail to have a man on the throne of*

> Israel.' 6 **But if you or your sons at all turn from following Me, and do not keep My commandments** and My statutes which I have set before you, but go and serve other gods and worship them, 7 then I will cut off Israel from the land which I have given them; and this house which I have consecrated for My name I will cast out of My sight. Israel will be a proverb and a byword among all peoples. 8 And as for this house, which is exalted, everyone who passes by it will be astonished and will hiss, and say, 'Why has the Lord done thus to this land and to this house?' 9 Then they will answer, 'Because they forsook the Lord their God, who brought their fathers out of the land of Egypt, and have embraced other gods, and worshiped them and served them; therefore the Lord has brought all this calamity on them.' "" (1 Kings 9:3-9 NKJV)

1 Kings 9:3 above is particularly important, for it shows that even Yahweh uses "for ever" to mean for a long time. Yahweh knew He would allow Rome to destroy the temple a few decades after Yeshua's death. Verses 4-9 above are included to show God attached an "if" to this promise. "if" you obey, "then" I will have My name there forever. So "for ever" here from the mouth of Yahweh meant "as long as you keep your covenant with Me.

> "6 Then King Rehoboam consulted the elders who stood before his father Solomon while he still lived, and he said, "How do you advise me to answer these people?" 7 And they spoke to him, saying, "If you will be a servant to these people today, and serve them, and answer them, and speak good words to them, then they will be your servants **forever.**"" (1 Kings 12:6-7 NKJV)

"Forever" in the verse above clearly means until Rehoboam's death or his servants' deaths. There are many more instances of "for ever" not meaning eternity as we usually understand it today. We must be very careful of the Bible translation we use and even compare one translation with another and with many others to come to an accurate understanding of the Bible.

> "5 But I want to remind you, though you once knew this, that the Lord, having saved the people out of the land of Egypt, **afterward destroyed those who did not believe.** 6 And **the angels who did not**

keep their proper domain, but left their own abode, He has reserved in everlasting chains under darkness for the judgment of the great day; 7 as Sodom and Gomorrah, and the cities around them in a similar manner to these, having given themselves over to sexual immorality and gone after strange flesh, are set forth as an example, **suffering the vengeance of eternal fire."** (Jude 1:5-7 NKJV)

Are Sodom and Gomorrah still burning? No, so the term "eternal fire" cannot mean fire that burns forever. With a quick Google search of photos of Sodom and Gomorrah, we can see hundreds of current photos of the desert area where Sodom and Gomorrah existed in the past. We see with our own eyes that there is no fire of any kind burning there today.

*"17 Now the Lord had prepared a great fish to swallow Jonah. And Jonah was in the belly of the fish **three days and three nights.**"* (Jonah 1:17)

*"1 Then Jonah prayed to the Lord his God from the fish's belly. 2 And he said: "I cried out to the Lord because of my affliction, And He answered me. "Out of the belly of Sheol I cried, And You heard my voice. 3 For You cast me into the deep, Into the heart of the seas, And the floods surrounded me; All Your billows and Your waves passed over me. 4 Then I said, 'I have been cast out of Your sight; Yet I will look again toward Your holy temple.' 5 The waters surrounded me, even to my soul; The deep closed around me; Weeds were wrapped around my head. 6 I went down to the moorings of the mountains; The earth with its bars closed behind me **forever;** Yet You have brought up my life from the pit, O Lord, my God. 7 "When my soul fainted within me, I remembered the Lord; And my prayer went up to You, Into Your holy temple. 8 "Those who regard worthless idols Forsake their own Mercy. 9 But I will sacrifice to You With the voice of thanksgiving; I will pay what I have vowed. Salvation is of the Lord." 10 So the Lord spoke to the fish, and it vomited Jonah onto dry land."* (Jonah 2:1-10 NKJV)

The Bible itself says Jonah was in the belly of the fish for three days and three nights. This is clearly only three days! Yet I think we can all understand why Jonah felt like that was for ever.

> *"1 After these things I heard something like a loud voice of a great crowd in heaven, saying, "Hallelujah! Salvation and glory and power belong to our God; 2 because His judgments are true and righteous; for He has judged the great harlot who was corrupting the earth with her sexual immorality, and He has avenged the blood of His slaves shed by her hand." 3 And a second time they said, "Hallelujah!* **Her smoke rises up forever and ever.**" *4 And the twenty-four elders and the four living creatures fell down and worshiped God who sits on the throne saying, "Amen. Hallelujah!" 5 And a voice came from the throne, saying, "Give praise to our God, all you His slaves, you who fear Him, the small and the great.""* (Revelation 19:1-5 LSB)

There seems to be some debate over exactly what city, nation, or religion this "great whore" is. Nevertheless, in Revelation 21, Yahweh creates a totally new heaven and earth. Will this "great whore" city or nation be kept burning and refueled through eternity on the new earth? That seems totally unimaginable. This just has to mean something else, like it will never be forgotten or rebuilt.

> "8 But for the cowardly and unbelieving and abominable and murderers and sexually immoral persons and sorcerers and idolaters and all liars, **their part will be in the lake that burns with fire and brimstone, which is the second death.**"" (Revelation 21:8 LSB)

Note that this verse says that for these unsaved humans **"their part will be in the lake,"** which does not specify for how long, but for these lost, unsaved humans, it is called "**the second death**." Sometimes the truth just stares us in the face! The Bible says God is not the author of confusion.

> "33 for **God is not a God of confusion** but of peace, as in all the churches of the saints." (1 Corinthians 14:33 LSB)

Does it make any sense at all, does it sound true at all, to say that when God says, "This is the second death," He means "where you will never die or suffer death, but will be tortured forever and ever and ever?"

> "14 Then death and Hades were thrown into **the lake of fire. This is the second death, the lake of fire.**" (Revelation 20:14 LSB)

We have examined "for ever," and have seen that it does not always mean for all eternity. Let's now examine another term used to support eternal torture: "everlasting."

What Does Everlasting Mean in the Bible?

As happens often, some of the verses below you have seen before, but with a different focus. Our focus now is on the word "everlasting" and how it is used in the Bible.

The first time the word "everlasting" is used in the KJV Bible is in the first book of the Bible, Genesis. And it calls the rainbow a sign of an everlasting covenant with all mankind, that He will not destroy all creatures with a flood again.

> *"15 and I will remember My covenant, which is between Me and you and every living creature of all flesh; and never again shall the water become a flood to destroy all flesh. 16 **So the bow shall be in the cloud, and I will look upon it, to remember the everlasting covenant between God and every living creature of all flesh that is on the earth.**" 17 And God said to Noah, "This is the sign of the covenant which I have established between Me and all flesh that is on the earth.""* (Genesis 9:15-17 LSB)

> *"1 "Now at that time, Michael, the great prince who stands guard over the sons of your people, will stand. And there will be a time of distress such as never happened since there was a nation until that time; and at that time your people, everyone who is found written in the book, will be rescued. 2 **And many of those who sleep in the dust of the ground will awake, these to everlasting life, but the others to reproach and everlasting contempt.**"* (Daniel 12:1-2 LSB)

The following selection is important, for it contains both "eternal" and "everlasting," describing what seems to be the same thing.

> "31 When the Son of Man comes in His glory, and all the holy angels with Him, then He will sit on the throne of His glory. 32 All the nations will be gathered before Him, and He will separate them one from another, as a shepherd divides his sheep from the goats. 33 And He will set the sheep on His right hand, but the goats on the left. 34 Then the King will say to those on His right hand, 'Come, you blessed of My Father, inherit the kingdom prepared for you from the foundation of the world: 35 for I was hungry and you gave Me food; I was thirsty and you gave Me drink; I was a stranger and you took Me in; 36 I was naked and you clothed Me; I was sick and you visited Me; I was in prison and you came to Me.' 37 "Then the righteous will answer Him, saying, 'Lord, when did we see You hungry and feed You, or thirsty and give You drink? 38 When did we see You a stranger and take You in, or naked and clothe You? 39 Or when did we see You sick, or in prison, and come to You?' 40 And the King will answer and say to them, 'Assuredly, I say to you, inasmuch as you did it to one of the least of these My brethren, you did it to Me.' 41 "Then He will also say to those on the left hand, 'Depart from Me, you cursed, into the **everlasting fire** prepared for the devil and his angels: 42 for I was hungry and you gave Me no food; I was thirsty and you gave Me no drink; 43 I was a stranger and you did not take Me in, naked and you did not clothe Me, sick and in prison and you did not visit Me.' 44 "Then they also will answer Him, saying, 'Lord, when did we see You hungry or thirsty or a stranger or naked or sick or in prison, and did not minister to You?' 45 Then He will answer them, saying, 'Assuredly, I say to you, inasmuch as you did not do it to one of the least of these, you did not do it to Me.' 46 **And these will go away into everlasting punishment, but the righteous into eternal life.**"" (Matthew 25:31-46 NKJV)

While the everlasting fire prepared for the devil and his angels is not our focus, we have no reason to believe it means anything other than what "everlasting" means in other usages. "Everlasting punishment" does sound like it means never-ending, but do consider that a punishment that is never rescinded or cancelled is everlasting. That does not necessarily mean the actual active phase of the punishment is never-ending. Death is an end.

> *"5 For the living know that they shall die: but **the dead know not any thing**, neither have they any more a reward; for **the memory of them is forgotten**."* (Ecclesiastes 9:5)

The following verse also has both "eternal" and "everlasting" describing the same thing. This seems to me to be a great affirmation that the life Yahweh gives believers through Yeshua Hamashiach will never end.

> *"15 that whoever believes in Him should not perish but have **eternal life**. 16 For God so loved the world that He gave His only begotten Son, that whoever believes in Him should not perish but have **everlasting life**."* (John 3:15-16 NKJV)

> *"36 He who believes in the Son **has everlasting life**; and he who does not believe the Son shall not see life, but the wrath of God abides on him.""* (John 3:36 NKJV)

> *"14 but whoever drinks of the water that I shall give him will never thirst. But the water that I shall give him will become in him a fountain of water springing up into **everlasting life**.""* (John 4:14 NKJV)

> *"24 "Most assuredly, I say to you, **he who hears My word and believes in Him who sent Me has everlasting life**, and shall not come into judgment, but has passed from death into life." (John 5:24 NKJV)*

> *"27 Do not labor for the food which perishes, but for the food which endures to **everlasting life**, which the Son of Man will give you, because God the Father has set His seal on Him." 28 Then they said to Him, "What shall we do, that we may work the works of God?" 29 Jesus answered and said to them, "**This is the work of God, that you believe in Him whom He sent**.""* (John 6:27-29 NKJV)

Notice above that Yeshua calls believing in Yeshua "the work of Yahweh," so **having faith is a work**.

*"35 And **Jesus said** to them, "I am the bread of life. He who comes to Me shall never hunger, and he who believes in Me shall never thirst. 36 But I said to you that you have seen Me and yet do not believe. 37 All that the Father gives Me will come to Me, and the one who comes to Me I will by no means cast out. 38 For I have come down from heaven, not to do My own will, but the will of Him who sent Me. 39 This is the will of the Father who sent Me, that of all He has given Me I should lose nothing, but should raise it up at the last day. 40 And this is the will of Him who sent Me, that **everyone who sees the Son and believes in Him may have everlasting life; and I will raise him up at the last day**.""* (John 6:35-40 NKJV)

*"43 **Jesus therefore answered** and said to them, "Do not murmur among yourselves. 44 No one can come to Me unless the Father who sent Me draws him; and I will raise him up at the last day. 45 It is written in the prophets, 'And they shall all be taught by God.' Therefore everyone who has heard and learned from the Father comes to Me. 46 Not that anyone has seen the Father, except He who is from God; He has seen the Father. 47 Most assuredly, I say to you, **he who believes in Me has everlasting life**."* (John 6:43-47 NKJV)

*"25 **Jesus answered** them, "I told you, and you do not believe. The works that I do in My Father's name, they bear witness of Me. 26 But you do not believe, because you are not of My sheep, as I said to you. 27 My sheep hear My voice, and I know them, and **they follow Me**. 28 And **I give them eternal life,** and they shall never perish; neither shall anyone snatch them out of My hand."* (John 10:25-28 NKJV)

The verses below again have both "everlasting" and "eternal" meaning the same thing.

*"22 But now having been set free from sin, and having become slaves of God, you have your fruit to holiness, and the end, **everlasting life**. 23 For the wages of sin is death, but **the gift of God is eternal life** in Christ Jesus our Lord."* (Romans 6:22-23 NKJV)

> *"13 I urge you in the sight of God who gives life to all things, and before Christ Jesus who witnessed the good confession before Pontius Pilate, 14 that you keep this commandment without spot, blameless until our Lord Jesus Christ's appearing, 15 which He will manifest in His own time, He who is the blessed and only Potentate, the King of kings and Lord of lords, 16 who alone has immortality, dwelling in unapproachable light, whom no man has seen or can see,* **to whom be honor and everlasting power.** *Amen.. Amen."* (1 Timothy 6:13-16 NKJV)

> *"8 in flaming fire taking vengeance on those who do not know God, and on those who do not obey the gospel of our Lord Jesus Christ. 9 These shall be* **punished with everlasting destruction** *from the presence of the Lord and from the glory of His power,"* (2 Thessalonians 1:8-9 NKJV)

If you are destroyed and then recreated, your destruction is not everlasting. If you are never recreated, then your destruction is everlasting. But it makes no sense that your destruction has been ongoing ever since, and will be going on forever.

> *"16 Now may our Lord Jesus Christ Himself, and our God and Father, who has loved us and* **given us everlasting consolation and good hope** *by grace, 17 comfort your hearts and establish you in every good word and work."* (2 Thessalonians 2:16-17 NKJV)

> *"20 Now may the God of peace who brought up our Lord Jesus from the dead, that great Shepherd of the sheep, through the blood of the* **everlasting covenant,** *21 make you complete in every good work to do His will, working in you what is well pleasing in His sight,* **through Jesus Christ,** *to whom be glory forever and ever. Amen. 22 And I appeal to you, brethren, bear with the word of exhortation, for I have written to you in few words.."* (Hebrews 13:20-22 NKJV)

> *"10 Therefore, brethren, be even more diligent to make your call and election sure, for if you do these things you will never stumble; 11 for so an entrance*

*will be supplied to you abundantly into the **everlasting kingdom of our Lord and Savior Jesus Christ**.*" (2 Peter 1:10-11 NKJV)

*"5 But I want to remind you, though you once knew this, that the Lord, having saved the people out of the land of Egypt, **afterward destroyed those who did not believe**. 6 And **the angels who did not keep their proper domain, but left their own abode, He has reserved in everlasting chains under darkness for the judgment of the great day;** 7 as Sodom and Gomorrah, and the cities around them in a similar manner to these, having given themselves over to sexual immorality and gone after strange flesh, are set forth as an example, suffering the vengeance of eternal fire."* (Jude 1:5-7 NKJV)

The verse above says **everlasting** chains, but only unto the judgment of the great day.

*"And I saw another angel fly in the midst of heaven, having the **everlasting gospel** to preach unto them that dwell on the earth, and to every nation, and kindred, and tongue, and people,"* (Revelation 14:6)

We have examined the terms "for ever" and "everlasting." Let's examine another term. Some say an unquenchable fire absolutely must burn forever and ever. Is that what the Bible says? Let's search the Scriptures to see what "unquenchable fire" truly meant to the authors who wrote the Hebrew and Greek words.

What Does Unquenchable Mean in the Bible?

From The American Heritage Dictionary: "unquenchable":
**"1. Impossible to slake or satisfy: unquenchable thirst.
2. Impossible to suppress or destroy: unquenchable enthusiasm."**

A person's unquenchable thirst is not eternal. It ends when they die. A person's unquenchable enthusiasm is not eternal. It ends when they die.

Unquenchable Does Not Mean Eternal.

"43 If your hand causes you to stumble, cut it off. It is better for you to enter into life maimed, rather

than having your two hands to go into **Gehenna,** *into the* **unquenchable fire**,*" (Mark 9:43 WEB)*

The verse above does associate Gehenna with a place of unquenchable fire. But what does that really mean? The American Heritage Dictionary says quench means the following (first 3 meanings).

"1. To put out (a fire, for example); extinguish.
2. To suppress; squelch:
3. To slake; satisfy:"

The Lake of Fire cannot be put out except, of course, by God. Think of how we use the words, even today. If the firefighters pour water on the forest fire, use their other fire-fighting techniques, and stop the fire, we say they put out the fire, or quenched the fire. But if the forest fire was far out in the wilderness and no firefighter arrived, it would burn up the local trees, brush, grass, and other combustibles, and it would stop. No forest fire burns up the entire world. No forest fire burns forever. We do not say the fire burned down the entire forest, from river to river, then was "quenched." We would say it "burned itself out." We mean it burned up everything that was burnable, ran out of fuel, ran its course, and burned out naturally.

In modern times, firefighters called to a house fire usually have the equipment to quench the fire, putting it out by dousing it with water. But if a news article today talked of a forest fire that firefighters could not put out, they could rightfully call it an unquenchable fire. Does that mean that it will burn forever? No! It means people could not put it out. But after some time, it will have burned up all its fuel and will burn itself out.

In fact, according to "10 Strategies Firefighters Use to Fight Wildfires" by Brooks Hays, three of the wildfire fighting strategies have exactly that goal: to let the fire burn itself out until all the fuel is gone. They minimize the fire by using various techniques.

1. Control Line: "A fire line is when the barrier is scraped down "to mineral soil."

2. Burning Out: "To create a sturdy, fuel-free barrier, firefighters may use small torches to burn the brush just inside a control line."

3. Backburn: "Once a Control Line is established, firefighters may set a controlled blaze downwind of the main fire, just on the inside of the control line. Firefighters then push the new blaze back toward the main fire, burning up all the fuel that lies between the fire and the control line."

Fires need fuel. A fire God makes for the devil and his angels is unquenchable because God does not want it to go out. But when He has finished using it, He can let it burn out. Even after it was out, it was an unquenchable fire. No one could put it out. It had to burn out, or be put out by God Himself.

Greek Fire

Figure 11.1: Greek Fire
Attribution: (Unknown Artist - Public Domain)

Figure 11.1 shows Greek Fire being used to burn an enemy ship. WorldHistory.org's article on Greek Fire says, in part, that "Greek Fire was an incendiary weapon first used in Byzantine warfare in 678 CE. The napalm of ancient warfare, the highly flammable liquid was made of secret ingredients and used both in catapulted incendiary bombs and sprayed under pressure so as to launch flames at enemy ships and fortifications. It was also used with success in defensive situations. Greek Fire became the most devastating weapon of Christendom for over seven centuries and ensured that Constantinople resisted all comers."

The article on Greek Fire at https://allthatsinteresting.com/greek-fire says this. "Also called "sea fire" and "liquid fire" by the Byzantines themselves, it was heated, pressurized, and then delivered via a tube called a siphon. Greek fire was mainly used to light enemy ships on fire from a safe distance."

"What made the weapon so unique and potent was its ability to continue burning in water, which prevented enemy combatants from dousing the flames during naval wars. It's possible that the flames burned even more vigorously upon contact with water."

"To make matters worse, Greek fire was a liquid concoction that stuck to whatever it touched, be it a ship or human flesh."

Greek Fire was basically "unquenchable." Pouring water on it did nothing but spread it. It burned even while floating on water. Because of the great secrecy surrounding the formula for this weapon, scientists today can still not recreate Greek Fire. Even the enemies who happened to capture some Greek Fire and its delivery devices could not recreate the liquid.

It was truly unquenchable! But when it had totally burned up the ship it was thrown on, when it had totally burned itself up, consuming most or all of the ship with it, it burned itself out. It accomplished its purpose, finished its job, and burned itself out. It did not float on the water to the shore and somehow flow across the land, burning forever and ever.

It was unquenchable, but not eternal. It did not burn for ever and ever.

Yeshua used the term "is not quenched."

*"43 If your hand causes you to sin, cut it off. It is better for you to enter into life maimed, rather than having two hands, to go to hell, into the fire that shall never be quenched— 44 where 'Their worm does not die And the **fire is not quenched**.'" (Mark 9:43-44 WEB)*

John the Baptist used the term "unquenchable."

*"11 I indeed baptize you with water unto repentance, but He who is coming after me is mightier than I, whose sandals I am not worthy to carry. He will baptize you with the Holy Spirit and fire. 12 His winnowing fan is in His hand, and He will thoroughly clean out His threshing floor, and gather His wheat into the barn; but He will burn up the chaff with **unquenchable fire**.'" (Matthew 3:11-12 NKJV)*

Yeshua and John were using the common understanding of the Children of Israel at that time. None of them believed in eternal torment in fire in a place called hell. Remember that word hell did not even exist until 725 A.D. The Hebrew words that today are translated into "Hell" did not mean the same thing to them back then, as it does to us today.

Yeshua and John may have been referring to Isaiah 66:22-24, below.

> *"22 For as the new heavens and the new earth Which I will make shall remain before Me," says the Lord, "So shall your descendants and your name remain. 23 And it shall come to pass That from one New Moon to another, And from one Sabbath to another, All flesh shall come to worship before Me," says the Lord. 24 "And they shall go forth and look Upon the corpses of the men Who have transgressed against Me. For their worm does not die, And their **fire is not quenched**. They shall be an abhorrence to all flesh."* (Isaiah 66:22-24 NKJV)

Note that **the bodies above are "carcasses," dead bodies, not living bodies, not living beings being tortured,** yet it says "their worm shall not die." The word "worm" here cannot mean soul, for the soul does not stay in a dead body. But let us keep looking at the ancient Hebrew usage of the word "quenched."

> *"8 For the Lord has a day of vengeance, a year of retribution, to uphold Zion's cause.* **9 Edom's** *streams will be turned into pitch, her dust into burning sulfur; her land* **will become blazing pitch! 10 It will not be quenched night or day; its smoke will rise forever.** *From generation to generation it will lie desolate; no one will ever pass through it again."* (Isaiah 34:8-10 NIV)

Wow! Taken alone, those verses above say Edom will be burning blazing pitch (tar) that will never be quenched and will burn forever and ever. But if you do not take it out of context and read just the next 3 verses, look what happens to your understanding of "not be quenched" and "forever."

> *"11 The* **desert owl and screech owl will possess it; the great owl and the raven will nest there.** *God will stretch out over Edom the measuring line of chaos and the plumb line of desolation. 12 Her nobles will have nothing there to be called a kingdom, all her princes will vanish away. 13* **Thorns will overrun her citadels, nettles and brambles** *her strongholds.* **She will become a haunt for jackals, a home for owls."** *(Isaiah 34:11-13 NIV)*

Can these animals live in burning pitch (tar)? Can even thorns, nettles, and brambles grow in burning pitch? Would jackals and owls choose to live in "blazing pitch?"

When good King Josiah found the Book of the Law of Moses that had been lost and ignored, he asked Huldah the prophetess what the future of Judah would be.

> "16 thus says Yahweh, "Behold, I am bringing evil on this place and on its inhabitants, even all the words of the book which the king of Judah has read. 17 Because they have forsaken Me and have burned incense to other gods that they might provoke Me to anger with all the work of their hands, therefore **My wrath is set aflame against this place, and it shall not be quenched.**"" (2 Kings 22:16-17 LSB)

Judah had turned to idols and provoked God's anger. Is the wrath of God still upon Judah today? Judah is gone. That land is Israel today.

> "20 Therefore thus says Lord Yahweh, "**Behold, My anger and My wrath will be poured out on this place,** on man and on beast and on the trees of the field and on the fruit of the ground; **and it will burn and not be quenched.**"" (Jeremiah 7:20 LSB)

Are there no trees, no animals, and no fruit in the land that was Judah today? Below, Jeremiah 17:27 is about Judah not keeping God's Holy Sabbath Day.

> "27 But **if you do not listen to Me to keep the sabbath day holy** by not carrying a load and coming in through the gates of Jerusalem on the sabbath day, **then I will kindle** a fire in its gates, and **it will devour the palaces of Jerusalem and not be quenched.**"" (Jeremiah 17:27 LSB)

> "45 Yahweh's word came to me, saying, 46 "Son of man, set your face toward the south, and preach toward the south, and prophesy against the forest of the field in the South. 47 Tell the forest of the South, 'Hear Yahweh's word: The Lord Yahweh says, "Behold, **I will kindle a fire** in you, and it will devour every green tree in you, and every dry tree. **The burning flame will not be quenched,** and all faces from the south to the north will be burned by

> *it. 48 All flesh will see that **I, Yahweh, have kindled it. It will not be quenched.**""" (Ezekiel 20:45-48 WEB)*

Are Israel and the land that was Judah burning today? No! Are there any green trees and other plants growing in Israel today? Yes! In fact, since being reborn as a nation, there is a saying today that Israel has made the deserts bloom!

In the context of history, Israel, Judah, Jerusalem, and Edom did burn to the ground, but they are not burning today.

The fires in all these examples were not quenched, but did burn up the available fuel and then burn out as a result of natural processes. These fires accomplished what God wanted, then burned themselves out.

We can see the Bible in the Old Testament uses unquenchable to mean a fire that cannot be put out! It cannot be quenched by those who did not start it. But it finally consumes its fuel and burns out naturally, having completed the task it was set to do.

Deuteronomy 32:39 says only God can stop what God Starts. No one can quench a fire God has started until it has fulfilled God's purpose.

> *"39 See now that I, I am He, And there is no god besides Me; It is I who put to death and give life. I have wounded, and it is I who heal, And **there is no one who can deliver from My hand.**"* (Deuteronomy 32:39 LSB)

Psalm 50:22 says no one can save someone from the will of God. No one can put out a fire that God starts. He will let it burn until He is done with it.

> *"22 "Now consider this, you who forget God, Lest I tear you in pieces, and **there will be none to deliver.**"* (Psalm 50:22)

Daniel 4:35 says no one can affect what God has decreed. What He says **will** come to pass.

> *"35 All the inhabitants of the earth are reputed as nothing; and **he does according to his will** in the army of heaven, and among the inhabitants of the earth; and **no one can stop his hand**, or ask him, "What are you doing?""* (Daniel 4:35 WEB)

Isaiah 14:27 says no one can thwart God's plans or decrees.

*"27 For Yahweh of Armies has planned, **and who can stop it?** His hand is stretched out, and **who can turn it back?**""* (Isaiah 14:27)

Mankind can say, "We have the best fire department in the world, with 1,000 fire trucks, 1,000 firefighting helicopters, and 10,000 firefighters. We can put out your fire." God just laughs.

Carefully consider the fire of God when Elijah called on God to burn his sacrifice. The following is an exciting and glorious example of God lighting a fire that could not be quenched by any means until it had accomplished its assigned mission, its heavenly purpose.

"20 So Ahab sent a message among all the sons of Israel and gathered the prophets together at Mount Carmel. 21 And Elijah came near to all the people and said, "How long will you be limping between two opinions? If Yahweh is God, follow Him; but if Baal, follow him." But the people did not answer him a word. 22 Then Elijah said to the people, "I alone am left a prophet of Yahweh, but Baal's prophets are 450 men. 23 Now let them give us two oxen; and let them choose one ox for themselves and cut it up, and place it on the wood, but place no fire under it; and I will prepare the other ox and put it on the wood, and I will not place fire under it. 24 Then you call on the name of your god, and I will call on the name of Yahweh, and the God who answers by fire, He is God." And all the people answered and said, "That is a good word." 25 So Elijah said to the prophets of Baal, "Choose one ox for yourselves and prepare it first for you are many, and call on the name of your god, but place no fire under it." 26 Then they took the ox which was given them and they prepared it and called on the name of Baal from morning until noon saying, "O Baal, answer us." But there was no voice and no one answered. And they limped about the altar which they had made. 27 Now it happened at noon, that Elijah mocked them and said, "Call out with a loud voice, for he is a god; either he is occupied or relieving himself, or is on a journey, or perhaps he is asleep and needs to be awakened." 28 So they cried with a loud voice and gashed themselves according to

their custom with swords and lances until the blood gushed out on them. 29 Now it happened when noon had passed, that they prophesied until the time of the offering of the evening sacrifice; but there was no voice, no one answered, and no one paid attention. **30 Then Elijah said to all the people, "Come near to me."** *So all the people came near to him. And he repaired the altar of Yahweh which had been pulled down. 31 Then Elijah took twelve stones according to the number of the tribes of the sons of Jacob, to whom the word of Yahweh had come, saying, "Israel shall be your name." 32 And with the stones he built an altar in the name of Yahweh, and he made a trench around the altar, large enough to hold two seahs [7quarts] of seed. 33 Then he arranged the wood and cut the ox in pieces and placed it on the wood. 34* **And he said, "Fill four pitchers with water and pour it on the burnt offering and on the wood."** *And he said,* **"Do it a second time,"** *and they did it a second time. And he said,* **"Do it a third time,"** *and they did it a third time. 35* **And the water flowed around the altar and he also filled the trench with water.** *36 Now it happened at the time of the offering of the evening sacrifice, that Elijah the prophet came near and said,* **"O Yahweh, the God of Abraham, Isaac and Israel, today let it be known that You are God in Israel** *and that I am Your slave and I have done all these things at Your word. 37 Answer me, O Yahweh, answer me, that this people may know that You, O Yahweh, are God, and that You have turned their heart back again." 38* **Then the fire of Yahweh fell and consumed the burnt offering and the wood and the stones and the dust, and licked up the water that was in the trench.** *39 And all* **the people saw it and fell on their faces and said, "Yahweh, He is God; Yahweh, He is God.""** (1 Kings 18:20-39 LSB)

God's fire burned the sacrifice, the water on it, the wood of the fire, the stones of the altar, and the water that was in the trench. It could not be quenched. But it did not burn down the whole area. It burned what God wanted burned, and God let it burn out. It was unquenchable, but not eternal. It did not burn "for ever."

We will start the next section with an affirmation of what the Bible says over and over. The unrepentant sinner, the wicked, shall not be; they shall perish; they shall vanish away.

> *"10 Yet a little while and **the wicked man will be no more;** You will look carefully at his place, and **he will not be there.**"* (Psalm 37:10 LSB)

> *"20 **But the wicked will perish;** And the enemies of Yahweh will be like the glory of the pastures, **They vanish—in smoke they vanish away.**"* (Psalm 37:20 LSB)

Smoke Rises for Ever and Ever

Old Testament

Some use the idea of the smoke of sinners torment rising up for ever to try to prove the eternal torture of sinners in hell.
So let us see what the Bible says about smoke rising for ever. Smoke rising forever is mentioned only once in the Old Testament.

We have seen these verses about Edom before in our discussion about "unquenchable," but for now we are looking at them for what they say about **smoke going up for ever.** Idumea was another name for Edom, the land of the Edomites, the descendants of Esau.

> *"5 For **My sword** is satiated in heaven; Behold, it **shall descend for judgment upon Edom** [Idumea] And upon the people whom I have devoted to destruction. "* (Isaiah 34:5 LSB)

> *"8 For Yahweh has a day of vengeance, A year of recompense for the cause of Zion. 9 And its streams will be turned into pitch, And its dust into brimstone, And its land will become burning pitch. 10 It will not be quenched night or day;*
> ***Its smoke will go up forever.*** *From generation to generation it will be laid waste; None will pass through it forever and ever."* (Isaiah 34:8-10)

At first glance, this may give the impression that Edom (Idumea) will be burning for ever. But if you do not take it out of context and you read the next three verses, look what happens to your understanding of "its smoke will go up for ever."

*"11 **The desert owl and screech owl will possess it; the great owl and the raven will nest there.** God will stretch out over Edom the measuring line of chaos and the plumb line of desolation. 12 Her nobles will have nothing there to be called a kingdom, all her princes will vanish away. 13 **Thorns will overrun her citadels, nettles and brambles her strongholds.** She will become **a haunt for jackals, a home for owls.**"* (Isaiah 34:11-13 NIV)

Can these animals live in burning pitch (tar)? Can even thorns, nettles, and brambles grow in burning pitch? Would jackals, ravens, and owls choose to live in "blazing pitch?" Is the smoke of this rising today, 2,000 years later? Obviously, it is not.

So from the only verse in the Old Testament about smoke rising for ever, we see that it cannot mean the fire will go on forever and ever, or even that the smoke of that fire will rise forever and ever. It just has to mean something else since we can see the physical land today without fire or smoke. Perhaps God was just speaking poetically.

Have you ever said (or been tempted to say) to your teenage kid, after they disobeyed you, "You are grounded forever!" You do not mean "forever," and they know you don't mean "forever." But they don't even question you about it because they know that your saying "forever" is an exclamation point about how bad their act was and how righteously angry you are. And even a teenager understands that it was a serious infraction. but they also know two things are possible. First, you love them, and when your anger cools, you will forgive them and at some point cancel their "grounding." Or second, when they turn 18, become an adult, and move out to their own home, you cannot "ground" them anymore.

For those who turn and repent and love and obey God, I think the first happens. But if it does not, then the second happens with our death. When the punished person no longer lives, the punishment has done its job. It is finished.

Either of those, the poetic imaging of a physical thing to describe a spiritual thing or the punishment running its natural course, may be the explanation for why God can say "the smoke thereof shall go up for ever," when we can see that there is no real physical smoke going up anymore in Idumea (Edom).

So we find no verse in the Old Testament clearly stating that unrepentant sinners will be tortured forever and ever in fire.

New Testament

Smoke going up forever is mentioned only two times in the New Testament.

> "9 Then another angel, a third one, followed them, saying with a loud voice, "If anyone worships the beast and his image, and receives a mark on his forehead or on his hand, 10 and he also will drink of the wine of the wrath of God, which is mixed in full strength in the cup of His rage, and he will be tormented with fire and brimstone in the presence of the holy angels and in the presence of the Lamb. 11 And **the smoke of their torment goes up forever and ever;** they have no rest day and night, those who worship the beast and his image, and whoever receives the mark of his name."" (Revelation 14:9-11 LSB)

The phrase in the verses above, "no rest day and night," is still of some concern, but forever and ever is the adjective phrase after "smoke of their torment," not the "no rest" phrase. Nevertheless, we must keep that phrase in mind.

The following is not about the smoke of those burning in hell but about Babylon, the Great Whore of the End Times. Do you think God will have the smoke of this great city or nation rise for all eternity, even in the new heavens and new earth?

> "1 After these things I heard something like a loud voice of a great crowd in heaven, saying, "Hallelujah! Salvation and glory and power belong to our God; 2 because His judgments are true and righteous; for He has judged the great harlot who was corrupting the earth with her sexual immorality, and He has avenged the blood of His slaves shed by her hand." 3 And a second time they said, "Hallelujah! **Her smoke rises up forever and ever.**"" (Revelation 19:1-3)

So we have seen the idea of smoke going up forever in the New Testament also, but this does not definitively prove people are tortured forever and ever in fire. We saw that the Old Testament was the same, so we see no clear proof of eternal torture in the entire Bible.

The Worm Dieth Not

In the Old Testament, the phrase "worm will not die" is used only once. The phrase "worm dieth not" is not in the Old Testament.

> "22 "For just as the new heavens and the new earth Which I make will endure before Me," declares Yahweh, "So your seed and your name will endure. 23 And it shall be from new moon to new moon And from sabbath to sabbath, All mankind will come to worship before Me," says Yahweh. 24 "Then they will go forth and look On the corpses of the men Who have transgressed against Me. **For their worm will not die And their fire will not be quenched;** And they will be an object of contempt to all mankind.""" (Isaiah 66:22-24 LSB)

The thought of being burned alive while at the same time being eaten alive by worms has got to be one of the most horrific descriptions of what people think hell is like.

In the New Testament, the phrase "worm dieth not" is used only in three verses, all in Mark: Mark 9:44, Mark 9:46, and Mark 9:48. "Where their worm dieth not, and the fire is not quenched" is quoted the same in all 3 verses. This appears to be Yeshua quoting Isaiah 66:24.

> "42 Whoever will cause one of these little ones who believe in me to stumble, it would be better for him if he were thrown into the sea with a millstone hung around his neck. 43 If your hand causes you to stumble, cut it off. It is better for you to enter into life maimed, rather than having your two hands to go into Gehenna, **into the unquenchable fire,** 44 'where their worm doesn't die, and the fire is not quenched.' 45 If your foot causes you to stumble, cut it off. It is better for you to enter into life lame, rather than having your two feet to be cast into Gehenna, into **the fire that will never be quenched— 46 'where their worm doesn't die, and the fire is not quenched.'** 47 If your eye causes you to stumble, cast it out. It is better for you to enter into God's Kingdom with one eye, rather than having two eyes to be cast into the Gehenna of fire, 48 'where their worm doesn't die, and the fire is not quenched.'" (Mark 9:42-48 WEB)

This could mean the maggots, the worms eating the dead bodies, will not be killed. It is inconceivable that it pictures worms eating a living body. And if the fire mentioned is a flaming fire that can consume dead bodies, how could any worms live?

Indeed, picture a raging flame that people kindle under a funeral pyre to consume the dead body relatively quickly. Wikipedia says the open-air funeral pyres burned in India today take about six hours to consume a body, whereas a cremation in a modern gas crematorium takes about 90 minutes to consume an average adult.

No worm could exist for more than a few minutes in that, even buried deep in the human body, such as a parasitic worm.

But the picture of a slow-burning, low-level, smoldering fire burning trash and drying out, then slow-burning dead bodies, would fit how a trash dump like Gehenna would burn.

The Cambridge Bible for Schools and Colleges commentary on Isaiah 66:24 says that the worm and the fire are descriptive of the two common ways to dispose of dead bodies: burying and burning. Cremation and interment are still the only two ways mankind disposes of dead bodies today, in the twenty-first century.

Verses That Say Souls Live For Ever in Hell

Some Bible verses, when read in isolation or cherry-picked out of the entire Bible, can seem at first glance to mean there is a place called hell in which sinners will burn forever and ever. But we must always take the sum total of All scriptures, in context.

> "24 "Then they will go forth and look On the corpses of the men Who have transgressed against Me. For **their worm will not die And their fire will not be quenched**; And they will be an object of contempt to all mankind.""' (Isaiah 66:24 LSB)

The verse above is here only for those who would otherwise complain that I missed one. Please read the above verse carefully and note that it does not say they will be tortured forever, but the fire will not be quenched, which means put out. It is the lake of fire, which John calls the Second Death. We know it will not be put out or quenched. If you throw wood into a fire that is not quenched, the wood burns up, but it does not burn forever, even though the fire is not quenched. Also, their "worm shall not die" does not say soul or spirit. Will you let one (1) verse that is at best nebulous outweigh dozens and dozens of very clear verses to the contrary? Dozens and dozens of verses say the unrepentant sinner will die!

> "40 And the King will answer and say to them, 'Assuredly, I say to you, inasmuch as you did it to one of the least of these My brethren, you did it to Me.' 41 "Then He will also say to those on the left hand, 'Depart from Me, you cursed, into the

> ***everlasting fire prepared for the devil and his angels:***" (Matthew 25:40-41 NKJV)

Again, the verse above is here only for those who would otherwise complain that I missed one. But note that it says only that the humans will be thrown into the fire. This does not mean that they will not be consumed and destroyed. It says the fire is everlasting. But the Bible clearly says man is not immortal.

> "*43 If your hand causes you to stumble, cut it off. It is better for you to enter into life maimed, rather than having your two hands **to go into Gehenna, into the unquenchable fire, 44 'where their worm doesn't die, and the fire is not quenched.'** 45 If your foot causes you to stumble, cut it off. It is better for you to enter into life lame, rather than having your two feet to **be cast into Gehenna, into the fire that will never be quenched— 46 'where their worm doesn't die,** and the fire is not quenched.' 47 If your eye causes you to stumble, cast it out. It is better for you to enter into God's Kingdom with one eye, rather than having two eyes to be cast into the Gehenna of fire, 48 '**where their worm doesn't die, and the fire is not quenched.'** For everyone will be salted with fire, and every sacrifice will be seasoned with salt.*" (Mark 9:43-49 WEB)

"Their worm doesn't die." What does that really mean? Does that obscure statement overpower about sixty Scriptures that clearly say sinners die, are destroyed, and are burned up? "The fire is not quenched" is confirmed by Matthew 25:41 "41: Then shall he say also unto them on the left hand, Depart from me, ye cursed, into **everlasting fire, prepared for the devil and his angels**:" But remember what forever or everlasting can mean in the Bible. It can mean until the end of an age.

> "*19 "Now there was a rich man, and he habitually dressed in purple and fine linen, joyously living in splendor every day. 20 But a poor man named Lazarus was laid at his gate, covered with sores, 21 and desiring to be fed with the crumbs which were falling from the rich man's table; besides, even the dogs were coming and licking his sores. 22 Now it happened that the poor man died and was carried away by the angels to **Abraham's bosom,** and the rich man also died and was buried. 23 And **in***

> ***Hades he lifted up his eyes, being in torment,*** *and *saw Abraham far away and Lazarus in his bosom. 24 And he cried out and said, 'Father Abraham, have mercy on me, and send Lazarus so that he may dip the tip of his finger in water and cool off my tongue, **for I am in agony in this flame.**' 25 But Abraham said, 'Child, remember that during your life you received your good things, and likewise Lazarus bad things. But now he is being comforted here, and you are in agony. 26 And besides all this, between us and you there is a great chasm fixed, so that those who wish to come over from here to you are not able, and none may cross over from there to us.' 27 And he said, 'Then I am asking you, father, that you send him to my father's house— 28 for I have five brothers—in order that he may warn them, **so that they will not also come to this place of torment.**' 29 But Abraham *said, 'They have Moses and the Prophets; let them hear them.' 30 But he said, 'No, father Abraham, but if someone goes to them from the dead, they will repent!' 31 But he said to him, 'If they do not listen to Moses and the Prophets, they will not be persuaded even if someone rises from the dead.""*
(Luke 16:19-31 LSB)

    This parable, in Luke 16:22, is the only place in the Bible that mentions "Abraham's Bosom." This one (1) verse is problematic. But it stands as one against the many, many above that clearly say the exact opposite. It also does not address how long the rich man had been there or was going to be there. It does not say for eternity. This is before the Great White Throne Judgment. Are people thrown into hell at death, brought out for the judgment, and then thrown back in?

    The following verses at first seem to say that those who worship the beast, the antichrist, will be tormented forever and ever. But it says, "The **smoke of their torment** goes up for ever and ever." The Lake of Fire does burn forever, and its smoke will go up forever. That does not mean they will be alive in that fire and smoke for ever and ever.

> *"9 Then another angel, a third one, followed them, saying with a loud voice, "If anyone worships the beast and his image, and receives a mark on his forehead or on his hand, 10 and he also will drink of the wine of the wrath of God, which is mixed in full strength in the cup of His rage, and **he will be***

> ***tormented with fire and brimstone*** *in the presence of the holy angels and in the presence of the Lamb. 11* ***And the smoke of their torment goes up forever and ever; they have no rest day and night, those who worship the beast*** *and his image, and whoever receives the mark of his name.""* (Revelation 14:9-11 LSB)

Some use Revelation 20:10 to say it proves that humans will be tortured forever in the Lake of Fire. They say the first beast, the antichrist, and the second beast, the false prophet, are still alive in the Lake of Fire, burning and being tortured, when the devil is thrown in. The beast and false prophet were thrown into the Lake of Fire before the 1000 years. The devil is thrown in after the 1000 years, and Revelation 20:10 appears to say the beast and false prophet **are** still there, not destroyed. However, the word "are" is not in the Greek manuscripts. Many translations add the word "are," but a number of translations do not and try to stay more true to the original language. For example, the following list is not complete, but is a sampling.

> *"10 And the devil, who deceived them, was thrown into the lake of burning sulfur, where the beast and the false prophet* ***had been thrown****. They will be tormented day and night for ever and ever."* (Revelation 20:10 New International Version)

> *"10 And the devil who had deceived them was thrown into the lake of fire and sulfur, into which the beast and the false prophet* ***had already been thrown****. There they will be tormented day and night forever and ever."* (Revelation 20:10 Berean Study Bible)

> *"10 And the devil who had deceived them was thrown into the lake of fire and sulfur where the beast and the false prophet* ***were****, and they will be tormented day and night forever and ever."* (Revelation 20:10 English Standard Version)

> *"10 Then the Devil, who deceived them, was thrown into the lake of fire and sulfur, where the beast and the false prophet* ***had already been thrown;*** *and they will be tormented day and night forever and ever."* (Revelation 20:10 Good News Translation)

*"10 The devil, who deceived them, was thrown into the fiery lake of sulfur, where the beast and the false prophet **were also thrown**. They will be tortured day and night forever and ever."* (Revelation 20:10 GOD'S WORD Translation)

*"10 And the devil who deceived them was cast into the lake of fire and brimstone, where **[are]** both the beast and the false prophet; and they shall be tormented day and night **for the ages of ages**"* (Revelation 20:10 Darby Bible Translation)

The brackets show the word "are" was added by translators. This may have been to perpetuate the eternal torture deception.

*"10 And the Devil, who had been leading them astray, was thrown into the Lake of fire and sulphur where the Wild Beast and the false Prophet **were**, and day and night they will suffer torture **until the Ages of the Ages**."* (Revelation 20:10, Weymouth New Testament (WNT))

So we see that translators, who had a preconceived notion that humans had spirits that could not die, added the word "are" to make the sentence sound better in English. However, we now see that their translation was then subject to their predilections. Those without that preconception do not add the word "are" and just say they were thrown there, leaving it open to the fact that they were destroyed there, in the Lake of Fire, called the Second Death.

Also, we can see from the last two translations that the Greek does not say they will be tortured "forever and ever," but more accurately, until "the ages of ages." This shows that "forever and ever" was a choice based on the translators' preconceived notions or traditions.

*"7 And when the thousand years are finished, Satan will be released from his prison, 8 and will come out to deceive the nations which are in the four corners of the earth, Gog and Magog, to gather them together for the war; the number of them is like the sand of the seashore. 9 And they came up on the broad plain of the earth and surrounded the camp of the saints and the beloved city, and **fire came down from heaven and devoured them. 10 And the devil who deceived them was thrown into the lake of fire and brimstone, where the beast and the false prophet are also, and they will be***

tormented day and night forever and ever."
(Revelation 20:7-10 LSB)

This specifies only the Devil. The Beast and the False Prophet were thrown there. Remember, the word "ARE" is not in the original text. This verse is therefore not proof that the Beast and the False Prophet were still there, to be tormented forever in the Lake of Fire. The Beast and the False Prophet had been thrown into the Lake of Fire before, in Revelation 19:20.

There are differing opinions as to whether the Beast and the False Prophet are humans or spirits or demons. Those who say they are humans will use Revelation 20:10 to try to prove humans will be tortured forever in "Hell," the Lake of Fire. But let us not be drawn into never-ending rabbit holes by the fate of these two unknown entities. Let us not be derailed into endless studies that come to no solid conclusion.

The Great White Throne Judgment

We have read about this judgment before, above. We saw how it fits into the sequence of events after a human dies.
Here, our focus is on the outcome. What happens to the unrepentant sinner who dies in their sins?

The Great White Throne Judgment, the last judgment, is shown in Revelation 20:11.

> *"11 Then I saw a **great white throne** and Him who sits upon it, from whose presence earth and heaven fled away, and no place was found for them. 12 Then **I saw the dead, the great and the small, standing before the throne**, and books were opened; and another book was opened, which is **the book of life**. And **the dead were judged from the things which were written in the books, according to their deeds**. 13 And the sea gave up the dead which were in it, and death and Hades gave up the dead which were in them, and they were judged, every one of them according to their deeds. 14 Then death and Hades were **thrown into the lake of fire. This is the second death, the lake of fire**. 15 And **if anyone's name was not found written in the book of life, he was thrown into the lake of fire.**"* (Revelation 20:11-15 LSB)

Up until the Great White Throne Judgment in Revelation 20:11, only spirits were thrown into the Lake of Fire. But at the Great

White Throne Judgment, "every man" was judged. Those whose names will not be in the Book of Life will be thrown into the Lake of Fire.

What does the Bible call the Lake of Fire? **"This is the second death."** It is not called eternal torture for ever and ever. It is called the **second death!**

Do you agree that the Scriptures above say that lost humans who have died in unrepented sins and have not believed and obeyed Yeshua are thrown in the Lake of Fire, not Hell?

Would you agree that the overwhelming majority of verses say the fate of those who die in their sins is death?

Summary of Part II

We have seen that the First Deception, believing that some part of man is eternal, causes one to believe that the condemned will be tortured by Yahweh for ever and ever. This deception started in the Garden of Eden and caused the first sin, disobedience. Adam and Eve knew God, and He even walked with them in the garden. It was not a lack of faith in God, but disobedience, that caused the first sin. Salvation requires obedience!

We read in God's Word, the Bible, that God did not command people to torture children in fire; "neither came it into my mind." That is what mankind did to their children in the valley of Gehenna, to offer to the idol Molech.

> *"35 And they built the high places of Baal, which are in the valley of the son of Hinnom, to cause their sons and their daughters* **to pass through the fire** *unto Molech; which I commanded them not, neither came it into my mind, that they should do this abomination"* (Jeremiah 32:35 KJV)

> *"35 . . . nor did it enter my mind—that they should do such a detestable thing."* (Jeremiah 32:35 NIV)

> *"35 . . . nor had it entered My mind that they should do this repulsive thing."* (Jeremiah 32:35 AMP)

If you believe in a god who tortures people for ever and ever in fire, then you do not know Yahweh, the God of the Bible. If you believe this deception of eternal torture for ever and ever in fire, then at least some part of humans must be immortal from birth, because you then do not believe eternal life is a **gift** God gives you when you believe and obey Him.

*"23 For the wages of sin is death; but **the gift of God is eternal life** through Jesus Christ our Lord."* (Romans 6:23)

It is not a gift if all mankind already has eternal life from birth, either in the Kingdom of Heaven or in hell. If you believe in eternal torture in the fire of hell, then you are forced to believe unrepentant sinners have eternal life from birth since they don't receive it as a gift from God.

It is a double deception of circular reasoning. If we believe the devil's lie to Adam and Eve that they will not die, then mankind is immortal from birth. If mankind is immortal from birth, then the unrepentant sinner who dies in their sins and is sent to punishment must be punished forever and ever, as they cannot die because they are immortal.

But both are wrong.

Please read and consider all the verses above and more on this topic. What is your final conclusion?

CONCLUSION

Is God a good God? Is God a just God? Is God a kind God, full of loving kindness? Is God a merciful God, full of tender mercies?

We saw a scenario like this before. Imagine a child born in a non-Christian country, born into a good and kind family that taught them Islam, Hinduism, Buddhism, or any other religion, and who, by the reports of all people, was a good and kind child. Then they died as a teenager. Have you always felt a little uneasy with the idea that you have been taught, by almost all Christian churches, that a person in this situation will be tortured forever and ever throughout eternity by God? Does that seem to be an unjust judgment, an extremely harsh judgment, or just plain unfair? Is there any way you could think of that god as a loving god?

The Bible is clear: all who are not saved are thrown into the Lake of Fire. If you believe what you have been taught—that they have an immortal soul or spirit—then you must believe they will be tortured in fire forever.

Cities have incinerators in which they burn trash. It is said that if you are very close to a nuclear explosion, you will be almost immediately vaporized. Studies have actually been done on organic matter like waste food being thrown into lava. It is totally destroyed in a few seconds.

If you are thrown into the Lake of Fire, which almost undoubtedly will be much hotter than the fires used to burn criminals in the Middle Ages, it is a reasonable guess that you will die in a few seconds. While still not pleasant, there is no comparison between a few seconds and forever and ever.

Please pray to Yahweh and ask Him to lead you to understand the truth in His Word. Ask Him to break you free of **any deception** you are trapped in.

Believing this first deception destroys the foundational understanding that Yahweh, the living God of the Bible, is a good, fair, just, and kind God. Believing this first deception opens you up to believing other lies of the devil and of the world. Studying your Bible carefully and thoroughly and praying deeply all the time should open your eyes, let you realize you have been deceived, and help you break free of this first deception.

There is no support in the Bible for an immortal part of man. Therefore, there is no eternal torture anywhere, particularly not in the made-up place called hell.

We need to all repent of not believing God when He said, "You shall surely die." We need to repent of thinking He is the kind of God who would torture people forever.

This is only the first deception. There are more deceptions we must break free from, but those are for other books.

May the living God, Yahweh, guide you and open your heart and eyes to see the truths of the scriptures.

www.ingramcontent.com/pod-product-compliance
Lightning Source LLC
LaVergne TN
LVHW051825080426
835512LV00018B/2732